KT-166-584

First published in Great Britain in 1985 by the Scottish Mountaineering Trust

Second impression 1985

Revised edition 1986

Copyright © by the Scottish Mountaineering Trust

Bennet, Donald J.
    The Munros: The Scottish Mountaineering Club guide.
    1. Mountains — Scotland — Highlands — Guide-books
    2. Highlands (Scotland) — Description and travel —
    Guide-books
    I. Title        II. Scottish Mountaineering Trust
    914.11'504858        DA880.H7
    ISBN 0 907521 13 4

**Front cover:** Carn Mor Dearg from Na Gruagaichean
            *Photo: D.J. Bennet*

**Rear cover:** Looking south-west from the Bealach Bhearnais
            *Photo: R. Robb*

Cover Design by Graham Forsyth Wylie
Typesetting by Clarksons of West Calder
Colour separations by Arneg, Glasgow
Printed by Cambus Litho, East Kilbride
Bound by James Gowans, Glasgow

Distributed by **Cordee**, 3a DeMontford St., Leicester LE1 7HD.

# CONTENTS

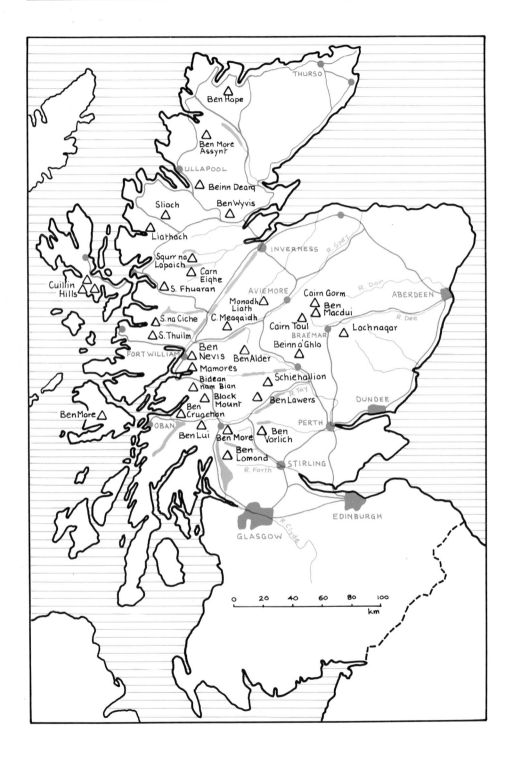

*The first Munroist, A.E. Robertson, and his wife en route to the Hebrides*                    *SMC Collection*

When Sir Hugh Munro published his first Tables of the 3000-ft mountains of Scotland in 1891 he can have had little idea of the influence that he was to exert on later generations of hill-walkers. He could hardly have expected that his own name would become synonymous with these mountains, nor could he have foreseen the numbers of climbers who, almost a century later, would be perusing his work and using his Tables as an inspiration for their hill climbing activities.

The publication of the first Tables in 1891 was the outcome of much painstaking research. Prior to that date no one knew exactly how many 3000-ft mountains there were in Scotland. It was thought by some that there were only about thirty. Early in its existence the Scottish Mountaineering Club set out to establish an accurate list, and Sir Hugh Munro, an original member of the Club and an experienced walker in the Scottish hills, was the right man for the task. The publication of his first Tables caused quite a stir, who would have thought that there were so many distinct mountains in Scotland, and soon the term 'Munro' was coined to denote them.

Munro was working on a revision of his Tables when he died in 1919, so he may not have been entirely satisfied with all the classifications in them. Later members of the Scottish Mountaineering Club have carried on the process of revision, partly in accordance with accurate aneroid measurements by early climbers and revised measurements of heights by the Ordnance Survey, and partly in an attempt to achieve a consistent distinction between Separate Mountains (which have by custom become known as the Munros) and Tops. However, no definitive criterion exists, and such distinction as does exist is based on the drop in height and the distance between adjacent summits, their character and the character of the intervening ground, and the time that might be taken to go from one to the other. This absence of an objective criterion for classifying Munros has given rise to many a controversy, but it is not the intention of this guide to become involved in this debate. We have taken the 1984 Revision of Munro's Tables as the basis for the list of mountains described in this book.

The publication of the Tables in 1891 must have acted as a stimulus to early climbers to ascend as many of the Munros as possible. The first to achieve the complete list, the first Munroist, was the Reverend A.E. Robertson, who in 1901 after what he himself described as 'a desultory campaign of ten years', climbed his last Munro, Meall Dearg on the Aonach Eagach. Thereafter twenty two years elapsed before the next climber completed the list, and for about sixty years the number of Munroists increased at the rate of only about one per year. However, nowadays twenty or thirty new names are added to the list of Munroists each year, and the number of climbers who are afoot in the Scottish mountains steadily ticking off the Munros is numbered in thousands. It is very much with them in mind that this book has been written.

A few words about the purpose and scope of this guide are in order. Each chapter describes the walking, or in some cases scrambling ascent of one or more Munros that can be climbed in a single day. The lengths of expeditions vary from the few hours needed to climb an easily accessible hill to the many

*On the ridge of the Five Sisters of Kintail*                                                    *D.J. Bennet*

hours required for a remote or distant group. In each case the choice of route has been influenced by the aim of using obvious lines such as footpaths, of avoiding unnecessary difficulties or long routes and of enabling the hill-walker to enjoy the best of the character and scenery of the mountains.

The descriptions in this book refer specifically to summer rather than winter conditions, and no snow or ice routes are described. However, winter routes on the majority of the Munros follow the same lines as summer ones, with the added hazards associated with snow or ice and the fact that footpaths may well be obliterated under snow. All remarks in this book about terrain, paths and routes refer to summer, and it must be remembered that many an easy summer hill-walk can become a serious climb on a snow or ice clad mountain. Summer scrambles such as the Aonach Eagach, Liathach or the Cuillins are likely to become technically difficult climbs in winter, and the winter hill-walker must have at his or her command skills and equipment far beyond those required in summer. Nevertheless, there can be no doubt that winter snows transform the Scottish mountains, enhancing their appearance and character as well as their difficulty, and giving them the character of much higher, grander peaks, as many of the winter photographs in this book show. No one can truly claim to know these mountains if he climbs them only in summer, and it behoves every Munroist that he should learn the rudiments of winter hillwalking to enjoy the enhanced pleasures of the winter hills.

It is assumed that users of this guidebook will also use the Ordnance Survey (OS) 1:50000 maps, as these are ideal for the hill-walker's needs. At the time of publication of this book most of the Highlands are covered by the Second Series and Landranger Series of these maps, but the southern edge of the Highlands are still covered by First Series maps which are enlargements of the earlier One Inch To The Mile maps, and contain the same detail.

Heights of Munros and Tops quoted in this guide are taken from the 1984 Edition of Munro's Tables. They do not all agree with the heights shown on the OS 1:50000 maps as in some cases other OS maps, such as the 1:25000, give more recently surveyed and presumably more accurate figures. Heights of passes, cols and bealachs quoted in the text are either taken from 1:50000 maps by reference to contour lines, or from surveyed heights shown on 1:25000 maps. All place names in the text and the specially drawn maps correspond with names and spellings in the OS maps.

The maps in this book are not intended to make the use of the OS map unnecessary, but rather to illustrate the text, and the detail shown on them is intended to be sufficient only to do this. Thus, for example, all footpaths are not shown, only those relevant to the routes being described.

*In the text, to distinguish between heights and distances, the abbreviation m (e.g. 150m) is used to denote a height, while the use of metre (e.g. 200 metres) denotes distance. Distances and heights are rounded up to the nearest ½km and 10m respectively, and times for ascents are calculated on the basis*

*Looking east from Am Bodach to peaks beyond Rannoch Moor*                    D.J. Bennet

*of 4½km per hour for distance walked, plus 10m per minute for climbing. The time thus calculated is rounded up to the nearest 10 minutes, but no allowance is made for stops or particularly rough or difficult terrain. (The preceding calculation is similar, but not identical to Naismith's time - honoured formula which is based on 3 miles per hour plus 2000 feet per hour for climbing). The times quoted in the text refer to ascents only, and the total time for the day's expedition must include stops and the descent. Where descriptions relate to the traverse of two or more Munros, times at each summit are cumulative from the day's starting point.*

It should be assumed that most of the Munros lie in privately owned estates in which stalking and shooting are important sporting and economic activities carried out in late summer and autumn. The culling of hinds may continue until the end of the year. Landowners and stalkers naturally discourage walkers from going onto the hills during these seasons, and urge them to seek information and permission from keepers and stalkers before setting out for the hills between mid-August and mid-October, or even later. There are exceptions, notably in National Trust for Scotland properties where there are no seasonal restrictions on climbing. Where such restrictions do not exist, this fact is stated in the text. Much Scottish hill country is used for sheep farming, and particular care not to disturb livestock should be observed in the lambing season, March to May.

The approaches to several of the remote Munros go for several kilometres along private and Forestry Commission roads, along which cars may not normally be taken. Often locked gates effectively bar access. In a few cases, e.g. in Glen Strathfarrar and Glen Elchaig, there are existing arrangements to permit motorists to use private roads, and in these two cases the present arrangements greatly assist climbers to reach remote hills. Elsewhere, for example in some Cairngorm glens, cars are not allowed along private roads and some very long walks are the result. The use of bicycles on these private roads is, however, normally allowed, and can considerably shorten climbing times.

All the expeditions described in the following pages are one-day trips, although some are very long days. In only a few cases is it positively advantageous to find overnight shelter in the hills. The youth hostels at Loch Ossian and Alltbeithe (Glen Affric) and one or two remote bothies are mentioned in the text as being useful in this respect, but otherwise a complete list of hostels, bothies and other accommodation is not considered necessary.

*Approaching the summit of Ben Cruachan from the west*                    *P. Hodgkiss*

## The Munros - A Personal View by Hamish Brown

'Only a hill, but all of life to me,
Up there, between the sunset and the sea.

Munro-bagging is now unashamedly a game climbers play. Gone are the days of clandestine expeditions and surreptitious ticking-off in the Tables. Even members of the Scottish Mountaineering Club do it. There are so many enthusiasts on the job nowadays that the truth has come out: climbing Munros is fun! It brings a drive and a discipline to wandering feet, it widens the appreciation of the Highlands and Islands, it lays up a store of experience and memories, it is open to all, it is freedom, health, awareness and joy - so small wonder that in this erratic, uncertain, nasty world many thousands have found the relaxation they crave in the hills and, within that sphere, Munro-bagging in particular.

A magazine once managed to misprint 'Munro-bagging', or else the editor had a sense of humour, so that it appeared as 'Munro-bogging'. This could be a new synonym, of course. The Munroist, perforce, meets plenty of bog, scree, water, wind, hail, rain, sleet and snow. Much as he may like a warm sleeping bag and a dram, he is quite likely instead to drag off his innocent friends to sample these outdoor delights, such is the magical motivation of the antique figure of three thousand feet. Not all Munros are equal of course, some are more equal than others and the Ordnance Survey will keep messing about with heights and producing new ones. Nothing is sacred. The term 'Munro' has even been filched by the perfidious Sassenach so that we hear of English Munros and the like.

The quest for the Munros ensures that any climber meets a great variety of experience. He may slither on wet quartzite for one tick on the list, and dance on sunny gabbro just a page later. Understandably some Munros are better than others: Beinn Teallach is a poor cousin of An Teallach, and no single Geal Charn (nor all of them) can rival Sgurr nan Gillean. Their diversity of character and geography is a bonus. The critic who decries walking the Munros because it means "climbing dozens of boring hills" is commenting not on the richness of the hills, but on his own dulled vision. No hill is dull between the sunset and the sea. By the time you have topped a hundred Munros (the incurable stage usually) you will know Scotland - and youself - in a fuller, richer way, I would claim, despite the odd drawbacks such as Scotland's meteorological instability or the presence of a few million midges with their piranha-like friendliness.

Munro-bagging has now become so popular that it receives the ultimate compliment of being parodied in the outdoor press. Even the national newspapers now use the term without any explanation. It has entered the vocabulary of the sitting-room. Every now and then we have a broadside fired into this ship of state. One magazine not so long ago had a letter demanding:"Why this mania for collecting

*The summit ridge of Beinn a' Chlaidheimh*                                    *H.M. Brown*

mountains like pelts? What is wrong with valleys and passes"?, and the writer continued in a very self-righteous way, boasting of not being a Munro-bagger. Well, I'm not a Munro-bagger either; I climb, ski, canoe, cycle, birdwatch, study hill flora and fauna, geology and history; I draw, paint and take photographs; I walk valleys and passes and enjoy lots more besides, as does every hillgoer in this country of ours, whether above or below the three thousand foot line. I don't know anyone who is only a Munro-bagger, though some do tend to become a bit single-minded after doing two hundred, nor do Munroists begrudge other hillmen their own particular game. Sir Hugh himself was a man of wide interests: swop his kilt and Balmoral bonnet for a cagoule and woollen tammy, and he'd be just another bearded lad at home in the Coe. The hills are more than the sum total of all our little games, and we do well to remember our lowly place.

Completing the Munros is apt to be a humbling experience, a poignant time with a layer of sadness below the icing on the celebratory cake. It has meant so much for so long. Only a succession of hills, but so much of life lies suddenly behind. Golden memories instead of brassy expectations, but it was worth every mile and every smile of the way.

There is a peculiar felicitous aptness about Munroing. It is a challenge, a big challenge, but just the right challenge. Were there fewer Munros it would be too easy; many more and it would be impossible for most ordered lives. There is just enough technical difficulty too. You cannot reach every Munro with hands in pockets. Sir Hugh himself never did manage the Inaccessible Pinnacle, largely due to bad luck, and I know quite a few folk who have "done them all except the In Pin". A certain pertinacity is essential in the game.

It is a game, remember. It is a British trait to take politics as a joke and sport seriously, but sometimes we need a reminder that dedication and delight can co-exist. People have gone round the Munros in summer and winter, as teenagers or septuagenarians, alone or in combinations of husband and wife, father and son, even man and dog. They have been done fast and slow, teased out over half a century or tramped in a single journey. They are all things to all men. Thank God for the Munros, however we approach them!

While this is very much a practical guide and has to be brief and to the point, the contributing authors are obviously enthusiasts. They know these mountains as first loves, despite other activities and other hills ranging to the ends of the earth. On their behalf I hope you find the climbing of these hills a joy shared and a fair addition to your "long, golden hills of memory". Only a hill, or two, or two hundred and seventy seven, it matters not. It's all of life - up there.

*The Arrochar Alps from Loch Arklet*                                     *D.J. Bennet*

# SECTION 1

### Loch Lomond to Loch Tay

*Looking north up Loch Lomond, Ben Lomond on the right*                    *D.J. Bennet*

**Ben Lomond;** 974m; (OS Sheet 56; 367029); M179; *beacon hill.*

Its isolated position at the southern edge of the Highlands makes Ben Lomond a conspicuous feature from many viewpoints, and from its summit there is an extensive view of both the Highlands and the Lowlands of Scotland. Although the mountain appears from many angles to be quite pointed, the summit is in fact a short level ridge curving round the head of the north-east corrie. Southwards the mountain throws out a broad grassy ridge towards the forest above Rowardennan, and this part of the mountain, above the forest, is National Trust for Scotland territory. To the north an extensive tract of featureless moorland extends towards Loch Arklet, and to the west, below the outlying spur called Ptarmigan, the Ben drops steeply in grand wooded crags to Loch Lomond.

The 'tourist route' starts at Rowardennan Hotel, or alternatively at the car park at the end of the public road just beyond the hotel. A broad path leads NE through the forest to emerge onto the grassy lower slopes of the S ridge. The path continues up to the level middle part of this ridge and N along its broad crest, giving delightfully easy walking. In due course the steeper cone of the summit is reached, and the path zig-zags up the stony hillside, bearing towards the NE to reach the summit ridge which is followed NW over a few small bumps to reach the top. (5½km; 940m; 2h 50min).

An attractive and much less frequented alternative route is the Ptarmigan ridge. Walk along the private road for 1km N from the car park, and climb the steep grassy hillside on the NW side of the stream N of Ardess. When the angle of the slope eases, bear N and climb the ridge to Ptarmigan, following narrow paths and sheep tracks. This route commands splendid views downwards across the steep wooded hillside of Craig Rostan to Loch Lomond far below. Beyond Ptarmigan the route goes NE across a featureless col to reach the NW ridge of Ben Lomond where a path leads to the top.

No restrictions in the stalking season.

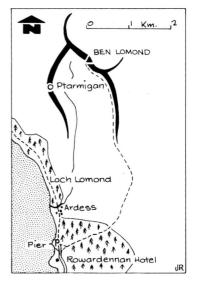

*Beinn Bhuidhe from the east*                                    *P. Hodgkiss*

**Beinn Bhuidhe**; 948m; (OS Sheet 50; 204187); M212; *yellow hill.*

Beinn Bhuidhe is the highest point between Glen Fyne and Glen Shira. It is an isolated mountain whose summit forms a ridge running from south-west to north-east, but it is so surrounded by lower ridges on its south side that it cannot be seen from the head of Loch Fyne. Only from further down the loch is there a view of the mountain, and from the north and east the isolated summit shows up well.

The shortest approach to Beinn Bhuidhe is up Glen Fyne, but the road up this glen is private and cars are not permitted along it. Start at the head of Loch Fyne and walk or cycle 7km up the glen to the house at Inverchorachan. Just beyond the house take to the steep slopes of Beinn Bhuidhe, climbing up the S bank of the stream which tumbles down the hillside. Just below the point where this stream emerges from a tree-filled gully cross to the N side and bear NW up steep grass and bracken, climbing steadily to about 600m.

Once the upper corrie is reached, it is possible either to bear W by a little stream towards the lowest point of the ridge between Beinn Bhuidhe and its lower NE top, or alternatively climb the pleasant SE ridge of this top, on which there is some enjoyable scrambling. Once the main ridge of Beinn Bhuidhe is reached at the col ¾km NE of the summit, a well marked path leads to the top which is crowned by an Ordnance Survey pillar. (10km; 950m; 3h 50min).

The alternative approach to Beinn Bhuidhe goes up Glen Shira, but the road in this glen is also private and the distance to be walked is slightly longer than the Glen Fyne approach. By way of compensation, however, Glen Shira is beautifully wooded for much of its lower reaches. Walk up the road on the SE side of the glen which leads to the Lochan Shira dam as far as the bridge over the Brannie Burn. Then climb the long, grassy and rather uninteresting ridge ENE over Tom a' Phiobhaire and Stac a' Chuirn to Beinn Bhuidhe, (14km; 970m; 4h 50min). The combination of the Glen Fyne and Glen Shira routes, plus a short bus journey along Loch Fyne, gives a good circuit of the mountain.

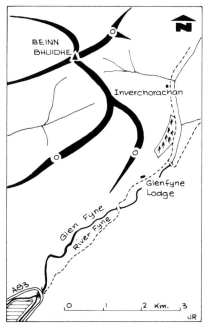

*Beinn Narnain from Beinn Ime*                                    *P. Hodgkiss*

**Beinn Narnain**; 926m; (OS Sheet 56; 272067); M255; *meaning unknown.*
**Beinn Ime**; 1011m; (OS Sheet 56; 255085); M115; *butter hill.*

The Arrochar Alps are a fine little group of mountains north and west of Arrochar, the village at the head of Loch Long. The main cluster of peaks lies opposite the village - The Cobbler, Beinn Narnain and A'Chrois, with Beinn Ime the highest, hidden behind this trio. These are rugged and rocky peaks with bold outlines, particularly so The Cobbler which not being a Munro does not feature in this guidebook.

The route to Beinn Narnain starts at the head of Loch Long just SW of the turn-off to Succoth farm. A path on the NW side of the road leads steeply uphill through the forest and onto the open hillside, following the line of an old rail-track as the many concrete blocks show. At the top of this track continue NW up the broad ridge on steep grass, following a faint but discernible path and turning a rocky barrier to the right to reach the knoll of Cruach nam Miseag. Beyond a slight dip the ridge becomes much steeper and quite rocky. Follow the path up through a few little crags to the base of the Spearhead, the prominent rock prow which crowns the ridge. Finally, climb a short gully on the right (N) of the Spearhead to arrive suddenly on the flat stony plateau of Beinn Narnain about 100 metres E of the trig point which marks its summit. (3km; 950m; 2h 20min).

To continue to Beinn Ime go W down a short boulder slope and then a broad grassy ridge to the Bealach a' Mhaim, a wide flat col. From there climb NNW up the long grassy rise to Beinn Ime. Near the top follow a path leftwards (NW) to the summit where the trig point surmounts a cairned crag. (6km; 1320m; 3h 40min).

Return to the Bealach a' Mhaim and bear S for a few hundred metres to the col at the head of the Allt a' Bhalachain (the Buttermilk Burn). Go SE across the boggy col to find the start of a path on the NE side of the burn which is followed down past the Narnain Boulders to a dam. There go NE along a horizontal track for ¾km to reach the uphill route at the top of the concrete staircase, and descend this to Loch Long.

No restrictions on access in the stalking season.

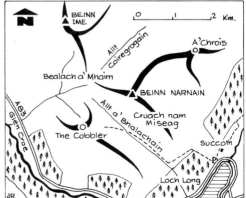

*Approaching Ben Vane from Inveruglas*                                                    *K.M. Andrew*

**Ben Vane**; 915m; (OS Sheet 56; 278098); M274; *middle hill.*

Among the Arrochar Alps, a group of mountains noted for their steepness and rugged character, Ben Vane is one of the steepest. Its south face rising above Coiregrogain has an angle of almost forty-five degrees for a height of 600m. On other sides it is less steep, but it is a very fine little mountain, almost the twin of the slightly lower, but otherwise similar A'Chrois on the opposite side of Coiregrogain.

The ascent is most frequently made from Inveruglas on Loch Lomond-side, starting just north of the bridge over the Inveruglas Water. The approach walk up the Hydro-Electric Board's private road to Coiregrogain is not particularly attractive, as huge pylons march alongside the road, and the Loch Sloy scheme (of which these pylons are part) is visually one of Scotland's most obtrusive hydro-electric schemes. 2km up this road turn left across the Inveruglas Water and continue for another few hundred metres before quitting the road.

The route to Ben Vane is now directly up the ESE ridge, an obvious route with some traces of a path. At first the ascent is up easy-angled grassy slopes which gradually steepen until many little crags and slabs seem to bar the way, but it is always possible to thread a route upwards following grassy gullies and ledges between the crags without the need for any scrambling. However, for those so inclined there are many opportunities for a little mild rock-climbing on the many outcrops. The angle of the ascent relents towards the summit, which is a little level plateau. At its S edge this plateau ends suddenly to reveal the long steep drop to Coiregrogain. (5km; 880m; 2h 40min).

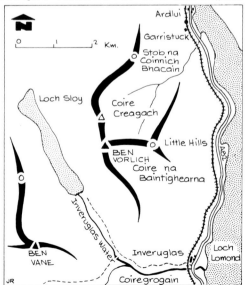

No restrictions on access in the stalking season.

Note: Car parking at the foot of the private road up Coiregrogain is strongly discouraged. The nearest car park is about ½km N opposite the Loch Sloy power station.

*Ben Vorlich from Loch Lomond, with Beinn Dubhchraig beyond*                    *D.J. Bennet*

**Ben Vorlich**; 943m; (OS Sheets 56 and 50; 295124); M224; *hill of the bay.*

Ben Vorlich is the northernmost of the Arrochar Alps, lying north-west of Inveruglas between Loch Lomond and Loch Sloy. The mountain is a long crescent-shaped ridge running roughly from south to north, with an eastward spur, the Little Hills, jutting out above Loch Lomond. To the north and south of this spur are Coire Creagach and Coire na Baintighearna. The west side of Ben Vorlich overlooking Loch Sloy is uniformly steep and craggy.

Surprisingly, considering that Ben Vorlich is very accessible and popular, there is no single route up it which is the most frequented to the exclusion of others. The mountain can be climbed equally well from Inveruglas and Ardlui by routes of similar length and character. From Inveruglas the two possible ways are either up to the Loch Sloy dam and from there up the steep hillside SW of the summit, or from the Inveruglas Water by the long undulating SE ridge. From Ardlui one route is by the Coire Creagach, starting at the 'cattle-creep' under the railway 400 metres S of Ardlui station, and following a track SW up the corrie on the NW side of the stream towards the upper corrie, from where the main ridge is reached 2km NNE of the summit. Another route is the NNE ridge, and this will be described in more detail.

Leave the A82 road 200 metres S of Ardlui station and take the private road past Garristuck cottage onto the open hillside. A well defined track, more used by sheep than by climbers, goes WNW up the grassy hillside, bracken covered in summer, to reach the main ridge above some prominent little crags just S of Stob an Fhithich. Turn SSW and climb the broad ridge over the top of Stob na Coinnich Bhacain, down across a flat grassy col and on up the final ridge, which is quite rocky in places, to the North Top of Ben Vorlich (931m). Continue along the dipping ridge to the summit cairn. (5½km; 1000m; 3h). The OS trig point is 100 metres further S and 2m lower, but it does command a fine view down Loch Lomond.

Another very attractive route of ascent, though possibly rather longer than those already mentioned, is the traverse of the Little Hills, the ridge which projects E from the summit towards Loch Lomond. The best starting point is about 1km S of Ardlui, and from there climb SW up a fairly easy-angled ridge to reach the first of the Little Hills. There turn W and continue up and down along the ridge to the summit. The views on this route, particularly S to Ben Lomond, are very fine.

No restrictions on access in the stalking season.

*Beinn Chabhair from Glen Falloch*                                        D.J. Bennet

**Beinn Chabhair**; 933m; (OS Sheets 50 and 56; 367180); M243; *possibly hill of the hawk.*

This mountain is situated at the head of the Ben Glas Burn, 4½km north-east of the head of Loch Lomond, from which it is not visible. One gets a fine view of Beinn Chabhair from Glen Falloch near Derrydarroch, from where its principal feature, the long north-west ridge is well seen, rising from the glen over many humps and rocky knolls towards the summit. The upper part of the mountain is quite rugged, there being innumerable rocky outcrops all round the summit, and in misty weather route-finding may be a problem.

Leave the A82 road at the foot of Glen Falloch near Beinglas farm. After crossing the bridge over the River Falloch follow the West Highland Way signposts round (not through) the farm over two stiles. Then climb steeply behind the farm, following a slanting path up the hillside dotted with birch and hawthorn until more level ground is reached above the falls of the Ben Glas Burn. Continue along the N side of the burn following narrow paths (which occasionally are lost in boggy ground) until Lochan Beinn Chabhair is reached. The upper 400m of the mountain rise above the lochan in grassy slopes broken by many rock outcrops. There is no single well defined route up this face, and the best line of ascent climbs diagonally NE from the lochan's outflow to reach the NW ridge just less than 1km from the summit. A faint path leads along the ridge, passing a small cairn shortly before reaching the summit, where the cairn stands on top of a small crag. (5½km; 920m; 2h 50min).

The ascent by the NW ridge past Lochan a' Chaisteal is a fine route, but is longer and more strenuous than the one just described on account of its many ups and downs.

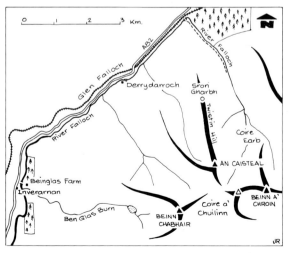

*Beinn a'Chroin and An Caisteal above the head of Glen Falloch*                    *D.J. Bennet*

**An Caisteal**; 995m; (OS Sheets 50 and 56; 379193); M144; *the castle.*
**Beinn a' Chroin**; 940m; (OS Sheets 50 and 56; 394186); M227; *hill of harm or danger.*

These two mountains stand close together above the headwaters of the River Falloch on the south-east side of the A82 road 6km south of Crianlarich. Typical of the hills in this part of the Southern Highlands, they are grassy on their lower slopes, and quite rocky high up near their summits.

An Caisteal has a well defined summit at the junction of its NW and NNW ridges, the latter being known as Twistin Hill. Southwards from the summit the SSE ridge drops to a col at about 825m below Beinn a' Chroin. This mountain has a 1km long summit ridge, with the highest point at the east end, and two lower cairned points to the west, one of them being the West Top, 938m. The west end of this undulating ridge drops steeply in broken crags above Coire a' Chuilinn.

To traverse these two mountains, leave the A82 road in Glen Falloch at (368238) near the obvious bend in the River Falloch. Follow the rough track under the railway, over the river by a bridge and up its W bank. Heading for An Caisteal first, leave this track after about 1km and climb S up the steepening grass slopes to Sron Gharbh. Follow a path along the ridge, Twistin Hill, which is level for some way and then climbs past a curious cleft across the ridge and over a rocky knoll to reach the summit of An Caisteal. (4½km; 830m; 2h 30min).

Descend the SSE ridge which is grassy at first; lower down there is a path through rocky outcrops. Cross the level col and climb the rocky NW end of Beinn a' Chroin's summit ridge, zig-zagging left then right to avoid crags. Continue along the undulating crest past two cairned points to the summit. (7½km; 960m; 3h 20min).

Go N from the cairn down the grassy ridge which drops to the stream junction in Coire Earb. Continue down the corrie, eventually joining the track on the W bank of the River Falloch.

Beinn a'Chroin can be equally well climbed from the east, approaching from Balquhidder along Loch Voil to the car park ¾km E of Inverlochlarig farm. From there walk W past the farm along a track on the N side of the river. In 3km cross the Ishag Burn and climb NW up steep grassy slopes, crossing a little knoll before reaching the broken crags just below the summit. (6km; 800m; 2h 40min).

*The ridge from Beinn Tulaichean to Cruach Ardrain*    H.M. Brown

**Beinn Tulaichean**; 946m; (OS Sheets 51, 56 and 57; 416196); M217; *hill of the hillocks.*

Beinn Tulaichean is at the south end of the long ridge which runs between Crianlarich and Inverlochlarig farm at the west end of the Braes of Balquhidder. The central and highest point of this ridge is Cruach Ardrain, and Beinn Tulaichean, although classified as a separate Munro, is little more than the outlying south peak of Cruach Ardrain. The broad grassy ridge which links the two mountains drops barely 120m from Beinn Tulaichean to the col ¾km north-west of its summit. On all other sides the mountain drops in long grassy slopes of uniform steepness above the Ishag and Inverlochlarig burns. Only high up near the summit are there areas of small crags and huge fallen boulders.

The ascent of Beinn Tulaichean from Inverlochlarig is a short and easy climb. Cars should be left at the car park ¾km E of the farm, and the SE flank of the mountain above the farm can be climbed anywhere by easy grassy slopes. High up the character of the climb changes as the route goes up among crags and boulders through which it is easy to find a way. The crest of the ridge is reached a short distance S of the summit, and it is only along the last couple of hundred metres of this ridge that there is any sign of a path. (4km; 810m; 2h 20min).

The continuation NW to Cruach Ardrain is straightforward. There is a path along this grassy ridge, and its crest should be followed until a point (marked by a small cairn) just W of Cruach Ardrain's summit is reached. Turn right at this point and climb about 70 metres E, passing two cairns, and beyond them reach the summit. (5½km; 1030m; 3h). On the return to Inverlochlarig from Cruach Ardrain the quickest route is back down the S ridge to the col, and then a descending traverse E towards the Inverlochlarig Burn where a track is reached leading down to the farm.

**Cruach Ardrain**; 1046m; (OS Sheets 50 and 51; 409211); M84; *stack of the high part.*

Cruach Ardrain is one of the most familiar of the mountains that encircle the village of Crianlarich. It has a fine pointed outline, enhanced in winter and spring when snow fills the steep Y-Gully on the north face above Coire Ardrain. The plan of the mountain itself is rather like the shape of the letter Y, with the summit at the junction of three ridges radiating NW, NE and S. The NE ridge drops steeply from the summit and leads to the rocky Top, Stob Garbh (959m); the S ridge leads to Beinn Tulaichean and the NW ridge which drops towards Crianlarich provides the usual route of ascent.

This route starts from the A82 road ¾km S of Crianlarich where a bridge over the West Highland Railway gives access to the forest which covers much of the N side of Cruach Ardrain. Once across the railway, bear right then back left through a wide clearing in the forest, following a path. After about 200 metres a broken fence is reached; turn right, uphill, along the line of fence posts through a narrow break in the closely planted spruce trees. At the upper edge of the forest, by a prominent boulder, turn SE up the grassy NW ridge to reach the Grey Height (685m), the first point on the ridge. For the next few

*Cruach Ardrain from the Grey Height*                    P. Hodgkiss

hundred metres the ridge is broad, grassy and featureless, and the next point Meall Dhamh (806m) is reached.

From this point quite a distinct path leads on, down for 50m at first, across a col and then steeply up the NW corner of Cruach Ardrain. The summit of the mountain may be confusing in thick mist. The route just described leads first to a flat top with two cairns about 25 metres apart. To the NE, across a slight dip in the ridge, is the true summit with a single large cairn. (4½km; 910m; 2h 30min).

From the summit the descent NE to Stob Garbh is very steep and rocky at first. To continue S to Beinn Tulaichean, return SW past the two cairns and descend about 70 metres in the same direction to a grassy ridge. Turn S along the crest of this ridge towards Beinn Tulaichean. The quickest return to Crianlarich is by the route of ascent.

No restrictions during the stalking season.

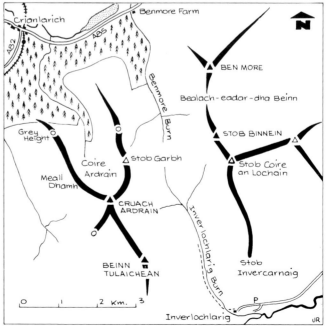

*Ben More and Stob Binnein from Strath Fillan*                              *H.M. Brown*

**Ben More**; 1174m; (OS Sheet 51; 432244); M15; *big hill.*
**Stob Binnein**; 1165m; (OS Sheet 51; 434226); M17; *either from Gaelic binnean meaning peak, or from innean meaning anvil.*

These two fine mountains, the highest south of Strath Tay, are among the best known and most popular in the Southern Highlands. From many viewpoints they appear as almost identical twin peaks, however Stob Binnein is more elegant, its ridges being better defined and the tip of its summit being cut away to form a little plateau. Ben More, with a few extra metres of height, certainly appears to be more bulky, particularly when seen from Glen Dochart near Crianlarich, for there it shows its full size above Loch Iubhair, and the ascent of that side of the mountain is a long unrelenting slog.

The traverse of the two mountains from the Braes of Balquhidder to Glen Dochart, or vice versa, is one of the classic hill-walks of the Southern Highlands, but it needs two cars or a helpful driver. If no such transport arrangements are available, then Benmore farm in Glen Dochart is the best point at which to start and finish the traverse.

The 'normal' route to Ben More starts from the A85 road at a stile over the fence 150 metres E of the farm. Once on the open hillside, climb SE up the ever steepening grass slopes of the NW shoulder of the mountain. High up a stone dyke is a useful landmark, the path being on its NE side. On its SW side there is a little corrie with steep slopes and crags at its head; a dangerous place in poor visibility. At the top of the dyke there are a few crags through which the path climbs before the angle of the slope eases below the summit, which is formed by a huge crag. (3km; 1010m; 2h 30min).

The descent from Ben More goes S for a short distance, then SW following an indistinct ridge before descending an open slope S to the wide flat col called the Bealach-eadar-dha Beinn, the pass between the mountains. The ascent of Stob Binnein is up the N ridge, a long uniform slope of moss and stones defined on its E side by the steep edge of the mountain's NE corrie. The cairn is at the S edge of the little summit plateau, which is surrounded by steep slopes and crags on all sides except the N. (5km; 1320m; 3h 20min). To return to Benmore farm, descend the N ridge to the bealach, and from there drop down NW to the Benmore Burn which is followed on its E bank down to the road.

An alternative route to Ben More from Glen Dochart which has more interest than the straight ascent from Benmore farm is the NE ridge. Start from the A85 road just E of the Allt Coire Chaorach bridge, 4½km E of Benmore farm. Follow the track on the E side of the stream into the forest, and after about 1km keep right to cross the stream (stepping stones may be helpful) and continue up the track S through the forest. It emerges at (458254) onto the open hillside. Keep on the right hand track up to the fence, then bear W to the crest of the NE ridge and follow this to the summit. At one point the crest of the ridge is quite rocky, but a traverse on the SE side avoids any difficulties. (5½km; 1010m; 3h).

*On the south ridge of Stob Binnein*                                    *D.J. Bennet*

The usual route to Stob Binnein from the S starts 2km beyond the W end of Loch Doine at the car park ¾km E of Inverlochlarig farm. From this point a path goes directly N to Stob Invercarnaig up steep grass with a few small crags high up. Once on more level ground above this slope continue NNW along a very pleasant grassy ridge with a well marked path to Stob Coire an Lochain (1068m), then down slightly and up a broad steepening ridge to the summit of Stob Binnein. (4½km; 1050m; 2h 50min).

No restrictions on access by the ascent route from Benmore farm during the stalking season

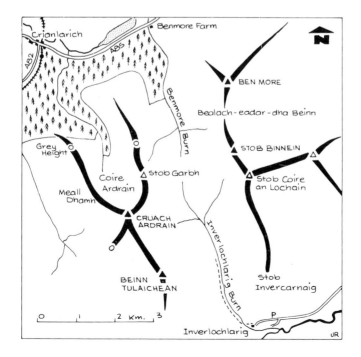

*Ben Lui from the River Cononish*                                      *P. Hodgkiss*

**Ben Lui (Beinn Laoigh);** 1130m; (OS Sheet 50; 266263); M27; *calf hill.*
**Beinn a' Chleibh;** 916m; (OS Sheet 50; 251256); M273; *hill of the creel or chest*

Ben Lui is in every respect one of the finest mountains in the Southern Highlands. By virtue of its height it stands high above its neighbours, and its splendid shape is unmistakable. In particular, the great NE corrie, the Coire Gaothaich, which holds snow most years from mid-winter to early summer, gives the mountain an Alpine character. The finest view of the mountain is from Strath Fillan, looking up the glen of the Cononish River directly at the steep NE face. From the west, low down in Glen Lochy, Ben Lui presents a very different aspect; the Ciochan Beinn Laoigh are prominent rocky knolls on the N side of the mountain from which the NNW ridge rises to the summit. From the west, also, its lower neighbour Beinn a' Chleibh is well seen, with its flat summit and long W ridge dropping to the forests of Glen Lochy.

The finest approach to Ben Lui, scenically at least, is the walk up the Cononish glen, but the subsequent traverse over Beinn a' Chleibh ends a long way from the day's starting point. For the shortest traverse of these two mountains the ascent from Glen Lochy by the Fionn Choirein, and descent by the same corrie is recommended.

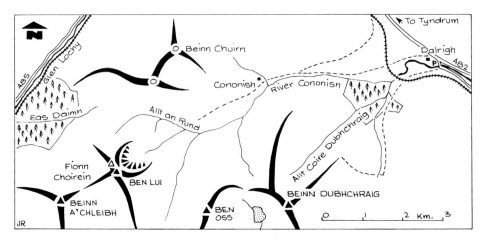

*Beinn a' Chleibh from the slopes of Ben Lui*                                    H.M. Brown

The Cononish approach to Ben Lui starts either at Tyndrum Lower Station or from the A82 road at Dalrigh (344291), and the two routes, both following private roads, converge 1 km before Cononish farm is reached. Continue past the farm along the forestry road which ends near the Allt an Rund. Cross this stream near a sheepfank and climb steeply by a faint track up the NW side of the stream which tumbles down from the Coire Gaothaich above. Once in this corrie bear N onto the NNE ridge, named Stob Garbh on the OS map, and climb this steep ridge to the N top and finally along the rim of the corrie to the summit. (9 km; 930m; 3h 40min).

The approach from Glen Lochy starts at a parking place for cars beside the A85 road at (239278). There is no footbridge over the River Lochy at this point, but the river is often easy to cross by stepping stones. There is a footbridge (not shown on the OS map) 1 km SW which provides a crossing if the river is in spate. Once on the S side of the river a well marked path is followed up the N side of the Eas Daimh through recently planted spruce forest. In 400 metres cross the Eas Daimh and continue E for another few hundred metres until a clear break in the trees leads SSE up to the open hillside and a stile over the fence. Once above the fence climb E up grassy slopes to the NNW ridge of Ben Lui which is followed over a series of rocky rises to the top. (4 km; 950m; 2h 30min). Descend SW down a wide uniform slope to the col at the head of the Fionn Choirein, and climb the broad ridge to the flat summit of Beinn a' Chleibh. (5½km; 1090m; 3h 10min). The safest descent, for the N and NE sides of Beinn a' Chleibh are very steep (in places precipitous) is to return to the col. From there descend by a short steep slope into the Fionn Choirein and continue down the grassy floor of the corrie well to the E of the stream to reach the stile over the forest fence crossed on the uphill route.

No restrictions in the stalking season.

*Ben Oss (left) and Beinn Dubhchraig from Loch Lomond*                    *D.J. Bennet*

**Ben Oss**; 1029m; (OS Sheet 50; 287253); M99; *loch-outlet hill.*
**Beinn Dubhchraig**; 978m; (OS Sheet 50; 308255); M171; *black-rock hill.*

These two mountains stand together several km west of Crianlarich between Glen Falloch and Strath Fillan. From the south, looking up Loch Lomond, they are well seen with Ben Oss showing a distinctive cone and Beinn Dubhchraig its craggy south face. From Strath Fillan, Ben Oss is almost hidden behind the shoulder of Beinn Dubhchraig which shows the whole of its north flank, the Coire Dubhchraig. This wide grassy corrie forms a great bowl between the N and NE ridges of Beinn Dubhchraig, and at its foot there is the pine wood of the Coille Coire Chuilc, a beautiful little remnant of the Old Caledonian Forest. The SE side of this corrie has recently been planted by the Forestry Commission, and a rough road climbs to about 500m on the NE ridge, providing an easy but not very aesthetic route to Beinn Dubhchraig.

The normal route for the traverse of the two mountains starts at Dalrigh in Strath Fillan (343291) where it is possible to drive off the new section of the A82 road and park at the old bridge over the River Fillan. Cross the river and follow the rough road on its S side W to a bridge over the railway. Beyond this, leave the road and head W (a faint track is marked by a few cairns) to the footbridge over the Allt Coire Dubhchraig. Once in the pine wood follow paths through the trees on the NW side of the burn to the upper edge of the wood where the deer fence is crossed by a stile. The route continues SW up the grassy corrie to reach the shoulder of Beinn Dubhchraig ¾km NW of the summit near a little lochan. The final climb is along a broad stony ridge at a very easy angle. (6½km; 800m; 2h 50min).

Return NW along the ridge to the shoulder and descend steeply for a short distance W to the col. The ridge to Ben Oss goes W for ½km to a small knoll, and then ¾km SW to the summit. (9½km; 1050m; 3h 50min). On the return it is advisable not to descend N from the Oss-Dubhchraig col as the ground is steep. It is preferable to climb about 120m to reach the shoulder of Beinn Dubhchraig and go down the corrie by the route of ascent.

The traverse of Beinn Dubhchraig and Ben Oss can be continued westwards over Ben Lui, and even as far as Beinn a' Chleibh, although one may finish a long way west of the day's starting point. There is, however, the Oban to Glasgow bus service which can be used for the return to Dalrigh. From Ben Oss descend the broad S ridge, bearing SW then W to a flat col at about 720m. Then climb the easy-angled S ridge of Ben Lui directly to its summit. (From Dalrigh: 13km; 1460m; 5h 20min). From there one can either return to Dalrigh by Cononish, or continue to Beinn a' Chleibh and descend to Glen Lochy by the Fionn Choirein, both these routes being described on the previous page.

Map on page 18.

The approach to Ben Vorlich from Ardvorlich                                    D.J. Bennet

**Ben Vorlich**; 985m; (OS Sheets 51 and 57; 629189); M161; *hill of the bay.*
**Stuc a' Chroin**; 975m; (OS Sheets 51 and 57; 617175); M176; *peak of harm or danger.*

These two mountains, standing on the southern edge of the Highlands, are among the most familiar in Scotland. From many viewpoints in the Forth Valley they are the most conspicuous features of the northern landscape. They form two parallel ridges running from south-east to north-west, separated by a col, the Bealach an Dubh Choirein, at a height of about 700m. Ben Vorlich appears from the south as a very sharp conical peak, and Stuc a' Chroin has a steep rocky buttress on its north-east side overlooking the Bealach.

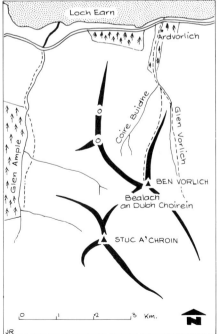

Of several starting points for the traverse, Ardvorlich on the S side of Loch Earn is probably the best. Go through the east gate of Ardvorlich House and follow the private road, becoming a rough track, S onto the open hillside in Glen Vorlich. The track ends after about 2km at the foot of Coire Buidhe, and a good path marked by a few wooden posts leads up the SE side of the corrie onto the NNE ridge of Ben Vorlich. Near the top of this ridge the path steepens towards the stony summit, marked by an OS pillar at its NW end, and 100 metres to the SE by a large cairn. (4½km; 890m; 2h 30min).

The route to Stuc a' Chroin is easy to follow, there being a line of fence posts down to the Bealach an Dubh Choirein. From there the first part of the climb to the Stuc is up a short boulder slope to the foot of the prominent buttress which is the true line of the connecting ridge. Its crest gives a good hard scramble, but a steep zig-zag path goes up about 30 metres to the right (NW) avoiding all difficulties. There is a cairn at the top of this buttress, and the summit of Stuc a' Chroin is about 300 metres S. (6½km; 1160m; 3h 30min).

To return to Ardvorlich, descend to the Bealach and then traverse horizontally N across the grassy hillside to reach the col at the head of Coire Buidhe. Continue down the SE side of this corrie to rejoin the track in Glen Vorlich.

*Ben Chonzie above Loch Turret*                                    A.C.D. Small

**Ben Chonzie (Ben-y-Hone)**; 931m; (OS Sheets 51 and 52; 774309); M246; *most probably mossy hill.*

This solitary Munro is the highest point of the extensive tract of flat-topped hills and high moorland between Strath Earn and Loch Tay. At the centre of this area, between glens Lednock, Turret and Almond, Ben Chonzie rises just sufficiently above its neighbouring hills to be the most prominent among them, although it does not itself have any outstanding character. The summit is a long broad ridge, and to its east there is a corrie ringed by grassy crags, but possibly the most noteworthy feature of Ben Chonzie is the large population of mountain hares which inhabit its upper slopes.

The normal approaches are from Crieff by Glen Turret, and from Comrie by Glen Lednock. Of the two, the latter is probably the easier, although longer, as it follows a track most of the way up the hill. From Invergeldie, 6km along the narrow public road up Glen Lednock, take the right-of-way to Ardtalnaig up the W side of the Invergeldie Burn. After 1½km, at the junction of tracks just beyond a gate, take the right hand one across the burn and follow it ENE up the hillside past shooting butts almost to the ridge. Then strike NE across heath and blaeberry covered slopes to the broad crest where a fence leads NW then NE to the summit. A large cairn gives some shelter in stormy weather. (6½km; 700m; 2h 40min).

Going by Glen Turret, drive as far as the car park at the Loch Turret dam, and take the track along the E side of the loch. Continue up the Turret Burn through an area of well-preserved moraines, and before reaching Lochan Uaine strike W up grassy slopes to the summit ridge where the previous route is joined. (6km; 570m; 2h 20min).

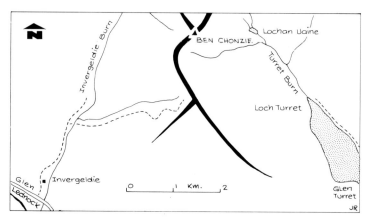

*Looking west from Meall Ghaordie towards the hills at the head of Glen Lochay*    *D.J. Bennet*

# SECTION 2

## Loch Tay to Rannoch Moor

*The Carn Mairg range from Glen Lyon*                                                                    *D.J. Bennet*

**Creag Mhor;** 981m; (OS Sheet 51; 695496); M167; *big rock.*

**Carn Mairg;** 1041m; (OS Sheet 51; 684513); M88; *may be hill of sorrow, pity or folly, or hill of the boundary, or perhaps from Gaelic marag, meaning pudding.*

**Meall Garbh;** 968m; (OS Sheet 51; 646517); M182; *rough hill.*

**Carn Gorm;** 1028m; (OS Sheet 51; 635501); M100; *blue hill.*

This group of hills is on the north side of Glen Lyon, and forms a great arc of broad high ridges above Invervar. The nature of the terrain along the tops is more characteristic of the Grampians or Cairngorms than the neighbouring Breadalbane mountains such as Ben Lawers; the ridges are wide and level, the corries easy-angled and devoid of crags. Only the lower slopes above Glen Lyon look impressively steep. The north side of the range drops gradually across wide tracts of moorland and forest towards Loch Rannoch. Between the four Munros the drops along the ridge are fairly small, although the distances are considerable, so that the traverse of all four is a good high-level expedition. It can however be shortened at almost any point by descending one of the easy corries or shoulders towards the Invervar Burn.

Start at Invervar in Glen Lyon, where the easiest place to leave a car is a few metres down the road which leads across the River Lyon to Inverinain. Take the track which starts directly opposite the telephone kiosk and leads N through the forest. In ½km the open hillside is reached and the track is followed for a further few hundred metres almost to the bridge over the Allt Coir' Chearcaill. Turn ENE and climb the ridge on the S side of this stream. There are traces of a path for much of the way, and the going is very easy, leading right to the first Munro of the traverse, Creag Mhor. The summit of this hill is a level grassy ridge with two tops a few hundred metres apart, the higher one being a little rocky tor. (4km; 790m; 2h 20min).

Descend grassy slopes NNW to the col at about 840m, and continue in the same direction up easy ground towards the E ridge of Carn Mairg. A dry stone dyke along this ridge is a useful landmark in mist. Once on the ridge turn W up a short stony slope to the big cairn on the summit of Carn Mairg. (6½km; 990m; 3h 10min). Descend NW and soon reach a line of rusty fence posts which mark the line of the traverse for the next few kilometres. For a short distance the NW ridge of Carn Mairg is quite narrow and bouldery, but it soon broadens out and bears W across a flat col to the short rise leading to Meall a' Bharr (1004m). This Top has a long level ridge, the summit being the cairn on a small rocky outcrop. Continue WNW then W, following the fence posts across a wide col and up to Meall Garbh whose flat stony summit has several cairns. Judgement as to which is the highest is difficult to make, the choice lies between one 70 metres S of the fence and another at the fence; the Munroist can decide for himself. (10½km; 1140m; 4h 20min).

*Carn Mairg from the east*                                           *J. Renny*

The line of fence posts which one follows on this traverse is one of the most unsightly and dilapidated on the Scottish hills; in places (such as the summit of Meall Garbh) there are large amounts of scrap iron lying about. Follow these posts W for only a few hundred metres further, then bear SW down to the next col at about 830m, marked by a cairn. Continue either over or round the little pointed Top of An Sgorr (924m) and climb quite steeply to Carn Gorm where at the top of the slope the OS trig point is reached, and a hundred metres further the slightly higher summit. (12½km; 1400m; 5h 10min).

Descend easy grassy slopes SE at first, then E to reach the Invervar Burn N of the forest. There is a footbridge across the burn at (659495), and on the NE side a good track leads back to Invervar.

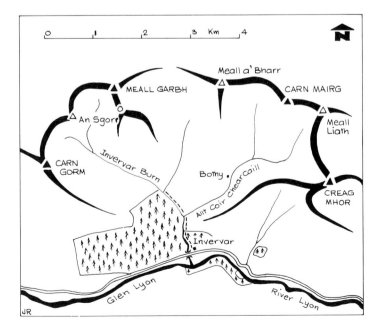

*Schiehallion from the River Tummel*                                     *D.J. Bennet*

**Schiehallion**; 1083m; (OS Sheet 51; 714548); M57; *the fairy hill of the Caladonians (acc. to W.J. Watson).*

Schiehallion is one of the best known of Scottish mountains by virtue of its striking appearance and isolated position in the centre of the Highlands. It is a conspicuous feature from many viewpoints; from the east and west it appears as a steep conical peak, but from the north or south its true shape is more apparent: a long whale-backed ridge dropping quite steeply to the west, but much more gradually to the east.

A narrow road leaves the A846 between Coshieville and Tummel Bridge and goes round the north side of Schiehallion to Kinloch Rannoch. 3km along this road there is a Forestry Commission car park just east of Braes of Foss farm. A plaque at this point commemorates the experiment carried out on the slopes of Schiehallion by Maskeleyne, once the Astronomer-Royal, to determine the earth's mass by observing the deflection of a pendulum caused by the mass of Schiehallion itself.

Starting at the car park, follow the route indicated to the 'Schiehallion path', and go WSW across the grassy moorland, past a prominent cairn, to join a track coming up from Braes of Foss. This track divides; keep heading W across the grassy lower hillside towards the mountain. Higher up, as the slope steepens, the route goes up peaty ground which has become badly eroded by the passage of many boots. In places the path along the E ridge is a trough in the soft ground. Higher up the ridge the terrain changes again, becoming very stony, and the upper part of Schiehallion is covered with angular quartzite boulders. The last 1½km of the route along the broad ridge is marked by many small cairns. (4½km; 760m; 2h 20min).

An alternative route, of rather similar character, starts NW of Schiehallion near Tempar, and goes up a track on the E side of the Tempar Burn leading to a bothy on the W side of the mountain. Leave this track after about 2½km and climb the NW ridge to the summit. (4½km; 880m; 2h 30min).

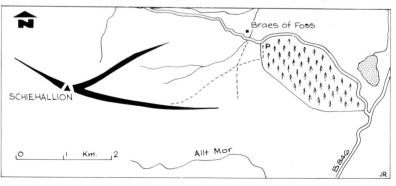

*Stuchd an Lochain*                                           *D.J. Bennet*

**Stuchd an Lochain;** 960m; (OS Sheet 51; 483448); M194; *peak of the little loch.*
**Meall Buidhe;** 932m; (OS Sheet 51; 498499); M244; *yellow hill.*

Far up Glen Lyon, just beyond Meggernie Castle, the Allt Conait, a tributary of the River Lyon, flows down from Loch an Daimh. Between this loch and Glen Lyon itself Stuchd an Lochain occupies a commanding position, its great bulk filling the westward view up the glen. On the north side of Loch an Daimh, Meall Buidhe is rather an undistinguished hill, the highest point of a vast tract of high undulating moorland between upper Glen Lyon and Loch Rannoch. Loch an Daimh itself is the enlarged loch formed by raising the level of Loch Giorra and Loch Daimh, which are now one.

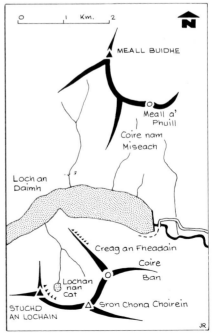

4km W of Bridge of Balgie in Glen Lyon a branch road leads to the dam at the E end of Loch an Daimh, and both hills are easily accessible from there. The loch is at an altitude of about 430m, so the amount of climbing on each is not great. In fact, the ascent of both in one day is no more strenuous than many a Munro by itself.

Climbing Stuchd an Lochain first, walk past the S end of the dam for 150 metres and climb a faint path up the steep grassy hillside to the S to reach the ridge above Coire Ban at a line of fence posts. These are followed W to Creag an Fheadain (867m), then SSW across a dip in the broad ridge to Sron Chona Choirein (c.920m), and then W and NW to Stuchd an Lochain, whose most interesting feature is its northern corrie holding the dark little Lochan nan Cat. (4½km; 600m; 2h). The return to the Loch an Daimh dam takes about an hour.

Starting again at the dam, this time at its N end, climb due N up easy slopes to Meall a' Phuill (878m), marked by two cairns. Continue W then NNW along the broad crest past some small cairns to reach the big cairn which marks the summit of Meall Buidhe at the N end of a level ridge 1km long. (4½km; 520m; 2h).

*The north side of Ben Lawers above Glen Lyon*                                    *J. Renny*

For much of its length, Loch Tay is dominated on its north-west side by the great sweeping slopes and high summits of the Lawers group. The name refers not only to the highest point, but to the whole range of seven distinct peaks, six of them Munros, linked by a twisting ridge 12km long which only once drops below 800m, the highest and most extensive mountain massif in the Southern Highlands. The range gives the impression of being very grassy, and this is certainly true of most of the peaks. Only in the north-east corrie of Ben Lawers itself, above Lochan nan Cat, are there crags of any size, and they too are vegetatious, of more interest to the botanist than the climber, for the whole area has a reputation for the wealth of its alpine flora.

Most of the south-eastern side of Ben Lawers, from the summit ridges well down towards Loch Tay, is owned by the National Trust for Scotland, so there are no restrictions on climbing on this side of the range at any time of the year. The Trust's Visitor Centre is high up on the road which crosses the west side of the range from Loch Tay to Glen Lyon, and it is a focal point for walkers, climbers and botanists on the mountain.

It is quite possible for any reasonably fit hill-walker, particularly if he has a co-operative car driver, to traverse all the peaks of Ben Lawers in a single day. However, such a degree of fitness and good fortune will not be assumed, and in the following descriptions the ascent of the six Ben Lawers Munros will be taken in three separate days, all of them quite short and easy, and allowing time for diversions to explore the range fully.

The traverse of the Ben Lawers group, starting and finishing at the same point, is probably best undertaken from Glen Lyon on the north side of the mountain. Leave the public road at Camusvrachan, cross the river and walk round to Milton Roro at the foot of the Allt a' Chobhair. Five of the six Lawers Munros are grouped round this stream and can be done in a long circuit, starting at Meall a' Choire Leith and ending at Meall Garbh. Only Meall Greigh lies outwith this ring of peaks, beyond Meall Garbh, and to include it and descend the Inverinain Burn to Glen Lyon adds several kilometres to an already long day.

**Meall Corranaich**; 1069m; (OS Sheet 51; 616410); M65; *perhaps notched, prickly, hooked or crooked hill, or possibly hill of lamenting.*

**Meall a' Choire Leith**; 926m; (OS Sheet 51; 612439); M257; *hill of the grey corrie.*

These two hills are at the western end of the Ben Lawers range, Meall Corranaich being on the main ridge which forms the watershed between Loch Tay and Glen Lyon, and Meall a' Choire Leith lying 3km to the north and outwith the territory of the National Trust for Scotland.

The nearest point of access for both hills is the summit of the narrow road which crosses the western end of the Lawers range from Loch Tay to Glen Lyon. Just north of Lochan na Lairige there is a prominent cairn above the road, and cars can be parked a few metres further west.

Going to Meall Corranaich first, cross rough moorland SE over peat hags to reach the Allt Gleann Da-Eig. Follow this stream uphill and gradually tend E to reach the SW ridge of Meall Corranaich which is followed to the top. (A shorter and steeper route goes directly up the W face of the hill). The small cairn stands close to the edge of the steep NE face. (3km; 520m; 1h 40min).

Continue N down the broad easy-angled ridge. In 1km this ridge splits, one branch going NNW and the other NNE, enclosing Coire Gorm. In misty weather be careful to keep to the NNE, as the other branch goes out along the wrong side of Coire Gorm. The route drops to a col at about 780m, beyond which the ridge merges into the flat-topped dome of Meall a' Choire Leith. (6km; 670m; 2h 30min).

To return to the day's starting point, descend SW from Meall a' Choire Leith, cross the stream in Coire Gorm and continue in the same direction to the Allt Gleann Da-Eig. Finally, climb gradually across rough peaty terrain to the col at (596419) and follow a track down to the road at the prominent cairn. The route described is almost entirely outwith National Trust for Scotland territory, and may be subject to restrictions in the stalking season.

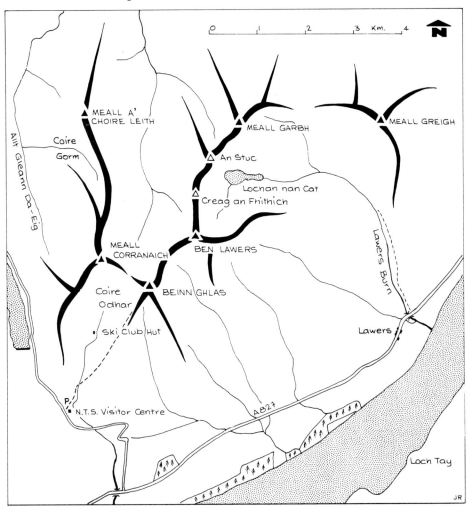

*Ben Lawers from the south-west ridge of Meall Corranaich*                    *D.J. Bennet*

**Beinn Ghlas**; 1103m; (OS Sheet 51; 626404); M45; *greenish-grey hill.*
**Ben Lawers**; 1214m; (OS Sheet 51; 636414); M9; *possibly from Gaelic Iabhar, meaning loud, describing the noise of a stream, or from ladhar meaning hoof or claw.*

These two Munros form the central and highest part of the range. They are best climbed from the National Trust for Scotland's Visitor Centre, which, being at a height of 450m, gives a good start for the climb. The road from Loch Tay to Glen Lyon is not kept open in winter, and in conditions of heavy snow the Visitor Centre may not be accessible by car.

Take the path (which for the first hundred metres or so is a timber walkway across boggy ground) NE up the W side of the Burn of Edramucky. In about ½km a signpost indicates the way to Ben Lawers across the burn to its E side. The path, which cannot possibly be missed in summer, goes NE up the grassy hillside onto the S ridge of Beinn Ghlas, and along this ridge, marked by many cairns and fading red paint marks. The summit of Beinn Ghlas has no cairn, but it is unmistakable for the drop on the N side is precipitous. (3½km; 660m; 2h).

Continue NE down the broad easy-angled ridge, following an obvious and much eroded path to the wide col at c.950m. For the first few metres on the Ben Lawers side the ridge is rocky, but thereafter the path continues up a wide grassy slope at a uniform angle to reach the summit where little now remains of the huge cairn that was once built to raise Lawers to the select company of Scotland's 4000ft mountains. (5km; 920m; 2h 40min).

The quickest return is probably by the same route. It is possible, but not particularly recommended, to avoid the reascent of Beinn Ghlas by going WSW from the Lawers-Ghlas col, descending slightly across the grassy hollow of the N corrie of Beinn Ghlas to reach the col at the head of Coire Odhar. There the old track down the E side of the corrie can still be discerned, and followed back to the Visitor Centre.

An attractive alternative route to Ben Lawers which avoids the summer crowds and eroded footpath of the way just described is to start at Lawers village, as the group of cottages and farms on the A827 road near the foot of the Lawers Burn is known. Follow the route described on the next page for Meall Greigh up the Lawers Burn and continue past the dam to Lochan nan Cat. This lochan is at the heart of the range, lying in a beautiful remote corrie above which Ben Lawers and its neighbouring Top An Stuc rise in steep craggy slopes. Climb S from the lochan to reach the ENE ridge of Ben Lawers and follow this to the summit. (7½km; 1000m; 3h 20min).

No restrictions on either of these routes in the stalking season.

Map on page 29.

*The ascent to Meall Greigh*                                                    *D.J. Bennet*

**Meall Greigh**; 1001m; (OS Sheet 51; 674437); M134; *hill of the horse studs.*
**Meall Garbh**; 1118m; (OS Sheet 51; 644437); M35; *rough hill.*

These two mountains form the north-eastern end of the great Ben Lawers range. Meall Greigh is the endmost point, well seen from the road near Lawers Hotel; it is a rounded mountain, grassy on all sides with a few small crags just E of the summit. Meall Garbh is not well seen from the road. Its craggy S face overlooks Lochan nan Cat, and with An Stuc and Ben Lawers it forms a grand semi-circle of steep mountainside enclosing this beautiful lochan. To the N it throws down two long grassy ridges, NNW and NE, to Glen Lyon.

The ascent of these two mountains can equally well be made from Glen Lyon or along the Lawers Burn above Loch Tay. The latter route has the advantage of giving very fine views of Ben Lawers rising above Lochan nan Cat; it starts from the A827 road at the bridge over the Lawers Burn where a private road leads uphill to Machuim farm. (There is limited roadside car parking, and space for 2 or 3 cars a short distance up the farm road). The route beyond the farm follows a good track along the edge of the fields with the fine larch-clad gorge of the Lawers Burn on the left. Once beyond the highest wall and into National Trust for Scotland territory it is quite possible to climb due N to the top of Meall Greigh over easy grassy slopes. Alternatively, the path up the Lawers Burn may be followed; contrary to the indication on the OS map, this path does not cross the burn, but remains on its NE bank. The S face of Meall Greigh is quite featureless, and in misty weather the stream which comes down this side of the hill may be a useful landmark to follow. The summit is a smooth rounded dome; there is a lower top with a small cairn about 150 metres NW. (4½km; 820m; 2h 30min).

The W ridge of Meall Greigh leading towards Meall Garbh is broad, grassy and featureless. In thick weather an accurate compass bearing is essential. Beyond the col (830m) the route continues more steeply up the grassy shoulder of Meall Garbh until the NE ridge is reached, and a fairly well marked path leads SW to the top where a tiny cairn is perched on the crest of the ridge. (8km; 1110m; 3h 40min).

On the descent it is best to follow, in part at least, the uphill route towards the Meall Greigh col, and then descend SE towards the catchment dam on the Lawers Burn. In this way the rather steep SE face of Meall Garbh is avoided.

No restrictions during the stalking season.

Map on page 29.

*The summit of Meall Garbh in the Tarmachans*                              *D.J. Bennet*

**Meall nan Tarmachan**; 1043m; (OS Sheet 51; 585390); M87; *hill of the ptarmigans.*

The Tarmachan Hills, as they are commonly called, are among the best known in the Southern Highlands, and the knobbly outline of their four peaks seen from the River Dochart at Killin is one of the most familiar of our mountain landscapes. They lie about 5km north of Killin and only the highest, Meall nan Tarmachan, is a Munro, the others being Tops. The southern front of the group overlooking Loch Tay has a discontinuous line of crags just below the summits along its entire length. The northern side drops steeply but less rockily to remote corries.

The nearest road approach to Meall nan Tarmachan is ½km NW of the National Trust for Scotland Visitor Centre on the road from Loch Tay to Glen Lyon. A rough road branches off to the SW and contours round the S side of the Tarmachans, but it is possible to drive only a short distance along it to a locked gate. Walk along the road beyond this gate for a few hundred metres, then climb W up easy grassy slopes to reach the broad SSE ridge of Meall nan Tarmachan. Follow this ridge over a small knoll (c.914m), and descend slightly to the col below the craggy SE face. Continue straight ahead up a steep slope to reach a grassy rake below the upper rocks, turn right (N) along this rising rake for about 150 metres and finally climb up steep grass on the left (W) to the summit cairn. (3½km; 600m; 1h 50min).

The return may be made by the same route, but this short outing hardly does justice to the Tarmachans. It is much better to continue the traverse over the three lower Tops. A broad grassy ridge leads SW from Meall nan Tarmachan to a col marked by two tiny lochans. From there a well defined narrow path leads up to the sharp rocky summit of Meall Garbh (1026m). Continue W along a narrow ridge and drop steeply to the next col. From there the ascent of Beinn nan Eachan (c.1000m) might be confusing in mist were it not for the path which twists and turns along the knolly ridge. Continue SW down a grassy slope to the level continuation of the ridge across the next col, and up to Creag na Caillich (916m).

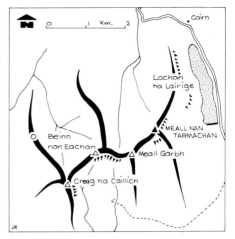

Return towards the col and descend SE into the grassy corrie to reach at (574373) a disused quarry and the road which leads in 4km back to the day's starting point.

*Meall Ghaordie from Glen Lyon*                                    *D.J. Bennet*

**Meall Ghaordie**; 1039m; (OS Sheet 51; 514397); M90; *possibly from Gaelic gairdean, meaning a shoulder, hand, arm.*

Meall Ghaordie rises between Glen Lochay and Glen Lyon, about 10km north-west of Killin. It is rather an isolated Munro, being far enough away from its neighbours, the Tarmachans to the east and Beinn Heasgarnich to the west to be usually climbed by itself. On the Glen Lochay side it has uniform featureless grassy slopes rising from glen to summit in a single sweep, and this aspect of the hill lacks character. On the north, overlooking Glen Lyon, there are two prominent spurs Creag an Tulabhain and Creag Laoghain which end steeply above the glen. The easiest and most usual route for the ascent is from Glen Lochay, although the approach from Glen Lyon is probably more interesting.

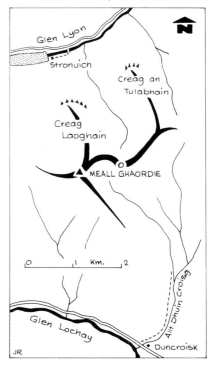

Start about 5km up Glen Lochay near Duncroisk. A short way along the road beyond the farm, on the NW side of the Allt Dhuin Croisg, a track leads through some fields onto the higher open hillside. Follow this track for about 1½km until, just beyond a sheepfank, a fence is reached. From there climb NW directly towards the summit up a broad shoulder of grass and heather. An iron post marks the way and then for several hundred metres the gradient is easy until some small outcrops of rock are reached, and just above them the summit appears. The OS trig point stands inside a fine circular cairn, a sheltered spot on a windy day. (4½km; 890m; 2h 30min).

*The upper part of the Sron nan Eun ridge leading to Creag Mhor*                    *G. S. Johnstone*

**Creag Mhor**; 1048m; (OS Sheets 50 and 51; 390361); M80; *big rock.*
**Beinn Heasgarnich**; 1076m; (OS Sheet 51; 413383); M61; *perhaps sheltering or peaceful hill.*

These two mountains of the Forest of Mamlorn are on the north side of Glen Lochay near its head, some 17 kilometres west of Killin. In common with many of their neighbouring hills in Breadalbane they are for the most part grassy, with no notable crags or rocky corries. Creag Mhor has two well defined ridges enclosing Coire-cheathaich at the head of Glen Lochay, and its north face immediately below the summit is fairly steep and rocky. Beinn Heasgarnich is a massive mountain of broad grassy ridges and corries, lacking outstanding features. There is a considerable area of peat moor at a height of about 650m just to the east of the summit.

The public road up Glen Lochay ends just beyond Kenknock farm. A private Hydro-Electric Board road climbs NW out of the glen at this point, crossing the east side of Beinn Heasgarnich at about 530m before dropping to Glen Lyon. If, as is sometimes the case, the gates on this road are not locked, there seems to be no objection to driving over it. Another rough private road continues up the glen.

To traverse the two mountains, Creag Mhor first, walk along the road up Glen Lochay beyond Kenknock for 5km to Batavaime. Climb the steep grassy hillside NW to reach the ESE ridge of Creag Mhor at Sron nan Eun, and continue up this ridge following traces of a path to the summit. (9km; 830m; 3h 30min).

To avoid the steep rocky descent of the NE face of Creag Mhor to the col at Lochan na Baintighearna, it is advisable to go NW then N for ½km down the broad ridge leading to Meall Tionail before turning E into the grassy corrie which leads down to the col at about 660m. From there the route to Beinn Heasgarnich climbs steeply at first up grassy slopes and continues along a broad undulating ridge to the flat summit. (13km; 1260m; 5h).

The quickest, if not quite the most direct return to the day's starting point is to descend E into the Coire Ban Mor and follow the Allt Tarsuinn across the peaty moor to the cairn at the summit of the Hydro-Electric Board road, and finally down this road to Glen Lochay.

*Beinn Heasgarnich from Coire Ban Mor*                              *K.M. Andrew*

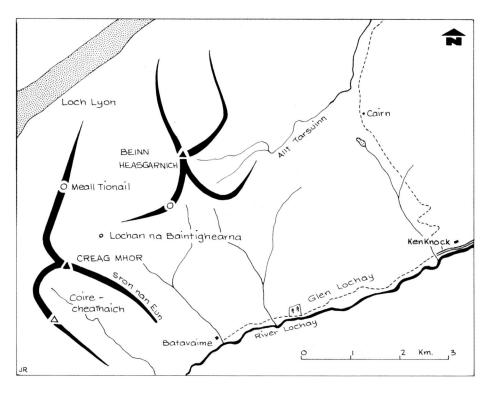

*Sgiath Chuil above Glen Dochart*                                    *D.J. Bennet*

**Meall Glas**; 960m; (OS Sheet 51; 431322); M193; *greenish-grey hill.*
**Sgiath Chuil**; 935m; (OS Sheet 51; 463318); M238 ; *back wing.*

Between Glen Dochart and Glen Lochay there is a range of low hills which to the east above Killin are little more than high moorland. Further west, Meall Glas and Sgiath Chuil are the only two Munros in this area, and they can be easily climbed together from Auchessan in Glen Dochart. From this glen both rise gradually from the wide strath over rough moorland to their steep upper slopes. Meall Glas shows a fairly continuous escarpment of steep grass and broken rocks around its southern flank, and Sgiath Chuil is characterised by its prominent summit rocks, resembling the prow of a ship.

From Auchessan follow a track on the E side of the unnamed stream which flows down from Creag nan Uan. This track ends once high ground is reached, and a course slightly W of N should be taken over rough featureless moorland to aim for the col just E of Meall Glas, where an easy grass slope leads up to the ridge. From there the summit of Meall Glas is a short distance W. (6km; 800m; 2h 40min).

Return E along the broad ridge, passing a prominent cairn at Pt.908m to reach Beinn Cheathaich (937m). The direct descent ESE from this Top is very steep, even rocky, for a short distance; however, a short diversion N before turning ESE avoids this minor difficulty. Lower down easy grassy slopes lead to the wide peaty col at the head of the Allt Riobain. The W face of Meall a' Churain (918m) rises directly above the col in uniformly steep grass slopes 300m high, and the summit ridge leading S to Sgiath Chuil is almost level. The cairn of this peak is right on the edge of the crag which is so prominent from below. (10½km; 1180m; 4h 20min).

The descent goes SW down easy grassy slopes towards the Allt Riobain, which can be followed downstream for about 1km before bearing away SW below Creag nan Uan to rejoin the uphill route.

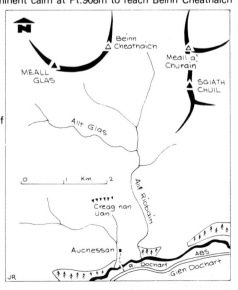

*Ben Challum at the head of Glen Lochay*                                      *D.J. Bennet*

**Ben Challum**; 1025m; (OS Sheet 50; 387323); M103; *Malcolm's hill.*

The north-east side of Strath Fillan between Crianlarich and Tyndrum is dominated by the slopes of Ben Challum, the largest and highest of the hills on that side of the strath. Seen from the south, from Crianlarich or the head of Glen Falloch, the main impression of the mountain is of the wide expanse of grassy hillside above the River Fillan, rising at an easy angle to the dome of the South Top (997m), behind which the true summit is hidden. The remoter side of the mountain above the head of Glen Lochay is very different, for the north face is steep and craggy.

The most convenient starting point in Strath Fillan is at Kirkton farm. (Cars should be left at the roadside before crossing the bridge over the River Fillan). Near Kirkton farm are the remains of St. Fillan's chapel, and nearby there are two old graveyards. From the chapel take the track uphill past the higher graveyard and cross the West Highland Line by an unofficial level crossing. Leave the track and strike NE directly uphill; there is no path, but none is needed for the walking is easy up grassy slopes, without much interest unless the day is clear enough to give views of the great mountains Ben More, Stob Binnein and Ben Lui on the far side of the strath.

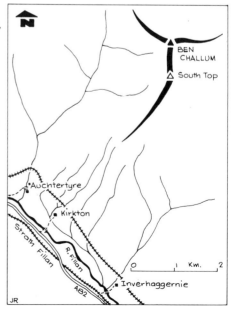

The route goes over flatter ground and a slight knoll, and a fence on the right hand side shows the way up the next rise. The fence ends abruptly, a few hundred metres further a small cairn is passed, and a short distance beyond it the South Top is reached, its summit being a large rock with a cairn nearby.

In clear weather the continuation to Ben Challum is obvious, but in a "white-out" the terrain may be confusing as a descent due N from the South Top would lead one astray. There is a little narrow hollow a few metres W of the South Top, and on its W side is the ridge leading onwards. Once on this ridge there are no route-finding problems, a gradual descent followed by a steeper ascent leads to the large summit cairn overlooking the steep N face. (5½km; 900m; 2h 50min).

*Beinn Dorain*                                                    *D.J. Bennet*

**Beinn Dorain;** 1076m; (OS Sheet 50) 326378); M62 *from Gaelic dobhran, may be hill of the otter but more likely hill of the streamlet.*
**Beinn an Dothaidh;** 1002m; (OS sheet 50; 332408); M130; *hill of the scorching or singeing.*

These two peaks are the southern half of the great semicircular range of mountains which overlook Loch Tulla and the headwaters of the Orchy. Beinn Dorain in particular, with its great upsweep above the West Highland Railway and its conical shape is one of the most familiar mountains in Scotland, in full view from the A82 road between Tyndrum and Bridge of Orchy. Beinn an Dothaidh may not be so spectacular in appearance, but it too presents an uninterrupted bastion above Loch Tulla, and has a fine corrie on its north-east face. The two mountains are easily accessible from Bridge of Orchy.

From the station car park go through the underpass and out onto the rising moorland. Bear left (NE) for 100 metres past a little fenced enclosure along a well-worn path which continues up the S bank of the Allt Coire an Dothaidh. High up the corrie the path becomes very faint; follow the stream which flows down from the steep Y-shaped gully on Beinn an Dothaidh until a line of rusty fence posts is reached, then bear SE up steep grass to reach the col between the two mountains, marked by a large cairn.

Going to Beinn Dorain first, there is a path to follow most of the way. Climb due S up an easy angled slabby ridge, the edge of a rocky escarpment. In a few hundred metres the rocks end, and the ascent continues up a broad grassy slope, bouldery high up, to a large cairn. This is not the summit, which is 200 metres further S beyond a slight drop in the ridge. (4½km; 890m; 2h 30min).

After returning to the col, climb NNE diagonally up the grassy S flank of Beinn an Dothaidh. The present edition of the OS map is not accurate in showing two tops, there are three, separated by only slight drops along the broad summit ridge. The highest point is the central one. (7½km; 1140m; 3h 40min). Return to the col and descend Coire an Dothaidh by the uphill route.

Map on page 41.

*Looking up the Auch Gleann to Beinn Mhanach*                                    *K.M. Andrew*

**Beinn Mhanach**; 954m; (OS Sheet 50; 373412); M205; *monk hill.*

The twin rounded summits of Beinn Mhanach and its slightly lower Top, Beinn a' Chuirn, are well seen looking up the Auch Gleann from the A82 road midway between Tyndrum and Bridge of Orchy. They fill the distant head of the glen 8km to the north-east, and occupy a remote setting behind the Bridge of Orchy mountains at the head of Loch Lyon.

Beinn Mhanach is a grassy hill, steep on its south side. The south-west end of Beinn a' Chuirn is even steeper, and craggy just below the top. Although the most direct approach seems to be up the Auch Gleann, another route which is slightly shorter in distance is from Achallader farm by Coire Achaladair, and this way enables the ascent of Beinn Mhanach to be combined with Beinn Achaladair.

For the Auch Gleann route cars must be left at the A82 road, as the side road down to Auch is private. Walk on past Auch, under the arches of the great viaduct of the West Highland Railway, and up the track in the Auch Gleann. This track crosses from one side of the Allt Chonoghlais to the other by fords several times. In wet weather, if the stream is in spate, the walker will be forced to stay on the SE side of the stream to Ais-an t-Sithein. Continue E on the N side of the Allt a' Chuirn, still following a rough track, to the watershed. Finally, climb the long, steep grass slope N to the flat summit of Beinn Mhanach. (9½km; 760m; 3h 30min).

The alternative route from Achallader Farm goes up the Coire Achaladair (see p.40). From the col at the head of the corrie traverse horizontally NE and follow a good sheep track (possibly an old stalker's path). This path crosses the grassy flank of Beinn Achaladair and drops gradually to the 620m col at (354418). From there follow a fence ESE to reach the flat col 1km W of Beinn Mhanach, and go up the broad mossy ridge to the summit. (8½km; 920m; 3h 30min). This route can very conveniently be extended by returning to the col at (354418), climbing NNW up Coire nan-Clach to Beinn Achaladair and continuing to Beinn a' Chreachain as described on the next page.

Map on page 41.

*Beinn Achaladair and Beinn an Dothaidh from Loch Tulla*         *H.M. Brown*

**Beinn Achaladair**; 1039m; (OS Sheet 50; 345434); M91; *from the name of the settlement, which is from early Celtic, meaning the field of hard water.*

**Beinn a' Chreachain**; 1081m; (OS Sheet 50; 373441); M59; *hill of the rock or hill of the clamshell.*

These two splendid mountains form the north-western perimeter of the Bridge of Orchy group of peaks, presenting a great curving rampart overlooking the Water of Tulla and the south-western corner of the Moor of Rannoch. Beinn Achaladair, in particular, has a continuously steep face above Achallader farm, and this face continues below Meall Buidhe to Coire an Lochain below the summit of Beinn a' Chreachain. The south-east side of these mountains is less impressive, forming a series of shallow grassy corries above Gleann Cailliche.

The traverse of these two mountains is best done from Achallader farm which is 1½km off the A82 road at the NE end of Loch Tulla. There seems to be no objection to cars being driven along the rough private road and parked just before reaching the farm.

Go S from the farm along a track, over the railway by a footbridge and up Coire Achaladair. There is a path on the W side of the stream, and the going is also very easy on the E side. It is quite possible to climb directly SE up the very steep slopes of Beinn Achaladair, aiming for the lowest point of the ridge between the two tops to avoid crags. It is easier, though longer, to climb up to the col at the head of the corrie and then turn N along the delightful grassy ridge to the South Top (1002m). Continue along the broad ridge to the summit of Beinn Achaladair, which is perched right at the edge of the steep NW face and commands a superb view in that direction. (7½km; 880m; 3h 10min).

Descend E along the edge of the crags of the NE corrie, and then drop steeply down among broken rocks to the 800m col at (353435). Here the ridge becomes broad and mossy again over the flat Top of Meall Buidhe (977m), then down for a short distance and finally up to the stony dome-shaped summit of Beinn a' Chreachain. (10½km; 1200m; 4h 20min).

Go down the NE ridge, which at one point is quite narrow, but perfectly easy. Near pt. 959m turn off to the WNW and descend grassy slopes, crossing the Allt Coire an Lochain just below Lochan a' Chreachain. Continue a descending traverse in the same direction through scattered birches and the fine old pine trees of Crannach Wood, a remnant of the Old Caledonian Forest. Cross the railway by a footbridge and go downhill towards the Water of Tulla to reach a track on the south side of the river which leads back to Achallader farm.

*Beinn Achaladair from Crannach Wood*                    D.J. Bennet

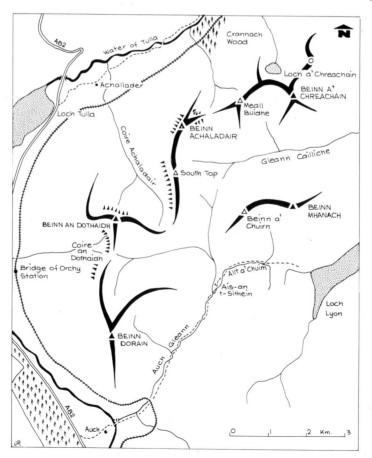

*Looking south-west from Bidean nam Bian to Ben Starav and Loch Etive*    *P. Hodgkiss*

# SECTION 3

### Strath Orchy to Glen Coe

*Beinn a' Chochuill from Beinn Eunaich*

*D.J. Bennet*

**Beinn a' Chochuill**; 980m; (OS Sheet 50; 110328); M168; *hill of the hood or shell.*
**Beinn Eunaich**; 989m; (OS Sheet 50; 136328); M152; *fowling hill.*

These two hills are joined at a bealach of 728m and are the highest points on a long ridge of 12km between Loch Etive and Glen Strae. Beinn a' Chochuill has a long, fairly level spine running from east to west, joined to the Ben Cruachan massif to the south by a bealach at 550m. Beinn Eunaich has a more pyramidal shape and is well seen from the main A85 road west of Dalmally. With the exception of Beinn Eunaich's west ridge, both hills give easy going on short grass, and both provide magnificent views of Ben Cruachan's majestic peaks and ridges.

Start from the B8077 road 2½km WNW of Dalmally at (137287) where a rough road leads off W across a cattle-grid and through a stand of Scots pine. Follow this road N skirting Castles Farm to the left to reach the Hydro-Electric Board road (gated) which traverses NW across the lower slopes of Beinn Eunaich. (The lower portion of this track is not shown on the Ordnance Survey 1:50000 map, but it is shown correctly on the One Inch to the Mile Tourist Map 'Ben Nevis and Glen Coe'). From the gate follow the track for 3km, climbing gradually, until less than ½km beyond a bridge the track divides. Take to the hillside of Beinn a' Chochuill and climb steeply NNW. The open grassy slopes gradually steepen and form an ill-defined ridge which leads to the E fore-top (896m). Beyond, the main ridge climbs very gradually W for 1km to the summit of Beinn a' Chochuill. (5½km; 930m; 2h 50min).

To continue the traverse to Beinn Eunaich, retrace the route back to the 896m fore-top, and drop down the ridge ENE to the bealach at 728m. Above, the W ridge of Beinn Eunaich has a rightward turn at 800m and beyond that point grows rockier and steepens steadily almost to the cairn, set at the N end of a short plateau. (8½km; 1200m; 4h). Descend due S down the broad grassy ridge leading to Stob Maol. On this descent there are fine views of Loch Awe and the long parallel ridges of the Dalmally Horseshoe.

No access problems by the route described in the stalking season.

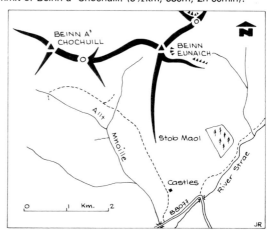

*Ben Cruachan from Beinn a' Chochuill*                                    *D.J. Bennet*

**Ben Cruachan**; 1126m; (OS Sheet 50; 069304); M31; *stacky hill.*

This sharp peak is the culminating point of a huge and complex massif, one of the finest and best known of Scottish mountains. It rises grandly above Loch Awe and its outlet through the Pass of Brander. The main spine of the mountain with its several peaks runs from east to west, and from it two arms go south enclosing an open corrie now dammed to hold the Cruachan Reservoir. Ben Cruachan itself lies at the junction of the westerly arm with the main spine, a peak with the classical form of four ridges rising from the four points of the compass to merge at the small top. Its north-west and north-east slopes fall very steeply into wild corries, and the uppermost 200m is composed of grey granite. With its high ridge of seven satellite peaks, Ben Cruachan is a very distinctive mountain as seen from other hills, and it is also prominent in views from the main A85 road between Tyndrum and Oban.

Start from this road several kilometres W of Dalmally in the Pass of Brander at the Cruachan Power Station. There are one or two roadside parking places nearby, but parking in the power station's Visitor Centre by climbers is apparently discouraged. Opposite the power station scramble under the left-hand arch of the railway bridge over the Falls of Cruachan burn, and immediately start climbing steeply up the path which goes along the W bank of the burn through open woodland of small oak, hazel and birch. The path leads up to more boggy ground above 300m and (although other paths lead up to the reservoir and along its W shore) the recommended ascent route strikes NW to the broad and grassy S ridge of Cruachan's southern Top, Meall Cuanail (918m). This ridge provides good views of lochs and islands, and there is a mere 70m of descent beyond Meall Cuanail before starting up the S ridge of Ben Cruachan. This ridge is littered with granite boulders through which a faint path leads intermittently to the sharp summit. (5km; 1200m; 3h 10min).

No access problems in the stalking season.

**Stob Diamh**; 998m; (OS Sheet 50; 095308); M141; *peak of the stag.*

This hill, one of Ben Cruachan's many peaks, lies near the east end of the main spine of the great massif, at the apex of an east-facing arc of peaks and ridges known as the Dalmally Horseshoe. To its north-east and south are two slightly lower satellites, Sron an Isean (966m) and Stob Garbh (980m). The circuit of these three peaks is over smooth terrain set at a generally easy angle.

Start 2½km WNW of Dalmally on the B8077 road where a gate at (134283) marks the beginning of an old railway track to a disused lead mine. Follow the track NW for 1km and continue in the same direction on a faint path to a bridge across the Allt Coire Ghlais at (120296). Due W there is some wet, humpy ground before the angle increases to lead onto the S arm of the Horseshoe. Above 450m the ridge levels out and there are fine views S to the crags of Beinn a' Bhuiridh. At 900m the ridge merges with that running S from Stob Garbh, and a faint path is joined leading N to this Top. The ground drops steeply for 60m N of Stob Garbh and then rises gradually to Stob Diamh along a broad ridge. (5km; 1000m; 2h 50min).

*Stob Diamh and the Dalmally Horseshoe*                    *J. Renny*

There is another steep descent of 100m ENE beyond Stob Diamh before the ridge rises to Sron an Isean. From this last Top an easy-angled descent follows its E ridge, eventually curving SE and latterly dropping S over steep grass slopes to the same wet humpy ground of the start and to another bridge at (122297) just below the confluence of the Allt Coire Ghlais and the Allt Coire Creachainn. From there the disused lead mine is several hundred metres SE.

No access problems in the stalking season.

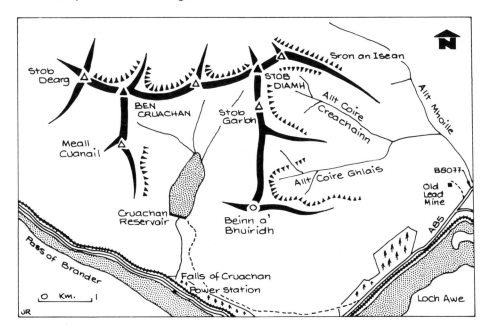

*Ben Starav from Glen Etive*                                                                    *A. Thrippleton*

**Ben Starav;** 1078m; (OS Sheet 50; 126427); M60; *origin unknown.*
**Glas Bheinn Mhor;** 997m; (OS Sheet 50; 153429); M142; *big greenish-grey hill.*

Both these hills stand up proudly at the foot of Glen Etive, and are well seen from the road near the foot of this glen. Ben Starav looks its full height and is clearly of great bulk, having a distinctive north ridge rising in one sweep from sea-level to summit. Glas Bheinn Mhor presents a classical pyramidal form with a very steep north face, but it can be seen to be really an incidental peak on the high ridge which extends east from Ben Starav.

From the Glen Etive road at (136467) where cars can be parked, follow a private track (not readily seen from the road) which drops E to cross the River Etive and reach the cottage of Coileitir. Continue SW along a path to the Allt Mheuran and SE to a bridge 200 metres upstream. Cross the bridge and continue along the path on the W bank for ½km before bearing right to gain the broad lower slopes of the N ridge of Ben Starav. The great length and height of this ridge is very noticeable, and its angle eases only at two shoulders at 500m and 800m. Steep slopes fall away on both sides until a parallel ridge merges with it at the 800m shoulder. The uppermost 200m steepens and is littered with granite boulders. There is a splendid view from the top, looking down Loch Etive to Ben Cruachan, and on a clear day further to the Paps of Jura. (5km; 1060m; 3h).

Starting S from the summit, and quickly veering SE, the Top of Stob Coire Dheirg (1068m) is soon reached, and ½km further ENE another little point is reached where the ridge turns ESE and drops to a bealach at 760m. Continue E, climbing over a minor grassy top (892m), dropping 70m and finishing up a broad rockier ridge to the summit of Glas Bheinn Mhor. (8½km; 1370m; 4h 10min).

Do not descend NNW from the summit of Glas Bheinn Mhor for the ridge in that direction is remarkably steep, possibly dangerously so if the grass is wet or there is snow. Instead, descend the E ridge until after ½km it is easy to drop down N into the corrie at the head of the Allt Mheuran and follow this stream back to Glen Etive by the path on its NE side.

*Glas Bheinn Mhor from Glen Etive*                                    G. Blyth

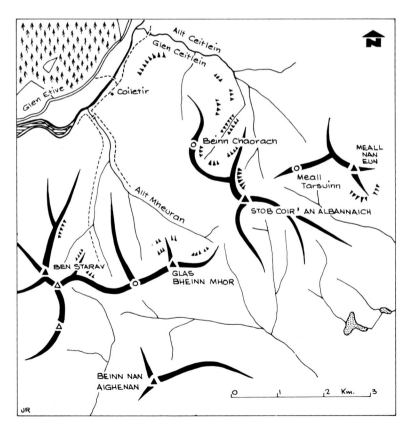

*Beinn nan Aighenan from the Starav-Glas Bheinn Mhor col*                    *D.J. Bennet*

**Beinn nan Aighenan;** 960m; (OS Sheet 50; 149405); M192; *hill of the hinds.*

A truly remote hill lying 6km south-east of the head of Loch Etive, and hidden behind other hills at the head of Glen Kinglass. It is bulky, with steep lower slopes and one distinctive high-level ridge running east from the summit over extensive pavements of granite.

Beinn nan Aighenan can be combined with Ben Starav and Glas Bheinn Mhor (qv), adding 4km and 500m of climbing to the traverse of those two mountains, or it may be climbed by itself. In the latter case the start is the same as for Ben Starav as far as the foot of the N ridge of that mountain. Proceeding to Beinn nan Aighenan, continue S up the W bank of the stream (not the Allt Mheuran) which comes down from the lowest point of the Ben Starav - Glas Bheinn Mhor ridge at (139424). There is a good path for a long way up into the corrie, and where it ends a faint path continues steeply up to the bealach at 760m on the ridge above.

In poor visibility very careful navigation is needed for the next section of the route, taking a slanting descent SSE across rough slopes and past a sprinkling of tiny lochans to the next bealach at 610m, 1½km NNW of Beinn nan Aighenan. Above, a craggy ridge climbs steeply SSE to the summit of the hill, from where there is a surprisingly open view E to Loch Tulla and Beinn Achaladair. (8km; 1100m; 3h 40min). Return by the same route, with another 150m of ascent to cross the ridge between Ben Starav and Glas Bheinn Mhor.

An alternative route to Beinn nan Aighenan from the east starts from Victoria Bridge near the west end of Loch Tulla, reached along the A8005 road from Bridge of Orchy. Although involving a long distance, this way makes use of the excellent track from Loch Tulla to Loch Etive, and provides splendid views of the remote southern corries between Ben Starav and Stob Ghabhar. From Victoria Bridge follow the track along the N side of the Linne nam Beathach to Loch Dochard and over the watershed to the headwaters of the River Kinglass. Descend about 1½km and 100m from the pass to a bridge across the River Kinglass and climb 300m of steep rough ground to reach the crest of the long E ridge of Beinn nan Aighenan. This ridge undulates and twists for 3km over pavements of cream coloured granite, over a fore-top to reach the summit. (13km; 1000m; 4h 40min).

Map on page 47.

*Approaching Stob Coir'an Albannaich from the south-east*                    P. Hodgkiss

**Stob Coir'an Albannaich;** 1044m; (OS Sheet 50; 169443); M86; *peak of the corrie of the Scotsmen.*
**Meall nan Eun;** 928m; (OS Sheet 50; 192449); M250; *hill of the birds.*

These two hills lie near the foot of Glen Etive and to its east. Stob Coir'an Albannaich rises so steeply from the glen that its summit cannot be seen above the lower slopes, while Meall nan Eun can be glimpsed at the head of the Allt Ceitlein. From the opposite viewpoint, however, near the west end of Loch Tulla, Stob Coir'an Albannaich shows its sharp pointed summit and Meall nan Eun appears as a great dome with a distinctive concave corrie on its south-east flank. These hills form the north-eastward extension of the great undulating ridge which starts at Ben Starav and separates Glen Etive from the streams flowing towards Glen Kinglass and Loch Tulla.

The starting point for the traverse is the same as for Ben Starav (qv), but after crossing the River Etive and before reaching Coileitir cottage strike SE uphill through open birch woodland. Climb up the SW side of the straight deep gully, the most prominent of several streams which tumble down this steep hillside. Above about 550m the climb becomes less steep as one reaches the broad NW shoulder of Stob Coir'an Albannaich, and the going is much easier up the broad ridge over extensive pavements of bare granite. At 850m a minor bump, Beinn Chaorach, is passed and after a short descent the route bears ESE up an open slope which converges to a narrow ridge where the large summit cairn of Stob Coir'an Albannaich stands above the granite cliffs of the NE face. (5km; 1040m; 3h).

The continuation to Meall nan Eun involves a series of 'dog-legs' that require accurate compass work in bad visibility, although the route is obvious in clear weather. From the summit of Stob Coir'an Albannaich descend E for less than ½km to a levelling in the ridge at 880m. At this point the cliffs on the N side of the ridge disappear and it is possible to go NNW steeply down mixed rock and grass to a bealach sprinkled with tiny lochans at 750m. Now turn ENE and climb over the top of Meall Tarsuinn (875m), descend to 790m and climb again to the rim of the summit plateau of Meall nan Eun, whose cairn lies some distance away to the SE. (8km; 1310m; 4h).

To return to Glen Etive go NW across the plateau and descend in the same direction to the headwaters of the Allt Ceitlein. Cross to the N bank to reach a path and easy going down to the Etive where the track leads back to the day's starting point.

Map on page 47.

*Stob a' Choire Odhair and Stob Ghabhar from Rannoch Moor*                    *D.J. Bennet*

**Stob Ghabhar;** 1087m; (OS Sheet 50; 230455); M54; *goat peak.*
**Stob a' Choire Odhair;** 943m; (OS Sheet 50; 258461); M223; *peak of the dun-coloured corrie.*

These two hills lie a few kilometres north-west of the west end of Loch Tulla, from where Stob Ghabhar in particular makes a fine sight through the fringe of mature Scots pine along the lochside. The approach to these hills is along the A8005 road from Bridge of Orchy past Inveroran Hotel to the end of the public road at Victoria Bridge. Stob Ghabhar is a well formed peak with deeply scalloped corries and its summit at the apex of three ridges. Stob a' Choire Odhair, with its south-east shoulder Beinn Toaig, though lower, is more prominent in views from the A82 road north of Bridge of Orchy.

From Victoria Bridge follow the track W along the N side of the Linne nam Beathach for 1½km to a small corrugated iron hut. Turn N and continue along a good, but sometimes very wet path on the E side of the Allt Toaig for a further 2km. At (252446) the path crosses a burn on whose W side a broad heathery ridge rises towards the summit of Stob a' Choire Odhair. Though not at first apparent, there is a well engineered stalker's path zig-zagging for 300m up this ridge, and this is followed. The path ends on bouldery ground and more open slopes lead to the stony summit of Stob a' Choire Odhair. (6km; 760m; 2h 40min).

Descend W along a broad ridge to the wide knolly bealach between Stob a' Choire Odhair and Stob Ghabhar at about 680m. Continue W gradually uphill for ½km, then turn SW and climb more steeply up rough slopes with some scree to reach the crest of a narrow ridge called the Aonach Eagach (991m). Turn W and follow a faint path on the left of the crest which avoids those sections of the ridge which are narrow and exposed, and require some scrambling. Two minor bumps on the ridge are passed before it merges with the SE ridge and this is climbed NW along the edge of the steep NE face of Stob Ghabhar to the top. (9km; 1220m; 4h 10min).

On the descent go down the SE ridge of Stob Ghabhar and continue to the flatter ground of the glen. If the Allt Toaig is not too full, cross it to rejoin the uphill path. Otherwise keep on the W side of this stream to the track from Clashgour farm down to Victoria Bridge.

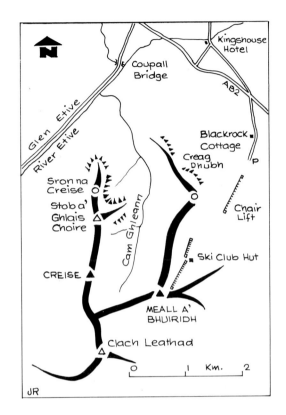

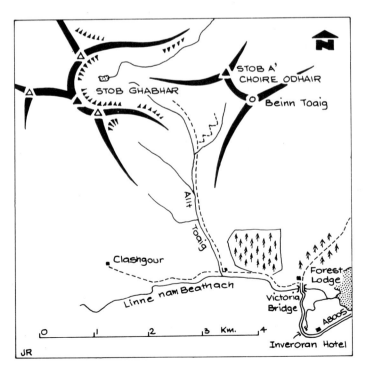

*The Black Mount and Meall a' Bhuiridh from Rannoch Moor*                    D. Scott

**Creise**; 1100m; (OS Sheet 41; 238507); M48; *origin unknown.*
**Meall a' Bhuiridh**; 1108m; (OS Sheet 41; 251503); M43; *hill of the bellowing (of the stags).*

These two mountains are the highest points at the northern end of that great range on the west edge of Rannoch Moor, the Black Mount. They form a horseshoe ridge overlooking the head of Glen Etive, and it is from there, near the point where the narrow road down Glen Etive leaves the A82, that the finest view of the group is had. All the peaks are visible, and the finest feature is the steep north-east face of Stob a' Ghlais Choire (996m), the north Top of Creise. Meall a' Bhuiridh is a particularly prominent mountain, fronting onto Rannoch Moor and having on the long-lasting snowfields of its north-east corrie the chair lifts and tows of one of Scotland's principal ski mountains. Behind it, Creise (which is not named on the Ordnance Survey 1:50000 map) is the highest point of the 3km long ridge which extends from Sron na Creise to Clach Leathad.

The traverse of this group is a fine mountaineering expedition, with river crossings and some steep scrambling to give it character and interest. These difficulties can be avoided, and in bad weather probably should be avoided, by an alternative route.

For the 'grand traverse', assuming fair conditions, start from the Glen Etive road just N of the bridge over the River Coupall and cross the River Etive. Bear S across the rough moor, crossing two burns, to reach the foot of the N ridge of Sron na Creise. Careful route finding will enable a way to be found up this fine steep ridge, and high up there is some good scrambling (avoidable on the left) before the top is reached. Now follow the broad rocky ridge S over Stob a' Ghlais Choire to Creise. (4km; 900m; 2h 30min). Continue S along the ridge for 600 metres to an almost imperceptible top (1068m), a little beyond which a spur falls steeply E. Descend this spur over granite boulders (faint path) to a well defined col, and climb the ridge leading ENE to Meall a' Bhuiridh. (6km; 1100m; 3h 10min). Descend N along the broad shoulder above Cam Ghleann, thus avoiding the machinery (and possibly crowds) of the ski slopes, and at Pt. 749m turn NW down the Creag Dhubh ridge to the moor and the re-crossing of the River Etive.

In bad weather, particularly if the River Etive is in spate, the preceding route may well not be possible. In that case start at the car park at the foot of the White Corries chair lift and climb the path under the lift to the more level slopes of Coire Pollach. Bear SW to reach the descent route described in the preceding paragraph and follow this in reverse to Meall a' Bhuiridh and Creise. Return by the same way.

Map on page 51.

*Beinn Sgulaird from Loch Creran*                                    *D.J. Bennet*

**Beinn Sgulaird;** 937m; (OS Sheet 50; 053461); M233; *origin unknown.*

Beinn Sgulaird stands at the head of Loch Creran, and forms a distinctive undulating ridge of granite running from south-west to north-east. Three km of this ridge lie above 800m, and although there are extensive grasslands on the lower western slopes, much granite is exposed elsewhere, particularly on the summit ridge and in the corrie on its north-west side, where smooth pink slabs drop steeply below the summit. There is a fine view of the mountain from the road on the north shore of Loch Creran.

In order to avoid walking through the policies of the house at Druimavuic, start from the A823 road about ¾km N at (011455) where there is a gate giving access to the wooded hillside. The mixed deciduous trees and conifers soon thin out, and above them climb ESE up steepening grass slopes to a minor top at 488m. A short, steep descent is followed by the continuation of the ridge, broad and grassy, until the first of the granite tops is reached, 863m, where there is a tiny lochan on the ridge between the two cairns.

Bear NE and descend a steep bouldery slope for 70m, then climb the rough, rocky ridge to the next top, 848m. Descend again quite steeply for 60m, and finally go up the narrowing ridge of granite slabs and boulders to the large summit cairn (5½km; 1110m; 3h 10min). Views to the west down Loch Creran include the island of Lismore and the hills of Mull and Morvern.

The return by the same route involves more ups and downs along the ridge, repaid in good weather by superb views. A quicker return to Druimavuic can be made by descending due W from the summit, steep and rocky at first, but then down easy grass slopes and through scattered birch woods to a hill track leading to Taravocan farm. From there a private road leads to the A828 near the day's starting point.

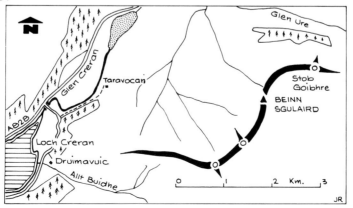

*Beinn Fhionnlaidh from the head of Loch Creran*                                                              *D.J. Bennet*

**Beinn Fhionnlaidh**; 959m; (OS Sheets 41 and 50; 095498); M196; *Finlay's hill.*

A shy hill lying to the west of Glen Etive, and only well seen from Sgor na h-Ulaidh or from Glen Creran to the south-west. It forms an east-west spine about 6km long, with steep and craggy slopes to the south and north, and the east end of the spine ends abruptly in a rocky bluff whose precipitous nature is only hinted at on the OS 1:50000 First Series map. Mainly composed of schistose rock, with bands of limestone providing the fertile basis for some rare alpines on the Glen Creran side. The summit ridge is bare and boulder strewn.

The shortest ascent route is from Glen Etive. From the A82 road drive almost 16km down the glen to within the second large afforestation where, 150 metres beyond the bridge over the Allt Charnan, there is a turn-off right to Invercharnan. Behind the house a Forestry Commission road leads SSW then WNW, parallel to the Allt nan Gaoirean, and it is followed for 3km to a sharp right turn. There on the left a path (marked by a small cairn) leads NW through a firebreak for 200 metres to a stile and the open hillside. Bear W, descending slightly to cross the Allt nan Gaoirean and climb the grassy hillside opposite towards the little col S of Pt 841m. (Shown as 821m on the First Series 1:50000 map). From this col climb N up stony slopes, then bear NW to reach the ridge of Beinn Fhionnlaidh, marked by a line of fence posts. Follow these W to a slight dip, at which point the fence-line turns S. Continue W then WSW up the narrowing ridge with an abrupt drop on its N side at the final steepening where, if the crest is followed, there are two short easy rocky steps to climb. (7½km; 960m; 3h 20min).

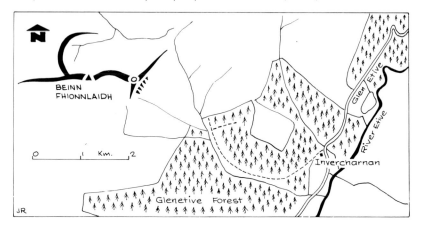

*Sgor na h-Ulaidh and Stob an Fhuarain from the east*                    J. Renny

**Sgor na h-Ulaidh**; 994m; (OS Sheet 41; 111518); M146; *peak of the treasure.*

Among the Glen Coe mountains, Sgor na h-Ulaidh is very much the forgotten and neglected one, hidden from the main road by the prominent projecting ridge of Aonach Dubh a' Ghlinne and lacking the bold features of Bidean nam Bian, in whose shadow it lies. However, it can be clearly seen from Beinn a' Bheithir, and from the hills on the south-east side of Glen Etive. Despite its retiring nature, Sgor na h-Ulaidh does have a distinctively mountainous character which is evident as one walks up the Allt na Muidhe into the wild glen which leads up to its steep northern face, and it is this glen which provides the usual approach.

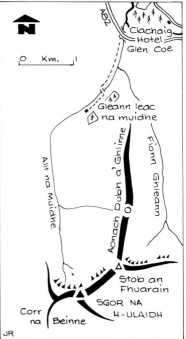

Start from the A82 road 2km W of Loch Achtriochtan along a Land Rover track that follows the W bank of the Allt na Muidhe for 1km before crossing to the E bank and continuing to the farmhouse of Gleann-leac-na-muidhe. The track continues for a further 1km, ending near a junction of streams where the glen turns S and Sgor na h-Ulaidh comes into view. Keep to the E bank of the burn and head S up the glen which is steeply enclosed by Creag Bhan and Aonach Dubh a-Ghlinne. After 1½km turn E and climb steeply up grass slopes riven by drainage channels of many little streams, and reach the ridge just N of the outlying Top of Stob an Fhuarain (968m). Traverse this peak and descend SW to the col at 860m; this col can be reached directly from the NW, but the final slope on that side is very steep and craggy. Continue SW up increasingly rocky ground to the cairn of Sgor na h-Ulaidh, which is on the brink of the steep N face. (6½km; 1040m; 3h 20min).

As an alternative to returning by the same route, continue W for ½km to the spur of Corr na Beinne and descend its steep N side to a col from which easy ground leads NE down to the head of the Allt na Muidhe.

*Buachaille Etive Mor*                                                          *J.E.S. Bennet*

**Buachaille Etive Mor, Stob Dearg;** 1022m; (OS Sheet 41; 223543); M106; *big herdsman of Etive, red peak.*

The Buachaille Etive Mor, and in particular its highest peak Stob Dearg, is one of the grandest and best-known mountains in Scotland, standing as it does in isolation and rising abruptly above the north-west corner of Rannoch Moor. The great walls, gullies and buttresses of Stob Dearg give that peak a decided air of impregnability, at least as far as the hill-walker is concerned, but the great cliffs which encircle the peak are breached on the north-west by Coire na Tulaich which gives a fairly easy walking route to the summit. The Buachaille Etive Mor is not just a single peak, but a 7km long ridge rising steeply above Glen Etive with three other peaks, Stob na Doire (1011m), Stob Coire Altruim (941m) and Stob na Broige (956m) along its length. The whole mountain is in National Trust for Scotland territory.

Start at Altnafeadh on the A82 road and follow the track down to the bridge across the River Coupall. Behind the white cottage of Lagangarbh take the right fork in the usually wet and muddy path, and continue SSW into Coire na Tulaich, crossing a burn and climbing up the path on its W bank. A few outcrops of rock call for a little easy scrambling, and the path ends at the foot of a scree slope at about 700m. Continue up the scree towards a narrowing gully which is probably best avoided by scrambling up rocky ledges on its E bank to emerge onto the broad ridge of the mountain at a flat bealach. Turn E and follow the path worn over pink rock and boulders, with many cairns, finally trending NE along the narrowing ridge to the summit. The view is extensive, most notable being the vast expanse of Rannoch Moor with the prominent peak of Schiehallion at its far edge. (3km; 750m; 2h).

The complete traverse of the ridge from Stob Dearg to Stob na Broige is a fine walk, and the return to Altnafeadh is best made by returning over Stob Coire Altruim to the col at (203531) between that peak and Stob na Doire. From there descend NNW to the Lairig Gartain and return along the path to Altnafeadh.

No restrictions on climbing at any time.

**Buachaille Etive Beag, Stob Dubh;** 958m; (OS Sheet 41; 179535); M197; *small herdsman of Etive, black peak.*

The Buachaille Etive Beag is in size and character the small brother of the Buachaille Etive Mor, and it has many similarities, both when seen from Rannoch Moor and from the lower reaches of Glen Etive. However, it lacks the grandeur of its big brother, and its highest point, Stob Dubh, is at the south-west end of its 4km ridge, the far end as seen from the A82 road. Only when seen from low down in Glen Etive does the Buachaille Etive Beag match its big brother in height and appearance. It lies entirely in National Trust for Scotland territory.

From the north the ascent route starts on the A82 road at (188563) where a signpost indicates the right-of-way 'Lairig Eilde to Glen Etive'. Follow the path SW for ½km, then turn uphill, traversing

*Buachaille Etive Beag from Glen Etive*                                    *D.J. Bennet*

towards the S and crossing two small burns, thus skirting beneath steeper and craggy slopes. At a third burn strike directly uphill to a well-defined bealach at 750m. A short diversion NE enables the Top of Stob Coire Raineach (925m) to be climbed. From the bealach climb SW up steepening rocky slopes to a little top (920m) beyond which, with one short descent, there is a level narrow ridge going for 1km to Stob Dubh. (4km; 740m; 2h 10min). There is a fine, though constricted view down Glen Etive.

A shorter route which might appeal to those staying in Glen Etive is the direct ascent of Stob Dubh from Dalness by its SSW ridge. This grassy ridge rises at a steady steep angle from the glen, and gives the climber no respite until he reaches the summit. (2½km; 870m; 2h).

No restrictions on climbing at any time.

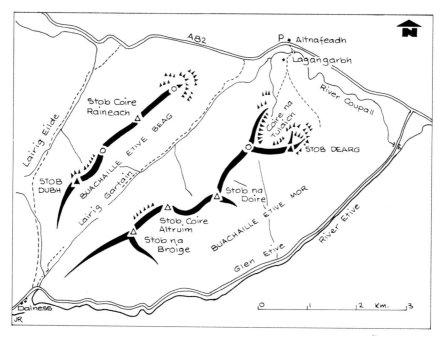

*Looking east along the Aonach Eagach towards Meall Dearg*                    D.J. Bennet

**Meall Dearg;** 953m; (OS Sheet 41; 161584); M208; *red hill.*

The north side of Glen Coe is hemmed in by the steep flanks of the Aonach Eagach, the notched ridge. From the roadside in the glen it is difficult to appreciate the true character of the ridge, its narrow crest and sharp pinnacles, and it is not easy to identify the individual summits along it. Meall Dearg is the lower of the two Munros on the Aonach Eagach, and is near its east end. Three sharp ridges culminate in its shapely top, and its south flank above Glen Coe is crag girt and riven by deep gullies, offering no easy route of ascent or descent. The usual route of ascent is from Glen Coe, but it involves first climbing Am Bodach (943m), the easternmost peak of the Aonach Eagach, and then traversing 1km of narrow ridge with a short section of easy rock climbing. A rope and a suitably experienced companion may be thought desirable.

Start at a car park on the A82 road a few hundred metres W of Allt-na-reigh at (173567) and take the signposted path which climbs steeply NE from the roadside. This path soon reaches the crest of the SE ridge of Am Bodach, and two possible routes are available. The more obvious is the direct ascent of the SE ridge, but it is in places steep and rocky, almost a scramble, though there is a path to follow, and higher up the angle eases and the ridge leads directly to the summit of Am Bodach. The alternative route follows the original path over the crest of the SE ridge into the narrow corrie on its E side. The path continues up the corrie on the W bank of the burn, fading as height is gained until only traces remain as the route veers NW to reach the main ridge at 800m. Once on the ridge turn SW and climb steepening slopes to the top of Am Bodach.

Descend WNW along the ridge and soon reach a sudden drop and a 20m scramble down polished rock. The route at this steep section starts on the N side of the ridge and works round to the crest where there is a steep descent of 3 or 4m on good holds. A path continues along the sharp ridge-crest, gradually climbing to a little top beyond which the final rocky slope leads to Meall Dearg. (3km; 870m; 2h 10min). This route is entirely in National Trust for Scotland territory, and there are no restrictions on access at any time.

An alternative route, involving no scrambling, starts at Caolasnacon on the A82 road between Glencoe and Kinlochleven, follows the Allt Gleann a' Chaolais to the col at the foot of the NE ridge of Meall Dearg, and continues up this ridge. (4½km; 910m; 2h 40min).

The classic traverse of the Aonach Eagach, one of the best ridge scrambles in Scotland, continues W from Meall Dearg. The next section along the ridge to the col below Stob Coire Leith involves a lot of excellent and in places exposed scrambling, up and down little gullies, slabs and chimneys, and round and over some little pinnacles. The route is obvious (in summer at least) and the rock is sound. From the col, where all difficulties end, there is a steep pull up to Stob Coire Leith followed by an easy and fairly level walk to Sgorr nam Fiannaidh.

*Looking west along the Aonach Eagach towards Sgorr nam Fiannaidh*                      *P. Hodgkiss*

**Sgorr nam Fiannaidh**; 967m; (OS Sheet 41; 141583); M183; *peak of the Fian warriors.*

This is the westernmost and highest peak of the Aonach Eagach ridge, separated by a drop of 100m from Stob Coire Leith (940m), the next Top along the ridge to the east. There is a sense of detachment about Sgorr nam Fiannaidh due to its position near the end of the ridge and the steepness of its flanks; on the south side above Glen Coe these slopes rise in a single steep and uninterrupted hillside 900m high. The summit provides a very fine view through the narrows of Loch Leven towards Garbh Bheinn in Ardgour.

Start the ascent from the A82 road in Glen Coe at the W end of Loch Achtriochtan, and climb due N up steepening grass slopes. With a little searching a faint path can be found for the first 150m, but higher up the climb becomes steeper and rougher and the uppermost 250m are composed of angular scree and boulders. The easiest ground is found by trending left to reach the ridge at about 900m a short distance W of the summit. (1 ½ km; 870m; 1h 50min).

Above Clachaig Hotel an obvious path scars the hill on the W side of the great tree-filled chasm of Clachaig Gully. This path is badly eroded with a lot of loose stones and rock which can be a hazard to climbers in the gully if dislodged, and despite its apparent popularity this route is not recommended. The south side of the Aonach Eagach is in National Trust for Scotland territory, and there is no restriction on climbing that side of the ridge at any time of the year. There may be restrictions on climbing on the north side during the stalking season.

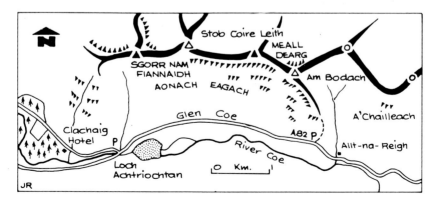

*Bidean nam Bian from Beinn a' Bheithir*                                        *G. S. Johnstone*

**Bidean nam Bian**; 1150m; (OS Sheet 41; 143542); M23; *peak of the mountains.*

The highest mountain in Argyll, Bidean nam Bian is a compact and complex massif, the name applying to the highest point as well as to the mountain as a whole. The main ridge is a north-facing arc with a subsidiary Y-shaped ridge projecting northwards to enclose three fine corries above Glen Coe. So high and steep are the peaks above the glen, the Three Sisters, that it is difficult to get a view of the summit of Bidean, which is hidden behind them, but from Loch Achtriochtan there is an impressive glimpse of the two huge buttresses beneath the summit. The two slightly lower Tops Stob Coire nan Lochan (1115m) and Stob Coire nam Beith (1107m) are more prominent when seen from the glen, both appearing as great rock peaks. The whole massif is rocky and steep-sided, and even the easiest walking routes to the summit of Bidean involve some mild scrambling.

Start just W of Loch Achtriochtan where the road to Clachaig Hotel leaves the A82. Climb over the wall at the W end of the bridge over the River Coe and follow the path on the W side of the burn coming down from Coire nam Beith. This path leads high up into the corrie, passing some fine waterfalls and at one point traversing across a steep rocky hillside where some easy scrambling is needed. At about 520m

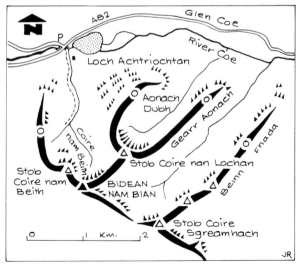

*The summit of Bidean nam Bian from the south-east, with the twin peaks of Beinn a' Bheithir beyond    K.M. Andrew*

there is a confluence of streams on the E of the path, and at this point, with the great rock cone of Stob Coire nam Beith directly ahead, there is a choice of routes.

One way goes SE, across a stream and up the corrie towards Bidean, still following a path with the great buttresses of Stob Coire nam Beith on one's right. Higher up, with the path fading, aim for the bealach at 1000m between Bidean nam Bian and Stob Coire nan Lochan, and climb steep boulder and scree slopes to reach that point. There turn SW and climb steeply and directly, passing the level shoulder at the top of the Diamond Buttress, to the summit of Bidean. (3½km; 1040m; 2h 30min).

The alternative route continues SSW from the confluence of streams in Coire nam Beith up a steepening slope of grass, boulders and scree to reach the main ridge of the mountain ½km WNW of Stob Coire nam Beith. Follow the path up the ridge to this peak, then SE to the W peak of Bidean, and finally a few hundred metres E to the summit. (3½km; 1080m; 2h 40min).

The N side of the mountain is in National Trust for Scotland territory, and there are no restrictions on climbing on that side at any time.

**Sgorr Dhearg;** 1024m; (OS Sheet 41; 056558); M104; *red peak.*
**Sgorr Dhonuill;** 1001m; (OS Sheet 41; 040555); M132; *Donald's peak.*

Beinn a' Bheithir, meaning hill of the thunderbolt, is a fine mountain rising above the narrows at the entrance to Loch Leven at South Ballachulish. Its two peaks lie on a long curving ridge which encloses north-facing corries, and except on their steepest slopes these corries are clothed with vast areas of conifers which cover the lower hillsides and extend high up into the heart of the mountain. Above the tree-line most of the ground is bouldery, that on Sgorr Dhearg being a pink quartzite, and that on Sgorr Dhonuill granite. There is a splendid view of the whole mountain from the A82 road near North Ballachulish, and there are superb views on a clear day from the summits, views which combine the mountains of Glen Coe and Lochaber with the seascapes to the west.

Leave the A828 road at (044595) about 1km W of the Ballachulish bridge and follow the minor road SSE for ½km to the group of houses at the foot of Gleann a' Chaolais where cars can be left. Continue S up the Forestry Commission road on the W side of the main stream, ignoring branch roads to the right. After 2km the road zig-zags up steeper ground, trending left past an old quarry and reaching a cross-road. Continue straight across and round another zig-zag until the road levels out at a concrete bridge and crosses a burn at (047569). Just E of this burn a cairn by the roadside marks the start of a path, cairned in places, which climbs SE through the trees onto the open hillside above the tree-line. Now climb S up rough grassland and boulders to the bealach (757m) between the two peaks of Beinn a' Bheithir.

*Sgorr Dhearg of Beinn a' Bheithir*                                    *K.M. Andrew*

From the bealach both peaks are easily reached along the main ridge of the mountain. There is a faint path up the stony ridge to Sgorr Dhearg. (5½km; 1000m; 3h). Return to the bealach and climb the ridge due W to a level section at 930m followed by a steep and narrow scramble to Sgorr Dhonuill. (7½km; 1250m; 3h 50min). Return to the bealach and descend by the route of ascent.

An alternative ascent of Beinn a' Bheithir, which can be combined with the above route to give a fine traverse, starts from Ballachulish. Go S from the school for 1km along a path, then climb SW up a steep and well defined ridge which leads to the main spine of the mountain a few hundred metres NE of Sgorr Bhan (947m), the north-east Top of Sgorr Dhearg. The ridge connecting these two summits forms a beautiful curving arc leading to Sgorr Dhearg (4km; 1040m; 2h 40min), and from there the traverse to Sgorr Dhonuill may be continued as described above.

No access problems in the stalking season.

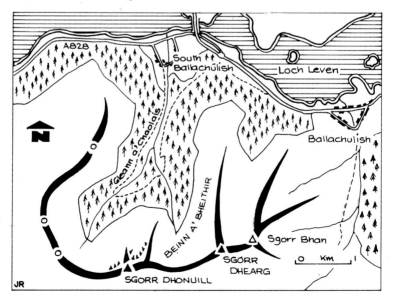

# SECTION 4

Loch Linnhe to Loch Ericht

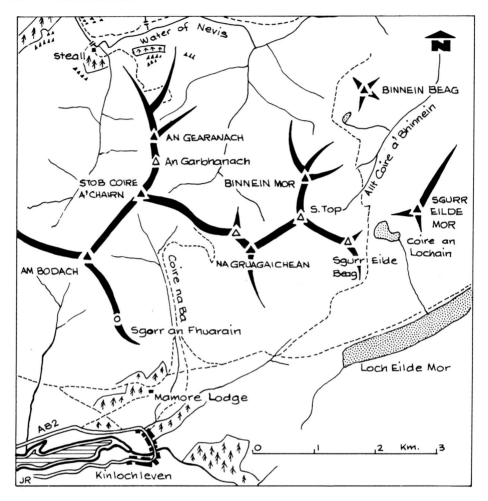

Between Loch Leven and Glen Nevis there stretches for 15 kilometres one of the finest mountain ranges in Scotland, the Mamores. Eleven Munros are linked by narrow curving ridges, their flanks scalloped by many corries, while through the mountains there is a remarkable network of stalker's paths, climbing up the corries and along the ridges, some of them taking spectacular lines across steep hillsides thus giving easy routes to many of the peaks.

There are three points of access to the Mamores that are particularly useful. On the south side one can start at sea-level from Kinlochleven, or drive up a rough road to Mamore Lodge at a height of 200m and park a car there for a small charge. From the lodge a Land Rover track traverses across the hillside, both to the east and west, at a height of about 250m, and gives access to the southern corries. If starting from Kinlochleven and heading for the eastern peaks, the following directions will be useful:-Leave the the A82 at the northern end of Kinlochleven, turning ESE along a street to reach a very simple white church in 250 metres (188623). From the E of the church a path starts N, soon turning E for 200 metres before descending to a bridge across a burn. Beyond, the path climbs through trees and, at their upper limit, forks. Take the right fork and follow it for 750 metres through humpy and undulating ground to a ford, beyond which is another fork. The left path goes N to the foot of Coire na Ba, the right path goes E towards Loch Eilde Mor, both paths joining the Land Rover track in a further few hundred metres. If heading towards the western peaks from Kinlochleven, follow the West Highland Way from the village school and climb diagonally NW up the wooded hillside, crossing the Mamore Lodge access road and reaching the Land Rover track higher up.

*Sgurr Eilde Mor above Coire an Lochain*                                        *G.S. Johnstone*

On the north side of the Mamores the public road up Glen Nevis gives access. Achriabhach is the starting point for the western peaks. Beyond there the road, very narrow and liable to congestion in summer, continues for a few kilometres to the car park at its end. From there walk through the magnificent gorge of the River Nevis to reach the upper glen and the eastern peaks of the range. This approach also serves for the Aonachs and Sgurr Choinnich Mor at the western end of the Grey Corries.

Many different combinations of Mamores can be climbed in a single day from one peak to all eleven. The latter is a magnificent traverse, but only for the very fit. It is not unduly difficult to do the lot in two or three days; however, in the following descriptions a more leisurely approach is taken, none of the expeditions described being at all long or strenuous.

**Sgurr Eilde Mor;** 1008m; (OS Sheet 41; 231658); M120; *big peak of the hind.*

This is the remotest of the Mamores, lying 6km north-east of Kinlochleven, and separated from the other peaks at the east end of the range by a low col at 740m. In appearance, particularly when seen on the approach from Kinlochleven, it is a steep conical peak of scree and quartzite boulders rising splendidly above Coire an Lochain. North-east from the summit the spine of the hill goes for 3½km towards the head of Glen Nevis, its crest paved with distinctive platelets of schist broken by outcrops of quartz.

Start from Kinlochleven or Mamore Lodge, and follow the Land Rover track E from the lodge to within 1km of Loch Eilde Mor (208635). There take the good stalker's path which climbs NE, quite gradually at first, then more steeply to reach Coire an Lochain where a high loch is set in a fine position among spectacular surroundings. Above the loch Sgurr Eilde Mor rises for 270m in uniformly steep scree slopes of rather uninviting appearance. Go round the N side of the loch and climb the easiest line up the fairly well-defined W ridge on steep and bouldery quartzite to the summit. (From Kinlochleven: 7km; 1010m; 3h 20min).

*Looking east from Squrr a' Mhaim to Binnein Mor*                          *D.J. Bennet*

**Binnein Mor;** 1128m; (OS Sheet 41; 212663); M30; *big peak.*
**Binnein Beag;** 940m; (OS Sheet 41; 222677); M228; *small peak.*

These two mountains lie north-east of Kinlochleven at the eastern end of the Mamore ridge. Binnein Mor is not only the highest, but also the finest of the range, having the classic mountain form of ridges and corries sweeping upwards to a narrow summit crest. From the north or south it appears as a single sharp peak, while from the east or west its level summit ridge gives it the appearance of a great tent. By comparison, Binnein Beag is small and quite different in shape, being a little conical peak. The two are separated by a high bealach at 750m.

The approach from Kinlochleven or Mamore Lodge follows the same route by track and stalker's path as that described for Sgurr Eilde Mor (qv) as far as Coire an Lochain. From there keep N along the path, dropping slightly, going left at a fork and descending NW for a further 100m. A rising traverse follows across the E face of Binnein Mor, crossing the headwaters of the Allt Coire a' Bhinnein to reach the wide bealach between the two peaks. Leave the stalker's path which has been followed to this point, and climb NE over scree and schistose boulders to the sharp summit of Binnein Beag. (9km; 1080m; 3h 50min). There is a splendid view - very open to the E towards the distant mass of Ben Alder, while the great bulk of Binnein Mor towers above in the SW.

Descend to the bealach and climb SSE to the toe of the ridge bounding the little NE corrie of Binnein Mor on its N side. This ridge is narrow and steep and gives an excellent scramble on sound schist. It emerges on the sharp summit ridge 200 metres N of the cairn. (11½km; 1460m; 5h). An easier alternative for the ascent of Binnein Mor is to traverse ½km SW from the bealach to reach the NNW ridge and climb the fine, but perfectly easy crest which curves up to the summit.

Continue S along the summit ridge to the South Top (1059m), and there turn SE down a broad ridge to another Top, Sgurr Eilde Beag (956m). From there descend SSE until at 840m a stalker's path is reached which leads in well engineered zig-zags down to join the path of the uphill route, and so back to Kinlochleven.

Map on page 64.

*Am Bodach from the head of Coire na Ba*                                    *D.J. Bennet*

**Na Gruagaichean**; 1055m; (OS Sheet 41; 203652); M71; *the maidens.*
**Stob Coire a' Chairn**; 981m; (OS Sheet 41; 185661); M165; *peak of the corrie of the cairn.*
**Am Bodach**; 1032m; (OS Sheet 41; 176651); M96; *the old man.*

These three peaks form an arc of ridges immediately north of Kinlochleven and make a natural traverse of not too great a length. Na Gruagaichean is particularly prominent when seen from the A82 road on the south side of Loch Leven, from where it has a huge tent-like appearance, and it is often mistaken for the hidden Binnein Mor. It has two tops separated by a rocky ridge which drops to a narrow gap. Am Bodach is another fine mountain with a particularly steep and rocky east face above the head of Coire na Ba. Between these two Stob Coire a' Chairn is a more modest peak situated at the point where the An Gearanach ridge runs out to the north. With the exception of the summits of Am Bodach and Na Gruagaichean, this part of the Mamore ridge is fairly grassy and gives easy walking.

Start from Kinlochleven or Mamore Lodge and reach the Land Rover track between Coire na Ba and Loch Eilde Mor as described for Sgurr Eilde Mor. From this track climb NE up steep grassy slopes for 500m to gain a stony ridge which leads N and narrows towards the summit of Na Gruagaichean. (4km; 1060m; 2h 40min). Descend very steeply NNW down a rocky slope to a narrow col and climb an equally steep ridge, very exposed on its NE side, to the North-west Top (1036m). Cross the short level summit and continue down the grassy ridge to the open bealach (783m) at the head of Coire na Ba.

Three stalker's paths converge at this point. Continue NW along one of them up the broad easy ridge to Stob Coire a' Chairn. (6km; 1300m; 3h 30min). Descend equally easily, crossing a small bump, to the next bealach from where the NE ridge of Am Bodach rises abruptly. This ridge is steep and rocky enough to make a pleasant scramble, and the angle is maintained almost to the summit cairn. (8km; 1550m; 4h 30min).

In descent follow the SSE ridge of Am Bodach towards the minor top of Sgorr an Fhuarain, which is best by-passed on the W. Grassy slopes lead easily SW down to the Land Rover track 1½km W of Mamore Lodge at the point where the path forming part of the West Highland Way leads down to Kinlochleven through open woodland.

Map on page 64.

*On the ridge between An Garbhanach and An Gearanach, looking towards Ben Nevis*    D.J. Bennet

**An Gearanach**; 982m; (OS Sheet 41; 188670); M162; *the complainer.*

An Gearanach is the northerly and highest point of the short narrow ridge which projects north from Stob Coire a' Chairn on the main spine of the Mamores. This latter peak is not named on the OS 1:50000 map; it is at (185661). The ridge passes over the rocky Top of An Garbhanach (975m) and for about a hundred metres at that point the crest is very narrow, rocky and exposed, falling steeply on both sides into narrow glens. The An Gearanach end is broader, grassy and perfectly easy, and north of this peak the ridge drops steeply towards Glen Nevis.

An Gearanach can be climbed equally well from Glen Nevis or, with rather more effort, from Kinlochleven. The Glen Nevis route starts at the car park at the road end and goes through the gorge, from where there is a magnificent view of the peak with its pendant waterfall. The path clings to the steep hillside, with crags above and the torrent of the River Nevis rushing below. Shortly after emerging onto the grassy flats of the upper glen, cross the river by a three-strand wire bridge and go E past the white climbers' cottage at Steall. Continue for ½km below the waterfall and past a wooded buttress until the path turns S up a little glen and becomes better defined. Climb the path in wide zig-zags until the last long traverse leads onto the NNE spur of An Gearanach, and follow this to the summit with fine views on either hand. (4½km; 850m; 2h 30min). The traverse along the narrow ridge to An Garbhanach is a pleasant airy walk, with some scrambling at its far end.

The alternative route from Kinlochleven involves first the ascent of the stalker's path up Coire na Ba (qv) to reach the main ridge SE of Stob Coire a' Chairn. From there either climb this peak and descend steeply NNE to the bealach below the craggy S end of An Garbhanach, or traverse below the NE face of Stob Coire a' Chairn to reach the bealach more directly. The ascent of An Garbhanach and its traverse are rocky, and some scrambling is involved before the ridge relents and leads easily to An Gearanach. (7km; 1130m; 3h 30min).

Map on page 64.

*Stob Ban from the east, with Mullach nan Coirean beyond*                    *D.J. Bennet*

**Mullach nan Coirean**; 939m; (OS Sheet 41; 122662); M231; *summit of the corries.*
**Stob Ban**; 999m; (OS Sheet 41; 148654); M138; *light-coloured peak.*

These two peaks lie at the western end of the Mamore ridge, and are most easily accessible from Glen Nevis. Mullach nan Coirean is a sprawling mass of grassy ridges enclosing several corries, as befits its name. Stob Ban makes a contrast with its shapely summit cone and fine line of buttresses and gullies on the north-east side of the peak. It makes a fine sight from the road near Glen Nevis youth hostel with its cap of quartzite looking curiously like snow in some lights. Though the Mullach is itself relatively shapeless, it does present an attractive profile when seen from the path through the Nevis gorge, and its summit is an unexpectedly rewarding viewpoint.

Start the traverse at Achriabhach in Glen Nevis from where access to the NNE ridge of Mullach nan Coirean can be gained through the forest. Go through the gate opposite the cottages and about 150 metres along the forest road take a path left (SW) through the trees to reach in about 300 metres the same road higher up. Turn left, round the next bend and then straight on NW to the road end at a stream. Climb up the path on the E bank of the stream out of the forest and then follow the fence SE to reach the NNE ridge of Mullach nan Coirean. This leads at an easy angle for 2½km to the summit. (4km; 890m; 2h 30min). There are fine views from this ridge of the great hump of Ben Nevis, and from the summit there is an equally fine view down Loch Linnhe.

To continue to Stob Ban, descend easy slopes SE along the rim of one of the northerly corries and follow an undulating ridge that goes SE and then S over a minor bump to the Mullach's South-east Top (917m). Beyond, the ridge becomes better defined and rockier, bearing NE over a minor top, then dropping E to the col (846m) between the two mountains. At this point the red granite rocks of Mullach nan Coirean suddenly change to the pale grey quartzite that gives Stob Ban its name. Finally, climb E then S more steeply up angular quartzite boulders along the rim of the NE cliffs to the summit of Stob Ban. (7½km; 1130m; 3h 40min).

In descent, follow the narrow shattered E ridge steeply down to grassier slopes, reaching a stalker's path near the col at the head of the Coire a' Mhusgain. Follow the branch of this path that goes N down the corrie on the E side of the stream, leading directly back to Achriabhach.

Map on page 71.

*Sgurr a' Mhaim (left) and Stob Ban seen from the Ben Nevis path*                    *P. Hodgkiss*

**Sgurr a' Mhaim**; 1099m; (OS Sheet 41; 165667); M49; *peak of the large rounded hill.*
**Sgor an Iubhair**; 1001m; (OS Sheet 41; 165655); M133; *peak of the yew.*

The dominating mountain in the western half of the Mamore range is Sgurr a' Mhaim, standing at the end of the longest of the arms projecting northward from the main ridge. There is a clear view of the peak from lower Glen Nevis, its great bulk fills the valley and the quartzite capping of its summit is very evident in certain lights. On its north and north-east sides there are two finely sculptured corries, below which the lower slopes of the mountain end abruptly in cliffs dropping into the Nevis gorge. To the south the connecting ridge between Sgurr a' Mhaim and the main spine of the Mamores is one of the finest sections of the range; it forms a sharp arête, the Devil's Ridge, which near its mid-point rises to the Top of Stob Choire a' Mhail, and continues to Sgor an Iubhair, a flat-topped summit on the main ridge. (Neither of these peaks is named on the Ordnance Survey 1:50000 map). The traverse of the Devil's Ridge is one of the highlights of hill-walking in the Mamores. Everyone will find it an exhilarating scramble, some may consider it to be a bit too exposed for their liking, but there are no real difficulties.

Start in Glen Nevis 300 metres E of Achriabhach and take the path up the E bank of the Allt Coire a' Mhusgain. After ½km leave the path and climb SE up the steep shoulder between the N and W faces of Sgurr a' Mhaim. Half way up, the zig-zags of a stalker's path on the W side of the shoulder give some respite from the steady steep climb, and at 800m the angle eases and the grassy slopes of the lower hillside give way to quartzite boulders and scree. Higher up the route follows the rim of the N corrie to the cairn of Sgurr a' Mhaim. (3km; 1050m; 2h 30min).

To continue the traverse, descend S down open slopes which soon converge to the narrow arête of the Devil's Ridge. Near the lowest point there are two short, exposed and slightly awkward sections where some might welcome the security of a rope. Continuing up the ridge, there is an airy climb up the very exposed crest to the Top of Stob Choire a' Mhail (980m). From there the route is much easier, descending to a broad col and climbing steeply up boulders to the flat top of Sgor an Iubhair. (4½km; 1190m; 3h).

Descend SW then W for 1km along a stalker's path to the col at the head of Coire a' Mhusgain, then turn N down the path in this corrie to return to Achriabhach.

*Looking along The Devil's Ridge from Sgurr a' Mhaim to Stob Choire a' Mhail*          *D.J. Bennet*

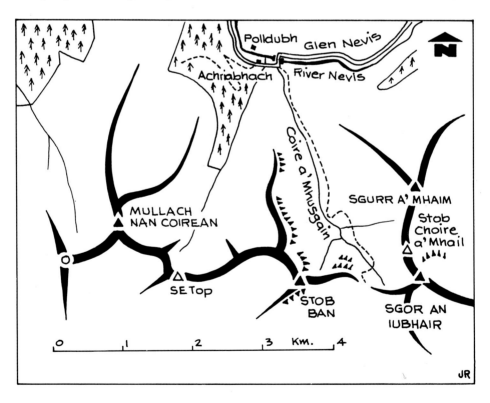

*Ben Nevis from the Carn Mor Dearg Arête*                                                                D. Scott

**Ben Nevis**; 1344m; (OS Sheet 41; 166713); M1; *possibly from an old Gaelic word meaning venemous.*
**Carn Mor Dearg**; 1223m; (OS Sheet 41; 177722); M7; *big red hill.*

For the average hill-goer, Ben Nevis is not just the highest mountain in the British Isles, its traverse combined with that of Carn Mor Dearg provides a taste of mountaineering amongst scenery of a magnificence not to be found elsewhere on the mainland of Britain. The two peaks form a vast horse-shoe facing north-west, with the simple shape of Carn Mor Dearg's slender ridge contrasting starkly with the huge and complex mass of Ben Nevis, whose north-east face presents the grandest array of cliffs of any Scottish mountain. Another contrast appears between the pink granite of Carn Mor Dearg and the grey andesite of the Ben, a contrast made more obvious by the great exposure of rock, boulders and scree on both mountains. Unfortunately, the hill-walker on the 'tourist route' up Ben Nevis gets little impression of its great mountain architecture, and one has to go round to the north-east side of the mountain, into the glen of the Allt a' Mhuillin, to appreciate the scale and grandeur of the mountain. For this reason the traverse from Carn Mor Dearg to Ben Nevis is recommended as the finest way for a fit and competent hill-walker to reach the summit of Scotland's highest mountain. The best roadside view is from the A82 a few kilometres north-east of Fort William, and even from a distance of several kilometres the scale of the cliffs in the great northern cirque can be appreciated.

The route to Ben Nevis starts at Achintee on the E side of the River Nevis and follows the excellent path which climbs across the flanks of Meall an t-Suidhe. The same path can be reached from the Glen Nevis youth hostel by a bridge across the river. After 2½km and 500m of ascent the path emerges onto the broad bealach holding Lochan Meall an t-Suidhe, and starts a series of uphill zig-zags with a long sweep NE. It is worthwhile following this first sweep as the short-cut involves very rough going. Above, the path crosses a deep gully, the Red Burn, and continues its zig-zags up increasingly bouldery ground to the extensive summit plateau. At the top there are the remains of the observatory, a small shelter, several cairns and a trig point, and a few metres to the north the cliffs drop vertically. In spring and early summer the cornices at the cliff-edge are likely to be dangerously unstable, so beware of approaching the edge too closely. (7km; 1340m; 3h 50min).

To reach Carn Mor Dearg, follow the Ben Nevis path as far as the bealach at Lochan Meall an t-Suidhe. Continue NNE along a level path to the N edge of the bealach and there, where the path turns ESE, descend NE across rough heathery ground to cross the Allt a' Mhuilinn near (154739). Now climb E up rough bouldery slopes for 600m to reach Carn Beag Dearg (1010m), and from there traverse the high ridge which stretches for 2km over Carn Dearg Meadhonach (1179m) to Carn Mor Dearg. (8km; 1450m; 4h 10min). The crest of this ridge provides easy walking and splendid views of the great cliffs of Ben Nevis's northern cirque.

To continue the traverse to Ben Nevis, follow the well-defined ridge S. After 200m of descent it sharpens to a narrow arête composed of huge granite blocks. Keeping to the crest makes for a fine scramble, but a faint path just below the crest on its SE side avoids the tricky sections and much of the

*Carn Mor Dearg*                                              *D.J. Bennet*

exposure. Throughout its length the Carn Mor Dearg Arête gives a superb view of the Ben's great ridges and corries, with the outline of the North-East Buttress growing more and more impressive. About 300 metres beyond the lowest point of the arête, at a level place below the final steep climb towards Ben Nevis, a post on the right-hand (N) edge of the ridge marks the start of a moderately easy descent into Coire Leis which might be used as an escape route in bad weather or failing light. However, if there is snow on the headwall of Coire Leis this descent is not advised unless the party has ice-axes or crampons. Above that point the arête merges into the bulk of Ben Nevis and it is worthwhile hunting for the faint path that climbs for 250m through the litter of giant boulders to the top. (10km; 1750m; 5h 10min).

No restriction on climbing during the stalking season.

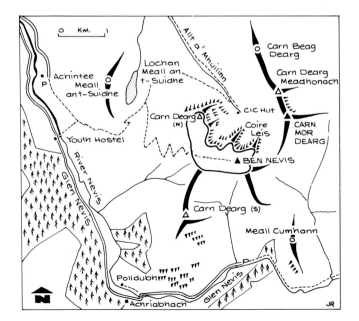

*Aonach Mor from Glen Spean*                                                    *D. Scott*

**Aonach Beag**; 1234m; (OS Sheet 41; 196715); M6; *little hill.*
**Aonach Mor**; 1221m; (OS Sheet 41; 193730); M8; *big hill.*

The Aonachs (as these two mountains are often called) form a great high ridge, several kilometres long from south to north, lying to the east of Ben Nevis and Carn Mor Dearg, and connected to the latter by a high bealach at 830m. Although the crest of the ridge, particularly on Aonach Mor, is fairly flat and broad, the slopes to east and west are very steep, forming wild and remote corries, so these two mountains call for respect, especially in bad weather. They make a fine natural traverse, best approached from Glen Nevis, although an ascent from the north is also possible. If transport arrangements permit, the complete traverse from south to north is the ideal expedition.

Aonach Mor is a long flat-topped mountain whose finest feature is its steep and scalloped east face which holds snow well into summer. Aonach Beag has a more rounded summit guarded by crags and corries on all sides. The best impression of this pair is gained from the Grey Corries from where their east facing corries are well seen, with Ben Nevis appearing over the connecting ridge.

Start from the car park at the end of the road in Glen Nevis and take the path through the Nevis gorge and along the N side of the Water of Nevis to the bridge across the Allt Coire Giubhsachan at the ruined Steall cottage. Above, to the NE, Aonach Beag forms a wide corrie, enclosed by its SW ridge on one side and the pointed Top of Sgurr a' Bhuic (965m) on the other. Bear NNE over hummocky gound and climb steeply towards the corrie for 1½km, trending N to reach the SW ridge of Aonach Beag. This ridge leads easily to the top. (6½km; 1100m; 3h 20min).

A longer and more scenic route bears more to the NE from the Steall ruin to reach the E ridge of Sgurr a' Bhuic. Traverse this Top and descend steeply NE along a rocky ridge with crags on the right to a col at 898m. Climb again to a small unnamed point (1049m), turn W over the Top of Stob Coire Bhealaich (1101m) and finally NW up stony ground to the summit of Aonach Beag. (8km; 1200m; 3h 50min).

To continue the traverse descend NW down rocky slopes that fall away to the right in steep crags, and reach the well-defined bealach at 1080m. Beyond, an easy rise over short grass leads in just over 1km to the cairn of Aonach Mor which, in poor visibility, may not be easy to find on the featureless area of the summit plateau. (From Aonach Beag, 1½km; 130m; 40min).

To return to Glen Nevis, retrace the route S keeping near the western cliffs of Aonach Mor for about 700 metres to (192722). At this point turn W down a steep, ill-defined spur to the bealach at 830m under Carn Mor Dearg. In bad visibility careful navigation is required for this descent as the ground on either side is very steep. Finally go S down Coire Giubhsachan to reach the path in Glen Nevis.

*Sgurr Choinnich Mor from the north-east*                                    *D.J. Bennet*

**Sgurr Choinnich Mor;** 1095m; (OS Sheet 41; 227714); M50; *big peak of the moss.*

This sharp and shapely peak lies directly north of the watershed at the head of Glen Nevis, and with its smaller companion Sgurr Choinnich Beag (966m) it marks the south-western end of the Grey Corries ridge. Sgurr Choinnich Mor has a narrow rocky summit ridge, dropping steeply on both sides, and it is the finest of the Grey Corries, comparable with Binnein Mor on the opposite side of Glen Nevis, and having the vast and steep corries of Aonach Beag close to the west to add to its mountainous setting.

Although Sgurr Choinnich Mor can be climbed from the north in combination with other peaks of the Grey Corries, that approach is quite long. A rather shorter route is from the car park at the road end in Glen Nevis. Follow the path through the Nevis gorge, and stay on the path along the N side of the Water of Nevis to the bridge over the Allt Coire Giubhsachan and the ruined cottage at Steall. Continue along the path for a further 2km until it leaves the main river to cross a minor side stream. Climb NNE up grassy slopes beside this stream to reach the bealach at the foot of the WSW ridge of Sgurr Choinnich Beag. Climb this ridge which steepens as it nears the distinctive Top. Descend E for 70m to a high col, and continue ENE up increasingly rocky ground to the summit of Sgurr Choinnich Mor. (8½km; 1030m; 3h 40min).

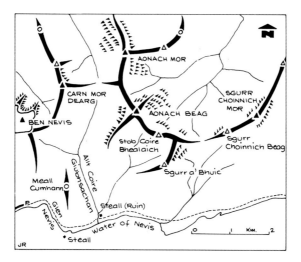

*Looking east along the ridge of the Grey Corries towards Stob Choire Claurigh*         *K.M. Andrew*

**Stob Choire Claurigh**; 1177m; (OS Sheet 41; 262739); M14; *claurigh is probably from Gaelic clamhras, brawling or clamouring.*
**Stob Coire an Laoigh**; 1115m; (OS Sheet 41; 240725); M37; *peak of the corrie of the calf.*

These two peaks are 3km apart at the ends of a high ridge to the south of Spean Bridge behind the extensive Leanachan Forest. They are part of the long chain of mountains extending eastwards from Ben Nevis over Aonach Beag and Sgurr Choinnich Mor. The pale grey quartzite screes which cover their higher slopes earn for them the name The Grey Corries, and when viewed in good lighting from the north-west, e.g. from the Commando Memorial above Spean Bridge, the aptness of this name is very apparent. The roll-call of two Munros and six Tops flatters to deceive, for their crest undulates gently, its lowest point being 980m, and it gives an excellent high level ridge walk.

The best approach is on the N side, from Corriechoille farm in Glen Spean which is reached from Spean Bridge by the narrow public road on the S side of the River Spean. The road which goes 2km S past the farm to the disused tramway is private, but at the time of writing no objection is made to driving up to the remains of the narrow gauge track that was laid to facilitate cutting the tunnel from Loch Treig to the Fort William Aluminium Works. Continue SE through the forest up the track which leads to the Lairig Leacach. In 1½km leave the forest and turn SSW up steep grassy slopes which continue unrelentingly for 600m to the first Top, Stob Coire na Gaibhre (955m). Beyond, the ridge becomes narrower with steep slopes on the left dropping into Coire na Ceannain with its almost perfectly circular lochan, and higher up past a minor bump it forms a narrow rocky crest for a few hundred metres before the summit of Stob Choire Claurigh is reached. (6km; 1020m; 3h 10min).

Turning WSW, the ridge undulates gently and a faint path eases the rough going over sharp and angular quartzite scree. From E to W the traverse includes the Tops of Stob a' Choire Leith (1105m), Stob Coire Cath na Sine (1080m), and Caisteal (1104m) before reaching the second Munro, Stob Coire an Laoigh, not named on the Ordnance Survey 1:50000 map, but notable for its dark northern cliff. (9km; 1220m; 4h 10min).

The ridge continues WNW to the Top of Stob Coire Easain (1080m) at which point a spur running N to the last Top, Beinn na Socaich (1007m) marks the line of descent. Continue along the broad spur for 1½km past this Top, then turn NE down into Coire Choimhlidh by grassy slopes. Cross to the E side of the Allt Coire Choimhlidh above the forest, and descend past a small dam to reach the end of the road. Go along this road for ½km and then turn NE along the clearing of the tramway back to the day's starting point.

*Stob Ban at the east end of the Grey Corries*                                    *N. Marshall*

**Stob Ban;** 977m; (OS Sheet 41; 266724); M173; *light-coloured peak.*

Stob Ban is a remote peak, far distant and invisible from any main road. It lies at the east end of the Grey Corries ridge, separated from it by a bealach of 800m, and it is only from viewpoints near the head of Glen Nevis or in the Lairig Leacach that one gets a vew of this solitary conical peak. Although it is grouped with the Grey Corries, and its Gaelic name is accurate, it is not included in the quartzite covering of the rest of the group, but lies within a band of schist.

The shortest approach is from Corriechoille farm in Glen Spean, as described for Stob Coire Claurigh (qv), by the track to the Lairig Leacach. Cross this pass and descend on its S side for 1½km to a small bothy from where there is a good view of Stob Ban. Beyond, the track fords a burn and forks; take the right fork and after 100 metres bear SW up the grassy hillside. At 650m the slope narrows to a ridge which at 750m levels to a flat shoulder before the final steep rocky rise to the summit. (9km; 790m; 3h 20min).

The return can be pleasantly varied by descending N over boulder scree to the 800m bealach. From there turn ENE and go down a giant's staircase of quartzite slabs which spills downwards for over 150m and gives an easy scramble when dry. Below, the burn leads back to the bothy and the short climb over the Lairig Leacach on the return to Glen Spean.

Stob Ban can be combined with the traverse of The Grey Corries. From the 800m bealach, a steep but straightforward ridge leads N and levels out to turn NW to the summit of Stob Choire Claurigh, where the traverse is joined.

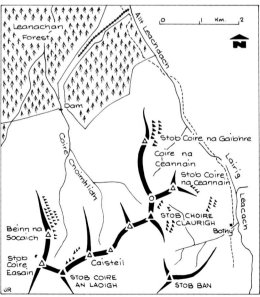

*Stob a' Choire Mheadhoin from Loch Laggan*                    *D.J. Bennet*

**Stob Coire Easain**; 1116m; (OS Sheet 41; 308730); M36; *peak of the corrie of the little waterfall.*
**Stob a' Choire Mheadhoin**; 1106; (OS Sheet 41; 316736); M44; *peak of the middle corrie.*

The Easains, as these two mountains are sometimes called, form a high ridge 10km long to the east of the Grey Corries. The two summits are near the middle of this ridge, and are separated by a col at 960m. To the east and west there are steep slopes, those to the east being particularly so and giving Loch Treig a fiord-like character. The two mountains are prominent in views from the south, appearing like twins, while from the north in Glen Spean there is a fine view of Stob a' Choire Mheadhoin, with Stob Coire Easain just appearing behind it. It is from Glen Spean that the two are most usually climbed, although a fine traverse can be made with the help of the West Highland Railway.

For the simple ascent, leave the A86 road in Glen Spean 7½km E of Roy Bridge and follow the narrow public road almost to Fersit near the N end of Loch Treig. Start climbing from the W bank of the River Treig near the outflow of the loch. Initially steep slopes lead W, but soon give out on a broad terrace above which a further 100m of climbing, skirting crags to the right, leads onto the crest of the NNE ridge of Stob a' Choire Mheadhoin. This long ridge is followed for 4½km up a series of rocky rises and level terraces to the final steep rise to the summit. (6km; 870m; 2h 50min). Descend SW down rocky ground to the col at 960m and climb the rocky ridge WSW to Stob Coire Easain. (7km; 1030m; 3h 20min). Return by the same route.

A rewarding way in which to traverse these peaks is to start from Corrour Halt on the West Highland Line, reached either by the northbound or southbound morning train. Follow the good track NW along the railway line and round the head of Loch Treig to Creaguaineach Lodge. 400 metres N of the lodge cross a bridge to the E bank of the Allt na Lairige and follow the path through a wooded gorge for 1km. Once on more open ground turn NNE and climb a ridge at a steady angle to a level shoulder at 900m. The ridge narrows, with crags falling to the right, and leads in a further 1½km to Stob Coire Easain. (11km; 870m; 4h). Continue the traverse over Stob a' Choire Mheadhoin to Fersit as described above.

Map on page 80.

*Looking south across the flat summit of Chno Dearg towards Meall Garbh; Beinn na Lap on the left*    *K.M. Andrew*

**Stob Coire Sgriodain**; 976m; (OS Sheet 41; 356744); M174; *peak of the corrie of the scree.*
**Chno Dearg**; 1047m; (OS Sheet 41; 377741); M82; *red nut (on early maps the name appears as cnoc dearg, red hill).*

Together with Chno Dearg's southern Top, Meall Garbh (977m), these hills make a natural and easy hill-walking circuit from Fersit, the small group of cottages reached by a minor road leaving the A86 7½km east of Roy Bridge. Stob Coire Sgriodain is quite a rugged looking hill on the east side of Loch Treig, dropping very steeply into the loch at an average angle of over 30°. Above 500m it forms a north-south ridge that is rough and craggy and has three distinct tops. This ridge curls round to the south-east and merges with Chno Dearg, a rounded and featureless hill with open and easy angled northern slopes. Both hills are well seen from the main road in Glen Spean.

Starting at Fersit, follow the forestry road E for almost ½km and then turn S up rough ground, usually wet and boggy for the first 1½km. Beyond a minor craggy top at 450m, the open slopes steepen to form a ridge with small crags which can easily be turned on one side or the other, and the next top, Sron na Garbh-bheinne is reached. A short level shoulder is passed, and the ridge narrows and rises to the summit of Stob Coire Sgriodain, from where there is a splendid view of the fiord-like Loch Treig. (4½km; 730m; 2h 20min).

A combination of knolly tops and two intervening drops makes the next section of the traverse confusing in bad visibility. Descend S for 60m to a pronounced col and turn SE up the South Top of Stob Coire Sgriodain (960m). Continue ESE over knolly ground and reach another distinct double-headed top (925m) in ½km. A short descent, still ESE, leads to an open col with a scatter of tiny lochans. Continue in the same direction, climbing easily to the crest of Meall Garbh, and turn S to reach the cairn on the S top. Return N then NNE across another open col above which easy slopes covered by dwarf vegetation lead to the flat, boulder-strewn summit of Chno Dearg. (8½km; 1020m; 3h 40min). Descend NNW down a wide grassy corrie in a direct line back to Fersit.

A fine traverse can be made by continuing from Chno Dearg to Beinn na Lap and Corrour Halt on the West Highland Line. Descend S from Chno Dearg into the corrie below the steep E face of Meall Garbh, cross the Allt Feith Thuill and climb the long easy-angled NNE ridge of Beinn na Lap. (14km; 1480m; 5h 40min). Descend SW down easy slopes to the end of Loch Ossian and follow the track for the last 1½km to Corrour Halt.

The train timetable should be consulted before doing this traverse as the return to Fersit involves taking the Fort William train to Tulloch and walking from there to Fersit.

Map on page 80.

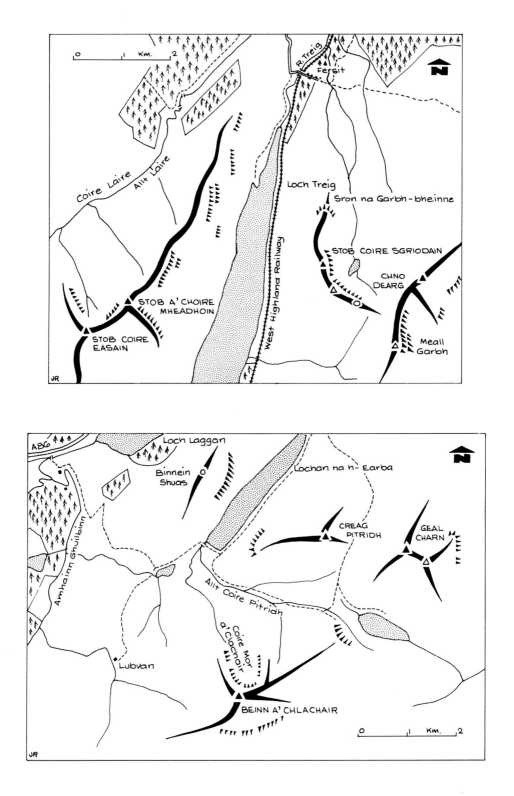

*Creag Pitridh and Geal Charn from Moy*                                        *H.M. Brown*

**Beinn a' Chlachair;** 1088m; (OS Sheet 42; 471781); M53; *stonemason's hill.*
**Geal Charn;** 1049m; (OS Sheet 42; 504812); M78; *white hill.*
**Creag Pitridh;** 924m; (OS Sheet 42; 488814); M260; *meaning uncertain, perhaps from the surname*
   *Petrie.*

This group of mountains lies south of Loch Laggan and is most readily approached from the A86 road. Beinn a' Chlachair is prominent in the roadside view from Moy, looking like a great whaleback with a prominent corrie scooped out of its north flank just below the summit. To its north-east Creag Pitridh is a much smaller peak with a pointed summit and broken crags on its west face overlooking Lochan na h'Earba. Between these two Geal Charn appears as rather a featureless flat-topped hill, but the best view of it is from the north-east, looking up the glen of the River Pattack from the vicinity of Laggan Bridge. The group is penetrated by an extensive system of estate roads and stalker's paths which makes access to the tops fairly easy, even though they are some distance from the road.

Leave the A86 at the concrete bridge 1km SW of the outflow of Loch Laggan near Moy, and follow the rough road up the E side of the Amhainn Ghuilbinn for about 1km. Then take a left turn (still on a dirt road) and go E for ½km, then go right along another track which leads horizontally round the base of Binnein Shuas to the SW end of Lochan na h-Earba. Leave the track (which continues along the loch) and follow a stalker's path SE up the Allt Coire Pitridh for about 1½km, then bear S up the very open slopes on the NE flank of Beinn a' Chlachair. Above 900m the ground levels out at a shoulder and the route bears round the rim of Coire Mor a' Chlachair over a waste of boulders, many of them of surprisingly regular shape. The large summit cairn is set a short distance back from the edge of the corrie. (9km; 840m; 3h 30min).

Return ENE along the broad ridge for almost 2½km, at which point the level shoulder ends abruptly above a large crag. Descend N and soon reach a stalker's path which forks a few metres lower. Take the right path and go N, climbing slightly to its highest point on the W flank of Geal Charn. Turn E and climb easy slopes of heath and boulders to the flat summit. (14km; 1150m; 5h 10min).

Retrace the route to the col W of Geal Charn and make the short, easy ascent of Creag Pitridh, keeping to the left of craggy ground. (16km; 1300m; 5h 50min). Descend SW to regain the stalker's path along the Allt Coire Pitridh, and return by the outward route.

*Beinn na Lap from Loch Ossian*                                    *P. Hodgkiss*

**Beinn na Lap**; 937m; (OS Sheet 41; 376676); M232; *mottled hill? (lap means a defective spot in a colour).*

Beinn na Lap may be classed as one of the easiest ascents among the Munros, although it does require a train journey to reach its foot. It lies 4km north-east of Corrour Halt, altitude 400m, on the West Highland Line and looms quite steeply above the northern shore of Loch Ossian. There is a clear view of the hill from Corrour, but from elsewhere its featureless whaleback is not readily identified.

Reach Corrour by either the south or north-bound train and follow the track E towards Loch Ossian. After 1¼km take the left fork on the track along the N side of the loch, and soon leave it to climb N on easy-angled slopes of dwarf vegetation. At 700m a broad ridge is reached and followed ENE to the summit of Beinn na Lap, which provides a remarkable contrast in views, with the wide expanse of Rannoch Moor to the SW and a complicated tangle of peaks around the northern arc. (5km; 540m; 2h).

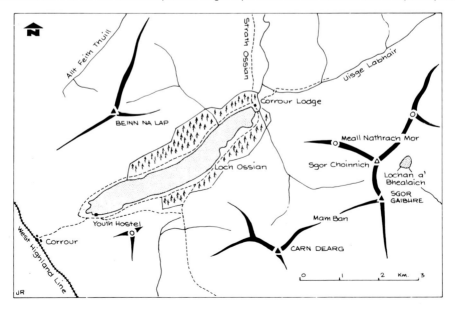

*The steep face of Sgor Gaibhre above Lochan a' Bhealaich*        *P. Hodgkiss*

**Sgor Gaibhre**; 955m; (OS Sheets 41 and 42; 444674); M203; *goat's peak.*
**Carn Dearg**; 941m; (OS Sheets 41 and 42; 418661); M225; *red hill.*

These hills, together with the Top, Sgor Choinnich (927m), make a fine round from Corrour Halt on the West Highland Line. It is quite a long circuit, and one may have to move fast to complete it between the morning and evening trains. Sgor Gaibhre and Carn Dearg lie between Loch Ossian and Loch Ericht and enclose in their open corries the gathering grounds for some of the largest herds of red deer in Scotland. In general they are rounded hills without distinctive features, and from Corrour there is not a clear view of them, but the two Sgors rise steeply above Lochan a' Bhealaich and present a bold profile when seen from the east. The total distance of 22km for this round is lightened by an excellent track for the first 7km and the smooth terrain of the hills themselves.

Follow the track ENE from Corrour Halt along the S shore of Loch Ossian to reach the cottages at the foot of the loch. Cross the bridge over the outflow, then immediately turn NE along a path to recross the river by a wooden footbridge and continue along the path W round a copse to reach open ground. (This avoids having to find a way through the forest at the E end of the loch). Bear SE and climb at an easy angle to a fore-top Meall Nathrach Mor, and beyond a short descent continue at an even easier angle to Sgor Choinnich. Descend S for 120m to a well-defined bealach and climb a broad steepening ridge to the summit of Sgor Gaibhre which provides a splendid view of Ben Alder and Loch Ericht. (12km; 720m; 4h).

Turn WSW and descend easy slopes of moss and heath to the broad bealach, the Mam Ban, riven by peat-hags. Continue in the same direction up Carn Dearg, climbing 220m to the cairn which overlooks the whole expanse of Rannoch Moor, while to the N the glacial trench of Strath Ossian is very prominent. (15km; 940m; 5h).

For the return to Corrour descend WNW, soon reaching an open corrie and in 2½km the path, known as The Road to the Isles, which can be followed W to the station.

**Beinn Eibhinn;** 1100m; (OS Sheets 41 and 42; 449733); M47; *delightful hill.*
**Aonach Beag;** 1114m; (OS Sheets 41 and 42; 458742); M38; *little hill.*

These two remote mountains lie in the hinterland between Loch Laggan and Loch Ericht, part of the range which forms the northern wall of the long glen cutting through the hills in a straight line from Loch Ossian to Loch Pattack over the Bealach Dubh. The only view of these hills from any public road is from the north, on the A86 near the west end of Loch Laggan, from where they can be seen rising beyond the forests of Glen Spean. Aonach Beag is a fine peak, with three well-defined ridges coverging at its top. Beinn Eibhinn is a more extensive mountain, with a level summit ridge curving round Coire a' Charra Mhoir and its south-west side forming a series of rounded ridges and open corries well seen from Loch Ossian.

The ascent of these two mountains can be made from Corrour Halt on the West Highland Line. Given clear visibility and good conditions underfoot, it should be possible to do the round trip comfortably between the morning and evening trains at Corrour, but attention must be paid to the clock and the railway timetable. Fortunately half the distance to and from the peaks is along the excellent track by Loch Ossian which makes for quick progress.

From Corrour Halt follow the route described for Sgor Gaibhre to the outflow of Loch Ossian. Take the path NE across the River Ossian, round the W side of the copse and continue along this path to the footbridge across the Uisge Labhair. A fair path continues up the N side of this stream past a fine rocky linn. After crossing the Allt Feith a' Mheallain head NNE up the grassy slopes of the rounded ridge Creagan na Craoibhe. Higher up the going becomes very easy on short heath and grass, past a huge rounded boulder on the crest to the Top of Meall Glas Choire (922m). Beyond a short drop into a square-cut col, easy slopes soon lead onto the stony summit ridge of Beinn Eibhinn, whose NE face drops steeply to Lochan a' Charra Mhoir. The summit cairn is at the E end of this ridge. (13½km; 730m; 4h 20min).

The narrow ridge continues NE in splendid surroundings, dropping 120m in a graceful curve before climbing again to Aonach Beag, whose summit is a small flat plateau. (15km; 860m; 4h 50min).

The best return is probably by the outward route over Beinn Eibhinn just described. It may be shorter in distance (though less pleasant) to descend fairly directly S from the summit of Beinn Eibhinn down steep, rough ground to reach the faint path beside the Uisge Labhair near the foot of the Allt Glas-choire.

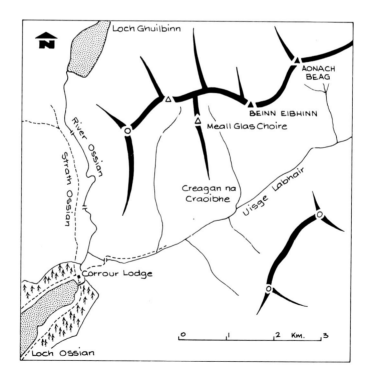

*Aonach Beag and Geal-Charn from Beinn Eibhinn*                     *J. Renny*

**Geal-Charn**; 1132m; (OS Sheet 42; 471745); M25; *white hill.*
**Carn Dearg**; 1034m; (OS Sheet 42; 504764); M95; *red hill.*

These hills lie in that great tract of land between Loch Laggan and Loch Ericht which is penetrated by no public roads. Geal-Charn is the highest point on the elevated ridge stretching from Strath Ossian to Loch Pattack, the north-easterly extension of Beinn Eibhinn and Aonach Beag just described, and Carn Dearg continues the range to its end above Loch Pattack. Geal-Charn has a large summit plateau surrounded by corries and steep hillsides, and it throws out two easterly spurs enclosing Loch an Sgoir. The southern one forms a well-defined Top, Sgor Iutharn (1021m), whose terminal ridge is the steep and narrow Lancet Edge. The ascent of this ridge and descent of the more northerly spur is a fine mountaineering expedition which can be continued over Carn Dearg.

The shortest approach, from Dalwhinnie, involves a distance of 40km for the round trip, and may entail a night out, possibly at Culra Lodge, a well situated bothy at the base of these hills. Alternatively, a bicycle can be used for 11km along the private estate road from Dalwhinnie to Loch Pattack as described for Ben Alder. (See p.86).

From the shed on this road ½km E of Loch Pattack take the path for 3½km SW across the level moor and along the SE bank of the Allt a' Chaoil-reidhe. Cross the stream by a footbridge near Culra Lodge and continue SW past this bothy on a parallel path for a further 3km to the crossing of the stream from Loch an Sgoir. Above and W, steep rough ground leads to the Lancet Edge, a ridge sharp enough to require careful scrambling, and providing magnificent views to the right of the waterfalls feeding Loch an Sgoir and left to the mass of Ben Alder. The ridge ends at Sgor Iutharn, beyond which the ground broadens and leads W across a wide col then NW up the final slope to the rim of the plateau which has to be crossed for 1km W to reach Geal-Charn's summit. (From Loch Pattack - 10km; 800m; 3h 30min).

To continue the traverse, cross the green fertile plateau ENE for 1km to reach the spur dropping steeply between the N and E corries. In poor visibility an exact compass bearing is needed to find the correct route. Descend to a narrow level ridge and climb a short way to an intervening Top, Diollaid a' Chairn (922m). Finally, a long, broad and stony ridge leads to Carn Dearg. (14km; 1000m; 4h 50min).

For the return descend due E to Culra Lodge and retrace the outward route.

Map on page 87.

*Ben Alder from Culra Bothy*                                            *R. Aitken*

**Ben Alder;** 1148m; (OS Sheet 42; 496718); M24; *from the Alder Burn, which may be from the Gaelic alldhobhar meaning rock water.*
**Beinn Bheoil;** 1019m; (OS Sheet 42; 517717); M110; *hill of the mouth.*

Ben Alder is one of the great remote mountains of Scotland, a vast high plateau surrounded by corries in the heart of the Central Highlands between Lochaber and the Cairngorms. For such a remote hill, however, there is a remarkable roadside view of it from Dalwhinnie, the eye being drawn 20km along the length of Loch Ericht to the expanse of its great north-eastern corries which hold snow into early summer. Other views from hills to the west tell more of the plateau-like form of Ben Alder, but only a circuit can reveal its enormous bulk and its fascinating complexity of ridge and corrie. By contrast, Beinn Bheoil has a simple north-south ridge, dropping steeply on both sides, but its position between Ben Alder and Loch Ericht gives it a very mountainous setting.

There is a strong mountaineering flavour to the traverse of these two peaks, and their remoteness may make necessary an overnight stop in the hills, possibly at Benalder Cottage or Culra Lodge. Alternatively, the use of a bicycle along the private road from Dalwhinnie to Loch Pattack brings them within easier reach on a long summer day. Ben Alder can also be climbed from Corrour Halt on the West Highland Line, but one would have to move very fast to do this between the morning and evening trains. For anyone staying at Loch Ossian youth hostel this constraint would not matter.

The Dalwhinnie approach starts just S of the station. Cross the railway and follow the estate road along the NW shore of Loch Ericht. There are locked gates, but a bicycle can be used as far as Loch Pattack, 3km W of Ben Alder Lodge and 11km from Dalwhinnie. Just before reaching this loch, at a large shed, take to a path which leads SW across wet level moorland to the E bank of the Allt a' Chaoil-reidhe. Follow this path, passing Culra Lodge on the opposite side of the stream, for about 7km until it reaches the burn flowing from the Loch a' Bhealaich Bheithe. Cross the burn and choose which of the prominent ridges above to climb: the Short Leachas lies SW and directly above, while the Long Leachas is reached by a traverse further W. Both are approached through thick boulder-strewn heather. The Short Leachas is steeper and involves frequent scrambling, while the Long Leachas is easier and has better situations. Both emerge onto the summit plateau near a minor top, beyond which 1km of stony and near-level ground leads SSW to the summit cairn. (From Loch Pattack - 10km; 750m; 3h 30min).

To continue the traverse, follow the rim of the great E corrie for 1½km, first S then SE to descend abruptly (still SE) down steep bouldery ground. Reach the glen falling S from the Bealach Breabag and climb NE up steep heather scattered with large boulders to reach the Top, Sron Coire na h-Iolaire (955m) which is a splendid viewpoint above Loch Ericht. Ahead, the spine of the hill stretches NNE for 3½km above 800m, dropping to 860m before rising to Beinn Bheoil. (14½km; 1030m; 5h). Follow the ridge N for a further 2km, then descend NW to reach the path returning to Loch Pattack. Altogether a very long expedition of 45km, half of which can be done by bicycle.

The ascent of Ben Alder from Corrour Halt follows the same route as for Beinn Eibhinn (qv) to the Uisge Labhair and continues up that stream for 5km. Cross the stream and work through peat hags to the foot of Ben Alder's broad W ridge, which is followed to the top. (16km; 750m; 4h 50min).

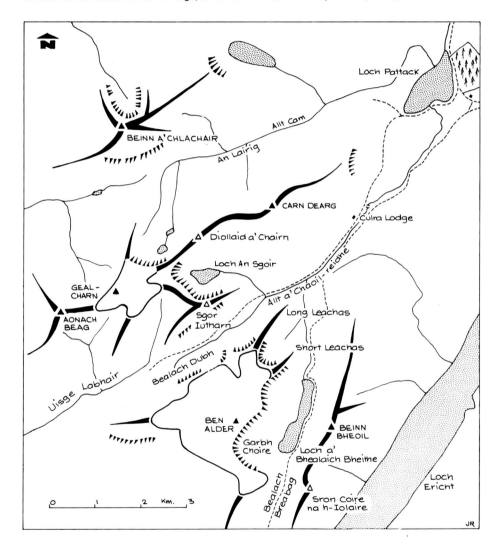

*Looking from Sron Coire na h-Iolaire to Loch Ericht and the Drumochter Hills*    W.D. Brooker

# SECTION 5

## The Drumochter Mountains

*Carn na Caim from the Allt Coire Chuaich Bothy*                                    *H.M. Brown*

**A' Bhuidheanach Bheag**; 936m; (OS Sheet 42; 661776); M235; *the little yellow place.*
**Carn na Caim**; 941m; (OS Sheet 42; 677822); M226; *cairn of the curve.*

These two hills are the highest points on the vast undulating plateau which extends north-east from the Pass of Drumochter to Loch an t-Seilich in the Gaick Forest. Both are flat-topped, and their most characteristic features when seen from the A9 road which runs along their western flank are the many shallow gullies and corries lining the hillside. A' Bhuidheanach Bheag lies well back from the edge of the plateau, and its summit is not visible from the road; Carn na Caim, on the other hand, is on the edge of the plateau and is the obvious rounded summit whose north and west sides are scalloped by shallow corries.

The two hills can be conveniently climbed together, and the best starting point is 1km N of Drumochter Lodge on the A9 at the foot of the Allt Coire Chuirn. Go through two gates in the deer fences onto the rising moorland beyond, and climb SE up the broad steepening ridge on the SW side of the Allt Coire Chuirn. The NE side of this ridge is cut away abruptly above the deep ravine of the Coire Chuirn. Beyond a narrow level section above 700m the ridge rises again to reach the flat grassy plateau.

This plateau lacks any distinctive features, so accurate map and compass work is essential in misty conditions, steering SE for 1½km to find the line of fence posts which leads to the summit of A' Bhuidheanach Bheag. (4km; 520m; 1h 50min).

Descend due N to the wide 830m col at the head of Coire Chuirn, and continue gradually uphill on the same bearing for 1¼km to reach the 902m knoll (this height is not shown on the First Series 1:50000 map). Continue NE over another knoll (914m), then slightly downhill and up again to Carn na Caim. (9½km; 700m; 3h 20min).

To return to the day's starting point, return SW along the plateau for 2½km to the 902m knoll and then go NW for about 200 metres to an old quartz quarry. Descend the track from this quarry for 1½km to the point where it turns N, and from there head directly back across the moor to the foot of the Allt Coire Chuirn.

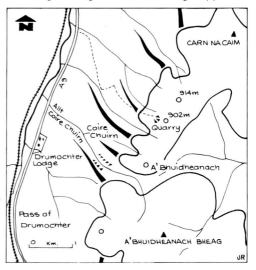

*A' Mharconaich with Sgairneach Mhor appearing over the Boar of Badenoch col,*     D.J. Bennet
*seen from the Balsporran Cottages.*

**Sgairneach Mhor;** 991m; (OS Sheet 42; 599732); M151; *big stony hillside.*
**Beinn Udlamain;** 1010m; (OS Sheet 42; 579740); M119; *gloomy mountain.*

These two mountains lie between the Pass of Drumochter and the middle part of Loch Ericht. Sgairneach Mhor is prominently seen as a high, rounded mountain from the A9 road east of Dalnaspidal, and is also well seen from further north framed by the col between A' Mharconaich and the Boar of Badenoch. From that direction its most obvious feature is its steep northern Coire Creagach. Beinn Udlamain, on the other hand, although the highest in this group of mountains, is screened by its satellites and is only visible from the A9 directly opposite the foot of Coire Dhomhain. The two mountains lie on either side of the head of this corrie, and can be easily climbed in a single expedition.

Leave the A9 opposite the entrance to Coire Dhomhain and cross the railway line to join the track up the corrie on the N side of the Allt Coire Dhomhain. Alternatively, start at the beginning of this track ½km further S on the A9. Follow the track into Coire Dhomhain for 1½km, then cross the stream to its S side and climb through grass and deep heather to a col on the E ridge of Sgairneach Mhor. From this col the ridge is rounded and easy-angled at first, but becomes steeper and narrower before reaching the summit round the edge of Coire Creagach. Alternatively, as the Allt Coire Dhomhain is difficult to cross when in spate, it may be necessary to walk 3km up the corrie before crossing the stream and climbing the ridge on the W side of the rocky edge of Coire Creagach. (5km; 550m; 2h 10min).

From the summit walk SW for ½km before turning due W to the col at the head of Coire Dhomhain. The slopes on the descent are featureless and in misty weather care should be taken not to be diverted S by the fall of the ground. From the col continue W to reach the crest of the S ridge of Beinn Udlamain, and follow the remains of a fence up this ridge to the summit. (8½km; 750m; 3h 10min).

Descend NE along the broad ridge, following the fence for 2km until the 860m col is reached. From there descend SE down easy slopes to reach the track in Coire Dhomhain. A' Mharconaich can be easily included by climbing NE from the col, still following the fence until it goes off leftwards, to reach the flat summit plateau of this hill. Descend steeply SE towards the Boar of Badenoch col and Coire Dhomhain.

**Geal-charn;** 917m; (OS Sheet 42; 597783); M272; *white hill.*
**A' Mharconaich;** 975m; (OS Sheet 42; 604764); M178; *the horse place.*

These two mountains lie west of the A9 road just north of the Pass of Drumochter. Geal-charn is a rounded mountain formed by a broad ridge running from south-west to north-east, and it has high on its shoulder some tall slender cairns, clearly visible from the road and looking like giant climbers. A' Mharconaich is a fine looking mountain seen from the road, with a very steep east face forming a high corrie just under the summit. They are both very accessible from the road, which is 425m above sea level, so their traverse is an easy day.

Leave the A9 at Balsporran Cottages, 3km N of Drumochter Pass, and cross the railway. Follow the path W, crossing the Allt Beul an Sporain, and then climbing directly up the broad NE ridge of Geal-charn through deep heather until above about 650m a faint path on the SE side of the ridge leads up past the tall cairns to the flat shoulder of the hill at 845m. Finally an easy stony slope leads to the summit of Geal-charn. (3½km; 500m; 1h 40min).

Descend the broad stony ridge S for 1½km to the col at 740m. From there climb SE up uniform grassy slopes, crossing the head of the Allt Coire Fhar to reach the flat summit plateau of A' Mharconaich. The summit cairn is at the NE end of this plateau. (6½km; 730m; 2h 40min). Descend N, steeply at first down rocky ground, then easily along the long NE ridge which leads directly back to the Balsporran Cottages, with some rough ground of peat bog and heather near the end. This rough ground can be avoided by dropping down on the N side of the NE ridge to cross the Allt Coire Fhar and continue along the path on its NW side, however if this stream is in spate the crossing should be made high up as there is no bridge.

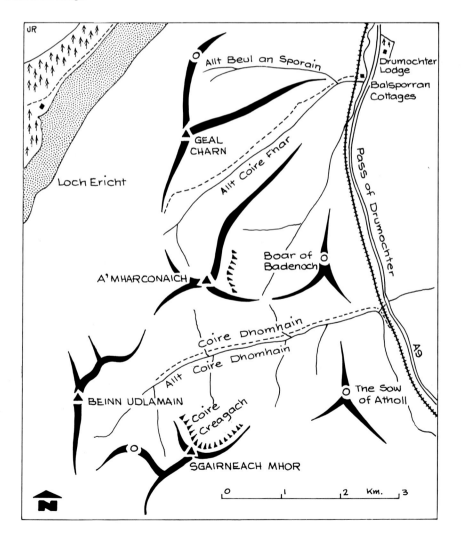

*Meall Chuaich from Loch Insh*                                      *D.J. Bennet*

**Meall Chuaich**; 951m; (OS Sheet 42; 716879); M209; *hill of the quaich.*

Meall Chuaich is at the northern end of the group of hills which form a great plateau to the north of the Pass of Drumochter and east of the A9 road. Its very roundness and isolation are its distinctive features, and as there is no higher ground for some distance to the north, east or west, it is a very good viewpoint.

Leave the A9 road just S of the Cuaich cottages where a rough private road passes through a locked gate. A short distance further another road is joined and followed E along the aqueduct which transfers water from Loch Cuaich to Loch Ericht. Continue past a small power station until ½km from the dam at Loch Cuaich, then turn E along a rough track past a small bothy towards Coire Chuaich. Soon after crossing to the N side of the Allt Coire Chuaich, leave the track and climb NE up the steep heathery hillside, aiming for the crest of the broad ridge where the going becomes much easier on grass and heath. Continue along the flat shoulder above Stac Meall Chuaich, and finally climb a steeper stony slope to the flat mossy summit of Meall Chuaich. (7km; 610m; 2h 40min).

Another possible approach to Meall Chuaich is up Glen Tromie, but the road up this glen is strictly private; a bicycle is therefore essential for the 10km from Tromie Bridge to Bhran Cottage. From there the ascent to Meall Chuaich goes up the broad, featureless NE ridge.

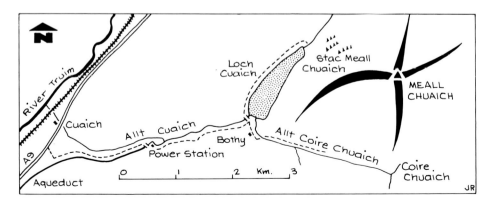

*Looking up Glen Shee towards The Cairnwell*                    *D.J. Bennet*

# SECTION 6

## The Grampians, Blair Atholl to Braemar

*Beinn a' Ghlo from Glen Fender*                                    *D.J. Bennet*

**Carn nan Gabhar**; 1129m; (OS Sheet 43; 971733); M29; *hill of the goats.*
**Braigh Coire Chruinn-bhalgain**; 1070m; (OS Sheet 43; 946724); M63; *upland of the corrie of round
    blisters.*
**Carn Liath**; 975m; (OS Sheet 43; 936698); M175; *grey hill.*

A beautiful, mysterious stony hill of many remote corries, Beinn a' Ghlo (meaning hill of the veil or
mist) is the finest hill in the Mounth from Drumochter to Aberdeen, apart from Lochnagar. It rises north-
east of Blair Atholl, a great complex range of ridges, summits and corries which looks particularly fine
from the Cairngorms.

The highest summit, Carn nan Gabhar, is the remotest, 12km from Blair Atholl as the crow flies, and
the finest way to it is the traverse of the other two Munros en route, starting with Carn Liath. From
Killiecrankie the pointed hill of Carn Liath with its grey screes looks more prominent than the higher tops
behind. It is best approached from Blair Atholl by the narrow road on the S side of Glen Fender; cars
should be left at the end of the public road near Loch Moraig, ¾km from Monzie Farm. Walk along the
track ENE towards Glen Girnaig for 2km to a little bothy, and then strike NE directly up the ever-
steepening slopes of Carn Liath. (4½km; 640m; 2h 10min).

Follow the twisting ridge N down to the col at 760m, and continue up the broad ridge of heath and
stones to Braigh Coire Chruinn-bhalgain. (7½km; 950m; 3h 20min). There is a fine view down into Glen
Tilt from this hill. Continue NE along the ridge for 1km before turning E to descend a grassy slope to the
next col at 847m. Climb ESE to the col between Carn nan Gabhar and Airgiod Bheinn (1061m; silver
mountain), and finally go NE along the broad easy-angled ridge to the top where there are two large
cairns. The highest point is at the NE end of this nearly level summit ridge, at a cairn about 200 metres
NE of the trig point and 9m higher. (11km; 1230m; 4h 30min).

The return to Loch Moraig can either be made by retracing the outward route along the ridges, or by
descending the stony SW shoulder of Airgiod Bheinn and traversing rough heathery terrain SW round
the foot of Carn Liath to reach the track between Glen Girnaig and Loch Moraig.

*Carn nan Gabhar from Braigh Coire Chruinn-bhalgain*                    W.D. Brooker

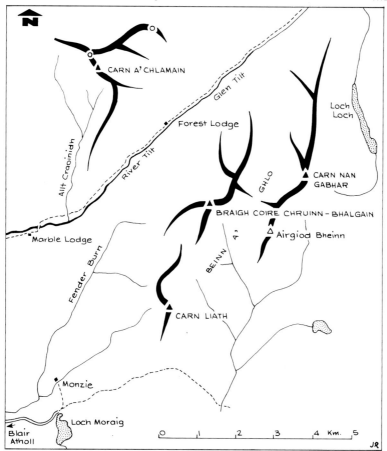

*Approaching Carn a' Chlamain from the south-east*                    *D.J. Bennet*

**Carn a' Chlamain**; 963m; (OS Sheet 43; 916758); M188; *hill of the kite or buzzard.*

This hill is the highest point of the undulating plateau, intersected by two or three deep glens, on the NW side of Glen Tilt. It has a pointed summit rising slightly above the general level of the plateau which makes it recognisable from a distance.

The approach is up Glen Tilt, and it is possible, on enquiry at the factor's office at Blair Castle, to obtain permission to drive up the private road from Old Bridge of Tilt to Forest Lodge. Alternatively, the walk up this very beautiful glen is full of interest and variety, and is well worth while.

If a car is taken, drive to Forest Lodge. At the end of the lodge wood a path zig-zags up the steep hillside on the NW side of the glen, offering an easy way up. This path, continuing at an easier angle beyond the edge of the plateau, passes close to the summit of Carn a' Chlamain on its N side. (4km; 660m; 2h).

If it is preferred to walk all the way, starting from Old Bridge of Tilt, either the road on the W side of the river, or the right-of-way on the E side may be taken. Continue up the glen until 1km beyond Marble Lodge where, after crossing the Allt Craoinidh, the ridge on the NW side of the glen is climbed. There is a fair path up the broad crest which gives good walking on short grass and heather, heading NE and then NW to join the previous route just before the summit of Carn a' Chlamain is reached. (12½km; 820m; 4h 10min).

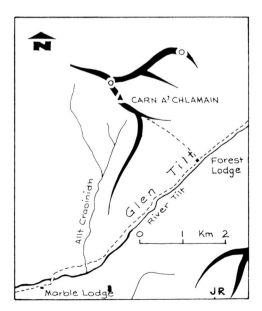

*The foothills of Beinn Dearg from Glen Tilt*                    *R. Simpson*

**Beinn Dearg**; 1008m; (OS Sheet 43; 853778); M121; *red hill.*

A pointed hill rising above a multitude of flat or rounded hills and peaty plateaux, Beinn Dearg stands north-east of Bruar Lodge in the middle of the Atholl deer forest, 12km north of Blair Atholl. It is a lone granite peak surrounded by a vast area of schist hills.

From Old Blair near Blair Atholl walk up the private road in Glen Banvie on the NE side of the Banvie Burn, and continue up the E side of the Allt an t-Seapail to the bothy beside the Allt Sheicheachan. An alternative route to this bothy is from Calvine on the A9 road, up the private road along Glen Bruar to join the above route at the Allt Sheicheachan. The path continues along the NW side of this burn to 800m on Meall Dubh nan Dearcag. From there an easy broad ridge leads N to the summit of Beinn Dearg up dwarf heath and the reddish-coloured screes which obviously give the hill its name. (14km; 890m; 4h 40min).

An alternative route of similar length and character also starts at Old Blair, but follows the high road on the W side of Glen Tilt through Blairuachdar Wood and up the Allt Slanaidh by a track ending at a bothy. Continue up the burn, bearing N across the shoulder of Beinn a' Chait to join the previous route at the col 2km S of Beinn Dearg.

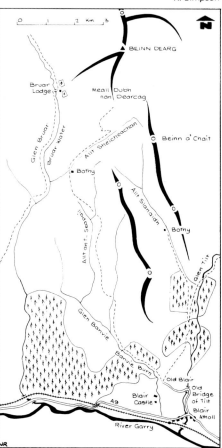

*Looking NW from Beinn a' Ghlo to the Tarf hills*                              W.D. Brooker

**An Sgarsoch;** 1006m; (OS Sheet 43; 933836); M124; *the place of sharp rocks.*
**Carn an Fhidhleir;** 994m; (OS Sheet 43; 905842); M145; *hill of the fiddler.*

These two very remote hills stand in one of the wildest and most inaccessible parts of the Highlands, more or less at the centre of the headwaters of the rivers Feshie, Geldie and Tarf. They are both smooth, gently-sloping hills, with rough heather and peaty ground on their lower slopes, but excellent walking on mossy turf on their upper parts.

They are a long way from any starting point, and a bicycle is a great help in reaching them. The three possible points of access to which cars can be driven are Linn of Dee, Achlean Farm in Glen Feshie and (with permission) Forest Lodge in Glen Tilt. The Linn of Dee approach is described; for most of the way from there to the hills there is a track which makes for fast walking, and although it is rough and stony in places it is negotiable by bicycle for much of its length.

The route follows this track along the N bank of the River Dee to the White Bridge, and then along the Geldie Burn to the ruined Geldie Lodge, 12½km from Linn of Dee. From there a bulldozed track climbs WSW, and it is followed to its highest point. Continue SW across peaty ground and climb the NE slopes of Carn an Fhidhleir, up grass and heather, to reach the N ridge near the summit. (18½km; 630m; 5h 10min).

Descend SSE along the broad ridge for 1km and then drop down the E side of the ridge to reach the 710m col. From there climb NE to the large cairn on the flat summit of An Sgarsoch. (22km; 930m; 6h 30min).

The easiest way back is due N, avoiding the steep NE corries which may hold snow drifts well into summer. Keep to the W of Scarsoch Bheag over peaty ground and reach the bulldozed track leading to Geldie Lodge.

The route from Forest Lodge in Glen Tilt starts up the zig-zag path to Carn a' Chlamain (qv). Once fairly level ground is reached at about 750m bear N across rough terrain of peat and heather, over the col between Carn a' Chlamain and Conlach Mor and descend to Tarf Bothy. This old shooting lodge is now in a ruined state, but one room is still weatherproof and provides good shelter. Cross the Tarf Water and go N up the Allt a' Chaorainn to the 710m col between An Sgarsoch and Carn an Fhidhleir from where the two hills are climbed. (From Forest Lodge to either hill: 11½km; 930m; 4h 10min).

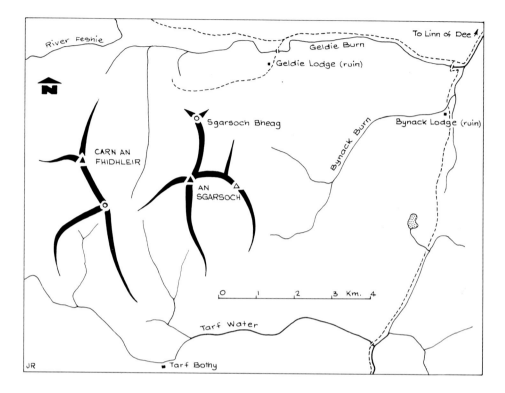

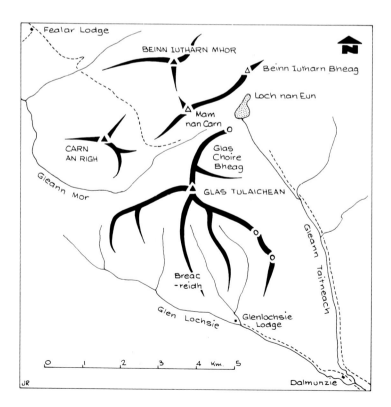

*Looking across the headwaters of the Tilt to Carn an Righ*                    W.D. Brooker

**Glas Tulaichean**; 1051m; (OS Sheet 43; 051760); M77; *from Glas-thulchan, green hills.*
**Carn an Righ**; 1029m; (OS Sheet 43; 028773); M98; *hill of the king.*

These two hills stand rather remotely between Glen Shee and Glen Tilt, and can most easily be reached up Glen Lochsie, an offshoot of Glen Shee. There is a private road from Spittal of Glenshee for 2km to Dalmunzie Hotel in Glen Lochsie, and it is normally permissible to drive along this road as far as the hotel.

Glas Tulaichean is a typical green Mounth hill, with crisp mossy turf and heath giving excellent walking on the upper slopes, and with green corries to the east. Carn an Righ is much more remote, the western outlier of the Glas Tulaichean and Beinn Iutharn Mhor group. It is a rounded hill, with much scree on its slopes.

From Dalmunzie, walk up the road past Glenlochsie Farm and along the track of the old railway which used to link Dalmunzie with Glenlochsie Lodge, a former deer-stalking lodge now in ruins. Now head NNW towards Glas Tulaichean, avoiding the little glens which are peaty and wet, and climbing along the crest of one of the broad ridges which lead to the summit. (7½km; 690m; 2h 50min).

To continue to Carn an Righ, go down the NNE ridge of Glas Tulaichean for 1km and then descend to the NW to reach the path on the S side of Mam nan Carn. Follow this path W for 1km to the col due E of Carn an Righ and climb to the summit up slopes of short heath and grass, mixed with stony patches. (11½km; 980m; 4h 20min).

On the return journey retrace the outward route for 2km and reach the 800m col at the foot of Glas Tulaichean's NNE ridge. Cross this col and descend by the Glas Choire Bheag into Gleann Taitneach where a bulldozed track has replaced the former path down this steep-sided glen. At the foot of the glen there are green spots where people once had their farms.

Map on page 99.

*Looking up the Baddoch Burn from Glen Clunie towards Sgor Mor*          A. Watson (sen)

**An Socach**; 944m; (OS Sheet 43; 080800); M221; *the projecting place.*

An Socach is a broad ridge rising between upper Glen Ey and the Baddoch Burn, several kilometres west of the A93 road from Perth to Braemar. The ridge is about 2km long between the east and west summits; the west summit is the higher, but its height is not shown on the OS 1:50000 map, and the name on this map appears (incorrectly) to apply only to the East Top (938m).

The shortest approach is from the highest point of the A93 road at the Glenshee Ski Centre. Follow the bulldozed track going NW up Butchart's Corrie, cross the Cairnwell-Carn Aosda col and descend W, traversing the heathery slopes and peat bogs N of Loch Vrotachan and across the upper Baddoch Burn.

The burnsides and ridges offer the best going across the peaty ground, and higher the walking is excellent on short heather up to the summit cairn. (6½km; 560m; 2h 30min). The 938m East Top lies 2km towards Glen Clunie, with very little drop along the ridge.

A more attractive approach to An Socach, avoiding the ski slopes, is up the Baddoch Burn from Glen Clunie. A road and then a bulldozed track lead far up into the upper part of the glen, where the previous route is joined. Another feasible route is from upper Glen Ey, possibly in combination with Beinn Iutharn Mhor.

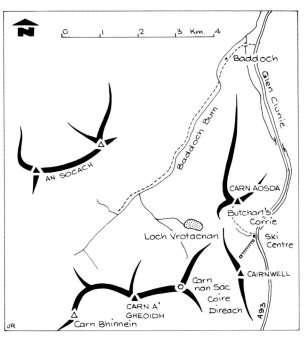

*Looking up Glen Ey to An Socach and Beinn Iutharn Mhor*                                    G. Nicoll

**Beinn Iutharn Mhor**; 1045m; (OS Sheet 43; 045792); M85; *probably from Beinn Fhiubharainn Mhor,*
   *big hill of the edge-point.*

   This is another green, rounded hill, the highest in the Mounth between Beinn a' Ghlo and Glas Maol.
Beinn Iutharn Mhor rises boldly in the view from upper Glen Ey, thrusting big shoulders out into the
glen. Glen Ey offers the most interesting approach.
   From Inverey cycle or walk up the road which starts on the E side of the Ey Burn (locked gate). This
road climbs through decaying birch woods past The Colonel's Bed, and higher up through beautiful
grassy haughs to the ruined Altanour Lodge, 8km from Inverey. From there continue up the Allt Beinn
Iutharn for a further 1½km, and then strike SW up the main shoulder of Beinn Iutharn Mhor. Heather
slopes lead to mossy turf higher up, and then to a flattish summit. (13km; 700m; 4h 10min). It is fairly
easy to take in the Tops of Mam nan Carn (986m) and Beinn Iutharn Bheag (953m) on the way back to
Glen Ey.
   These three hills can also be easily reached from Glen Shee, by driving to Dalmunzie Hotel and then
walking up the bulldozed track through Gleann Taitneach to reach Loch nan Eun, from where they are
easily accessible.

**Carn Bhac**; 946m; (OS Sheet 43; 051832); M216; *hill of peat-banks.*

   Straddling the Perthshire-Aberdeenshire boundary, Carn Bhac is the highest point of an area of rather
featureless rounded hills between the Tilt-Dee watershed and Glen Ey. The hill has two tops, the higher
being the NE one, though it does not have its height shown on the OS 1:50000 map. The name Carn
Bhac applies to both tops, especially the higher one, although on the map it appears to refer to the lower
top only.
   From Inverey take the road (locked gate) up the W side of the Ey Burn past the ruin of Loin-a-veaich.
Continue through a conifer plantation and by a bulldozed track leading up to the source of the Allt
Cristie Beag, S of Carn Liath, 6½km from Inverey. From there a long undulating ridge leads S over Geal
Charn, then to Carn Bhac, with peaty hollows but hard ground and wind-clipped heather on the crest of
the broad ridges. The 920m SW Top is reached first, and the summit is an easy 1½km to the NE. (12km;
600m; 3h 40min).
   Navigation in the Carn Bhac area is difficult in thick weather because of so much featureless peaty
ground.
   The return may be varied by descending NE from the summit to the Allt Connie, and going down this
stream to regain the Track on the N side of the Allt Cristie Beag.

*Looking south-east from Carn Bhac to The Cairnwell between An Socach and Beinn Iutharn Mhor*    W.D. Brooker

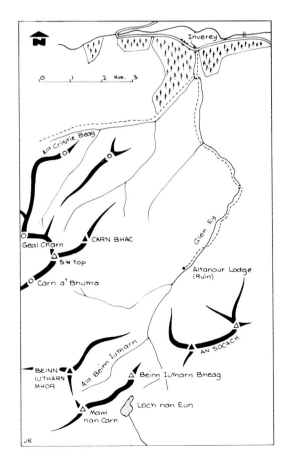

*The Cairnwell from Carn Aosda across Butchart's Corrie*                    *H.M. Brown*

**The Cairnwell**; 933m; (OS Sheet 43; 135773); M242; *from the Gaelic Carn Bhalg, hill of bags (referring to its shape)*.
**Carn Aosda**; 917m; (OS Sheet 43; 134792); M270; *hill of age*.
**Carn a' Gheoidh**; 975m; (OS Sheet 43; 107767); M177; *hill of the goose*.

These three hills lie on the west side of the A93 road from Perth to Braemar, and are most easily accessible from the summit of that road where the Glenshee Ski Centre has its many tows, lifts and bulldozed pistes.

The Cairnwell may be a dull-looking hill from this point on the road, but it stands out boldly in the view from Glen Shee to the south. Carn Aosda rises to the north of The Cairnwell, a heathery hill with pale grey screes on its bald top. Its flanks are scarred by bulldozed tracks and ski tows right up to the summit. Carn a' Gheoidh, on the other hand, is hidden from the summit of the road, being well to the west of its two neighbours.

The Cairnwell and Carn Aosda are the two most accessible Munros in Scotland, particularly The Cairnwell, for there is a chairlift which operates in summer as well as winter and goes up to 910m, a short distance from the summit. However, no true Munro-climber would use this form of uplift.

Going to The Cairnwell first, and starting just S of the Ski Centre, steepish slopes of short, dry heather and, higher up, wind-clipped heath and occasional patches of grey screes lead to the big summit cairn where there is also a small hut. (0.6km; 270m; 40min). It is a very good viewpoint, offering fine panoramas of the Cairngorms and down into Central Scotland.

Descend NNW past the top of the chairlift and along a broad ridge with snow-fences, and after 1km diverge W, just before reaching the Cairnwell-Carn Aosda col, and drop down to another col at 810m which is the lowest point betwen The Cairnwell and Carn a' Gheoidh. Continuing SW, the walking is easy up a gentle slope of crisp, mossy heath along the edge of the Coire Direach rocks, past Carn nan Sac (920m) and W to Carn a' Gheoidh across a little plateau. (4½km; 440m; 1h 50min).

Returning along the same route to the Cairnwell-Carn Aosda col, climb NE then E along the broad ridge of wind-clipped heath, passing the top of the ski tow in Butchart's Corrie, to reach the flat, stony summit of Carn Aosda. (9km; 570m; 3h). Descend S and return to the road by the bulldozed tracks at the foot of Butchart's Corrie.

Map on page 101.

*The White Mounth from the River Dee*                                    *A. Watson*

# SECTION 7

## The Mounth, Glen Shee to Lochnagar

*Glas Maol from Carn an Tuirc*                                                    *A. Watson*

Lying to the east of the A93 road over the Cairnwell pass, the sprawling Mounth plateau extends from Creag Leacach in the south-west and Driesh in the south-east for 20km to the north facing Lochnagar corries. Never falling below 800m, the outline of its continuous high ground widens and narrows in accordance with the glens and high corries which bite into the edge of the plateau; Callater from the west, Muick, Clova and Isla from the east. North of the Tolmount drove road, which crosses the Mounth from Callater to Glen Doll, the underlying granite yields a poorer soil and sparser vegetation than the grassier tundras to the south which are based on varied metamorphic rocks. No fewer than 13 Munros and 16 Tops are scattered on this part of the Mounth, and easy high level walking connects them all so that they may be done in various combinations. The routes suggested in the following descriptions involve a variety of approaches by different glens, and do not involve any particularly long days.

**Glas Maol**; 1068m; (OS Sheet 43; 166765); M67; *greenish grey bare hill.*
**Creag Leacach**; 987m; (OS Sheet 43; 155746); M157; *slabby rock.*

These hills lie east of the A93 road over the Cairnwell pass at the south-west corner of the great Mounth plateau. The bald dome of Glas Maol rises just south of the point where the plateau is pinched between the Garbh-choire and the Caenlochan Glen to form a narrow isthmus joining it to Cairn of Claise. Spurs project from the dome north-west to Meall Odhar, and south-east to Little Glas Maol. The main ridge extends south-south-west to Creag Leacach and beyond it for a further 5km over a series of lesser tops towards Glen Shee.

Start from the car park near the summit of the A93, and ascend to the E where a bulldozed track leads over a knoll and into a dip holding sundry buildings at the foot of the Meall Odhar ski-tows. In winter there are hot drinks and many people, but in summer these are replaced by an abandoned and desolate atmosphere. Continue up the stony slope, keeping well to the right of the ski-tow and cross Meall Odhar to a flat mossy col. From there a short but steep pull of 100m, with the edge of the Glas Choire just to the left, brings one to the dome of Glas Maol. The summit cairn lies ½km SE across the stony plateau. (3½km; 440m; 1h 30min).

The summit is wide, but from a short distance E of the cairn the fine grassy ridge which carries the Monega drove road over Little Glas Maol and along the curving rim of the Caenlochan corrie can be seen. To the SW schistose screes, blanketed in moss, slope down towards the ridge leading to Creag Leacach. The old fence is a convenient guide, and where it branches near a col take the right fork leading SW along the ridge which is unusually narrow for this part of the Grampians and even rocky in places, although mainly broken into large scree and boulders. The summit of Creag Leacach lies 1km along this ridge. (6km; 520m; 2h 20min).

Continue down the widening stony ridge to the South-west Top (943m) and then leave the crest to go NW down a fairly steep slope to reach the saddle behind the outlying knoll of Meall Gorm. From there

*Creag Leacach from the north*                                              *H.M. Brown*

descend NNE by a grassy re-entrant to the floor of the side valley below. Go downstream, crossing to the N side to join a path and cross the Allt a' Ghlinne Bhig by a footbridge to reach the A93. Walk up the road for 2km to return to the starting point.

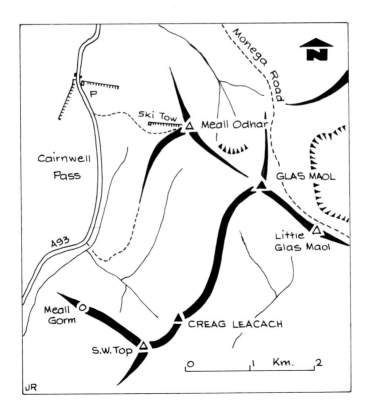

*Carn an Tuirc from the Glen Clunie road*                                   H.M. Brown

**Carn an Tuirc**; 1019m; (OS Sheet 43; 174804); M112; *hill of the boar.*
**Cairn of Claise**; 1064m; (OS Sheet 43; 185789); M68; *hill of the hollow.*
**Tolmount**; 958m; (OS Sheets 43 and 44; 210800); M199; *probably hill of the valley.*
**Tom Buidhe**; 957m; (OS Sheets 43 and 44; 214788); M200; *yellow hill.*

Of these four hills, Carn an Tuirc and Cairn of Claise overlook the head of Glen Clunie a few kilometres north-east of the Cairnwell pass, showing shallow grassy corries and rounded shoulders to the A93 road. Tolmount, a few kilometres east, stands at the head of Glen Callater with a steep craggy face above this glen, and Tom Buidhe to its south is a rounded swelling on the Mounth plateau. The four can be climbed in a round tour from the head of Glen Clunie.

Leaving the A93 road 2km N of the Cairnwell pass at (148800), descend a short distance to cross the Cairnwell Burn by the old bridge, a remnant of the 18th Century military road. Follow the Allt a' Garbh-choire stream E by a path for 1km and cross the tributary coming down from the NE. Then climb due E up heather, grass and areas of boulders to reach the flat stony summit of Carn an Tuirc. (3km; 510m; 1h 40min).

Continue E across the summit stonefield and, where the slope steepens towards Coire Kander, turn SE down a wide grassy ridge to the saddle from where Cairn of Claise lies 1½km SSE. Climb the easy slope to reach a line of fence posts which lead to the summit. (5½km; 620m; 2h 20min). A pleasant walk ENE down grassy slopes leads to a shallow peaty col from which a wide incline (it is hardly a ridge) leads to Tolmount. (8½km; 700m; 3h 10min). This summit stands near the edge of the headwall of Glen Callater, a steep mass of broken granitic slabs.

To the S the subdued eminence of Tom Buidhe swells from the tableland. It is best approached by returning down the wide incline and skirting round the upper part of a shallow green glen, one of the sources of the River South Esk, which separates Tolmount from Tom Buidhe. A short ascent SE up a grassy slope studded with occasional boulders leads to the rounded summit of the latter. (10km; 790m; 3h 40min).

Return due W along the highest ground over Ca Whims. After 2km bear SW, contouring at about 950m to avoid both Cairn of Claise and the steeper slopes dropping towards the Caenlochan Glen. This traverse is over tussocky grass and blaeberry, but leads to the smooth ground of the watershed in another 2km. Go SW along the fence line to the path of the Monega road, the highest drove route in the Highlands. This crosses the divide here and leads NW down the spur of Sron na Gaoithe. Leave this ridge to descend on the N flank just before the rocky knob at its termination. The path soon expires, but an easy grassy slope leads down to the Allt a' Gharbh-choire which must be crossed to gain the bridge at the starting point of the route.

*Looking south-west across the Mounth Plateau towards Glas Maol*                    A. Watson

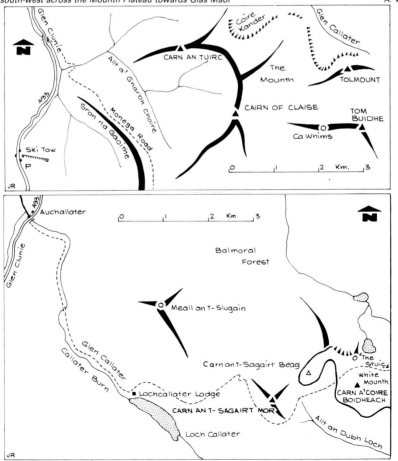

*The White Mounth from the road to Glen Gairn*                    *W.D. Brooker*

**Carn an t-Sagairt Mor**; 1047m; (OS Sheets 43 and 44; 208843); M81; *big hill of the priest.*
**Carn a' Coire Boidheach**; 1118m; (OS Sheet 44; 226845); M33; *hill of the beautiful corrie.*

Between the north facing corries of The Stuic and Lochnagar and the deep valley of Loch Muick and the Dubh Loch is the corner of the high Mounth plateau known as The White Mounth. To the east the Cac Carn Beag of Lochnagar is its highest point, while in the middle Carn a' Coire Boidheach rises marginally higher than the top of The Stuic just to its north. Westward the plateau begins to rise and fall into individual hills of which Carn an t-Sagairt Mor (or Cairn Taggart to give its anglicised name) is the highest.

It is possible to do these hills in a single long day from Glen Muick and include Lochnagar, Cairn Bannoch and Broad Cairn. However, this involves an excursion of nearly 30km, and it is more usual to enjoy them in shorter sections by the routes described here and in the following pages.

Start from the bridge at Auchallater on the A93 road and follow the estate road up Glen Callater for 5km to Lochcallater Lodge. (This is the first part of the Tolmount road leading to Glen Clova). Just outside the lodge enclosure a path strikes uphill before turning SE to traverse the hillside above Loch Callater, gaining height gradually. It bends NE below the small rocky bluff of Creag an Loch to gain a col below the W slope of Cairn Taggart. Follow the path up this slope by zig-zags until it starts to contour around to the SE, and then climb direct to the summit by the fence line. (9km; 680m; 3h 10min).

Continue NE, descending about 80m and reascending the same height to pass over the Top of Carn an t-Sagairt Beag (1044m) and reach the plateau rim ¾km beyond. The Stuic rises a little higher ½km E, and is well worth visiting for the view over its rocky corries to the Dee valley far below. An easy walk S for ½km over the sparse, stony tundra of the high plateau brings one to Carn a' Coire Boidheach. (11½km; 880m; 4h 10min).

Return by descending the slope W to intersect the path which leads SW, traversing the head streams of the Allt an Dubh-loch and then girdling the S side of Cairn Taggart on its way back to Glen Callater and finally the A93 road at Auchallater.

Map on page 109.

*Looking up Loch Muick towards Broad Cairn*                                    *A. Watson*

**Cairn Bannoch**; 1012m; (OS Sheet 44; 223826); M114; *possibly peaked hill, or may be from Gaelic bonnach a cake.*
**Broad Cairn**; 998m; (OS Sheet 44; 240815); M139.

The glacial valley which bites deeply into the eastern part of the Mounth plateau on the south side of Lochnagar forms a deep trough containing Loch Muick. Upstream the valley floor rises to a smaller upper basin holding the Dubh Loch. Broad Cairn stands at the southern edge of this upper basin, and with its north face of overlapping slabs it is a dominant feature on the approach from Glen Muick. Cairn Bannoch on the other hand, although near the south-west edge of the basin, is set back a little into the great plateau so that it is only distinguished from a number of other tops of comparable height by its small yet prominent summit cone.

From the car park at the end of the public road in Glen Muick, walk SW past Spittal of Glenmuick and after 1km take the path to the right which crosses the outlet of Loch Muick to reach the road on the W side of the glen. Continue along the loch-side to the Glas-allt-Shiel wood, and emerge on the far side of the plantation by a footpath. In another 100 metres or so take the right fork of the path and proceed up the valley of the Allt an Dubh-loch. To the right the Strulan burn cascades down its rocky bed in an attractive waterfall, while below on the left the Dubh-loch stream sluices over red granite in a succession of waterslides. Abruptly the Dubh Loch itself comes into view, said to be the lair of a notorious waterkelpie. The path peters out on the N side of the loch, however continue along easy if slightly boggy terrain upstream until the NW end of Creag an Dubh-loch has been outflanked and Cairn Bannoch itself can be seen. After passing a tributary that tumbles down over the slabs of Eagle's Rock high up on the right, cross to the S side of the Allt an Dubh-loch and ascend by another tributary which flows down behind Creag an Dubh-loch, until it is easy to gain the summit cone of Cairn Bannoch with its broken granite tor. (11½km; 610m; 3h 40min).

Proceed SE for 1km by easy walking over the undulating plateau to reach the Top of Cairn of Gowal (983m), and then go E, descending to a wide saddle before the gentle ascent to the boulderfield summit of Broad Cairn. (14km; 710m; 4h 20min).

Descend E down granite boulders to reach a rough path through rocks and heather. Lower down it becomes a bulldozed track, and after a further 1km a wooden stable shelter is reached. Continue E for 300 metres, then bear left along the path (called the Flash of Lightning) which slants down to reach Loch Muick near its head. The path continues along the shore of the loch through attractive scattered birches, and in 1½km merges with a bulldozed road which continues past the conifer plantation of Lochend to reach Spittal of Glenmuick.

Map on page 112.

*Lochnagar from Aberarder in Deeside*                    A. Watson

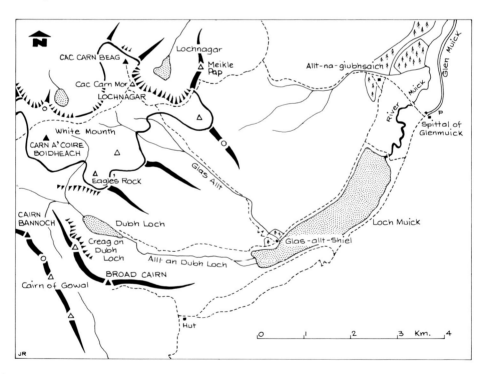

*The north-east corrie of Lochnagar*                                    *R. Robb*

**Lochnagar**; 1155m; (OS Sheet 44; 244862); M19; *named after Lochan na Gaire in the NE corrie, meaning little loch of the noisy sound.*

Located entirely in the royal estate of Balmoral, this fine complex mountain lies south of the Dee valley, and north-west of Loch Muick. Its summit crowns the northern rim of the great Mounth plateau which sweeps far southward to Glen Shee and the Angus glens. The true nobility of Lochnagar is best appreciated from the north, from Deeside or even better from the B976 Crathie to Gairnshiel road, from where its sharp summit and flanking corries can be seen rising above the lower slopes mantled by the ancient pinewoods of the Ballochbuie Forest.

Start at the Spittal of Glenmuick car park at the end of the public road on the E side of Glen Muick. Walk SW along the private road for 250 metres and turn right along the edge of the plantation to reach the other side of the glen at Allt-na-giubhsaich. Continue W along a path on the S side of the burn through the pine woods to reach a vehicular track, which is followed W for almost 3km to the col leading through to Gelder Shiel. Here take the prominent rough path WSW across a slight dip and then more steeply for 1 ¼ km to the last waterpoint of the Foxes' Well to the left of the path. The slope now relents before the steep ascent known as The Ladder, and a short diversion W to the col just S of Meikle Pap gives a splendid view of the great NE corrie of Lochnagar.

If there is old hard snow covering the steep slope of The Ladder, it may be safer to keep to the right among the boulders nearer the edge of the corrie, and at the top the summit ridge is reached. A short descent across a wide col and a climb of 70m lead to the almost level roof of the mountain. Finally, an airy walk of 1km along the rim of the corrie, past the cairn of Cac Carn Mor and the deep indentation of the Black Spout, leads to the summit cone of Cac Carn Beag (as Lochnagar's highest point is called) where the trig point stands on top of a granite tor. (9km; 800m; 3h 20min).

An enjoyable alternative descent route is by the Glas Allt, passing a pretty waterfall and then by steep zig-zags to the wood of Glas-allt Shiel. Continue by the road along the NW side of Loch Muick to Allt-na giubhsaich and cross the glen to the car park.

No restriction on climbing by the ascent route described above during the stalking season. Other routes should be avoided at that time.

*Driesh above the forested hillsides of Glen Doll*                    *J. Renny*

**Driesh;** 947m; (OS Sheet 44; 271736); M213; *from Gaelic dris, a thorn bush or bramble.*
**Mayar;** 928m; (OS Sheet 44; 241738); M248; *meaning obscure, perhaps from m'aighear, my delight, or from magh, a plain.*

The straightest and deepest of the Angus glens, its sides scalloped by many corries, Glen Clova slices north-westerly into the Eastern Grampians. At its head it forks into two branches, the northerly one being the glen leading to Bachnagairn, the southerly one Glen Doll. Both these branches are hemmed in by steep slopes and rocky bluffs, Glen Doll opening on its south side to form the wide amphitheatre of Corrie Fee. Driesh stands south of the mouth of Glen Doll, and 3km west Mayar rises from the plateau south of Corrie Fee.

There are extensive coniferous plantings in upper Glen Clova, and the route starts at the Forestry Commission car park ½km past Braedownie farm. Go W along the road past the youth hostel at Glendoll Lodge as far as a new bridge (unmarked on the 1:50000 map) at (276763). Cross the bridge and continue W along a forest road until the old hill path to Kilbo in Glen Prosen turns off SW. This path leads uphill until it crosses the Burn of Kilbo and emerges from the forest at a deer fence. Continue up the path along the steep side of the Shank of Drumfollow to the col between Driesh and Mayar. Turn SE then E to reach the summit of Driesh in 1½km of easy walking over a subsidiary top. (5½km; 700m; 2h 30min).

From Driesh one can see into the upper reaches of the Clova glens and identify the lines of the old drove roads crossing to Glen Muick and Braemar, and all the summits of the Mounth from Mount Keen to Glas Maol can be identified on a clear day.

Mayar is reached by returning to the col and following the line of the fence W over pleasant grassy tundra, taking care to avoid the festoons of old fence wire, a hazard for the unwary. (9km; 860m; 3h 30min).

Grassy slopes lead down NNE for 1km to the edge of Corrie Fee, from where descend on the SE side of the Fee Burn past small waterfalls. At the foot of the steepest section a path is reached and followed ENE down the lower corrie, over a stile and into the forest. This path develops into a forest road which continues down Glen Doll past the youth hostel to reach the car park.

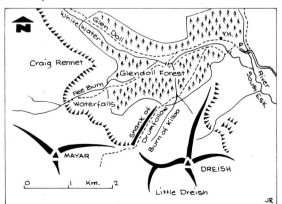

*The path from Mount Keen to Glen Mark over the Knowe of Crippley*                    *W.D. Brooker*

**Mount Keen;** 939m; (OS Sheet 44; 409869); M229; *from Gaelic monadh caoin, smooth or pleasant hill.*

This is the most easterly of all the Munros, and one of the most solitary. Its pointed dome is on the spine of the Mounth between the Dee valley and the Vale of Strathmore, and it is the highest summit east of Loch Muick. There are two commonly used approaches to Mount Keen, from Glen Esk to the south-east, and Glen Tanar to the north-east.

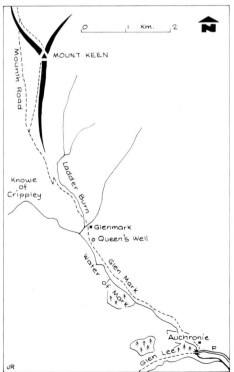

The Glen Esk route starts at a car park where the glen divides into Glen Lee and Glen Mark. Go W to the road junction and take the right fork up Glen Mark, continuing for 3½km to the Queen's Well, a monument which commemorates a visit by Queen Victoria. Bear right (N) past the last house in the glen and follow the track up the narrow glen of the Ladder Burn, climbing its W slope to emerge onto an undulating high moorland. The blunt cone of Mount Keen rises to the N, and the track leading towards it reaches a fork. The traditional Mounth Road goes due N and another path, more frequently used today, bears a little to the right to ascend Mount Keen. Just before the very large summit cairn there is a boundary stone with a large B carved on it. (9km; 680m; 3h 10min).

The other route starts at the end of the public road up Glen Tanar. From the car park at Glen Tanar House go past a sawmill and through a gate to the estate road up the N side of the Water of Tanar. This road passes through fine native pine woods for 6km, and for another 4km up the open glen, crossing the river twice. Cross the Water of Tanar for a third time at (407896) and ascend the Mounth Road S by a bulldozed track through heather clad slopes, diverging SE up the path to the summit of Mount Keen. (13½km; 760m; 4h 20min).

All these routes follow rights-of-way.

*Cairn Toul from Sron na Lairige*                                                    *D.J. Bennet*

# SECTION 8

## The Cairngorm Mountains

*Cairngorm winter landscape looking south from Cairn Gorm towards Derry Cairngorm*                    *A. Fyffe*

This vast high mountain range is divided into three main blocks or massifs by the Lairig Ghru and Lairig an Laoigh paths which run from south to north through glacially cut passes. To the east of the Lairig an Laoigh lie Beinn Bhreac, Beinn a' Chaorainn and the huge plateaux of Beinn a' Bhuird and Ben Avon. The middle block consists of the high ground above Strath Nethy and the deep basin of Loch Avon; it extends over Cairn Gorm to Ben Macdui and round to Beinn Mheadhoin in a great horseshoe, with offshoots to Bynack More, Derry Cairngorm and Carn a' Mhaim. West of the Lairig Ghru the largest of the three blocks extends across the grassy plateau of the Moine Mhor (the great moss) to the valley of the Feshie, and includes Braeriach and Cairn Toul facing Ben Macdui across the Lairig, and further south and west The Devil's Point, Beinn Bhrotain, Monadh Mor, Mullach Clach a' Bhlair and Sgor Gaoith.

Largely of intrusive granites, the Cairngorms are characterised by poor acid soils and bleak stony tundra, albeit richer and grassier on the western massif. Consequently the most attractive features tend to be in the corries and penetrating valleys where cliffs, streams and lochans create variety and interest, rather than on the high plateaux which, unless enlivened by tors, tend towards monotony.

Some of the summits of the Cairngorms may be approached from either Deeside or Speyside. Since both approaches are frequently used, brief descriptions of access routes from the two directions are included where appropriate.

In Deeside the common starting point for several of the peaks is the car park near the Linn of Dee at the end of the public road up Deeside. From there one rough private road continues up the River Dee towards the Lairig Ghru and distant passes leading to Glen Tilt and Glen Feshie; another private road leads north-west up Glen Lui to Derry Lodge and is the most important access route on the south side of the Cairngorms. On both these roads bicycles can be used to save some time.

From Speyside the Cairngorms appear as a great scarp, scalloped by corries and sliced through by the deep cleft of the Lairig Ghru, with the dark forests of Glen More, Rothiemurchus and Inshriach in the foreground. There are a number of suitable starting points for the mountains, those most frequently used being the car park at the end of the road to the ski slopes on Cairn Gorm and, for the western summits, the road up the east side of Glen Feshie as far as Achlean.

*Clach Choutsaich, one of the tors of Ben Avon*                    *W.D. Brooker*

**Ben Avon, Leabaidh an Daimh Bhuidhe**; 1171m; (OS Sheets 36 and 43; 132019); M16; *bed of the yellow stag.*

One of the most unusual mountains in Scotland because of the many strange granite tors along its skyline, Ben Avon is also one of the biggest in terms of its area of high ground, being a vast plateau stretching 12km from Glen Quoich in the south-west to Inchrory in Glen Avon far to the north-east. It is the most easterly mountain of the main Cairngorm range, and the most prominent of them when seen from lower Aberdeenshire or Banffshire.

Ben Avon can be reached from three points – Inchrory in Glen Avon to the north, Corndavon Lodge high up the River Gairn to the east, and Invercauld Bridge near Braemar to the south. All these routes are long, and the use of a bicycle along the private approach roads will shorten the walking distances.

The Invercauld Bridge route, which is probably the most used, starts from the A93 road a few kilometres E of Braemar. Turn up the public road to Keiloch where cars should be left. Continue on foot or by bicycle along the private road past Alltdourie for 6km up Gleann an t-Slugain, and onwards by the path past the ruins of Slugain Lodge to reach Glen Quoich. The path continues up the E side of this glen to end just beyond the huge boulder of Clach a' Chleirich. From there it is an easy climb up the narrowing grassy glen to the saddle at 970m called The Sneck, where a fine view opens out to the N into the wild corrie of Slochd Mor. Climb E up slopes of gravel and turf to the plateau, and then 1½km NE to the summit tor. (16km; 850m; 5h).

To vary the return route, one can keep high along the plateau on the E side of Glen Quoich, going S to the Top of Carn Eas (1089m), then SE to Creag an Dail Mhor (972m) before descending SW to Glen Quoich and the ruined lodge at the head of Gleann an t-Slugain.

The northern approach starts at Tomintoul, driving a few kilometres up Glen Avon to the locked gate at Birchfield (167148). Continue on foot or bicycle along a good road to Inchrory Lodge. About 1km further leave the gravel road and climb the stalker's path up the northern spur to Meall Gaineimh to gain the vast tor-studded plateau which undulates SW for another 4km to the summit. (17½km; 870m; 5h 20min. 9km may be done by bicycle).

*Beinn a' Bhuird and Ben Avon from Invercauld*                    A. Watson

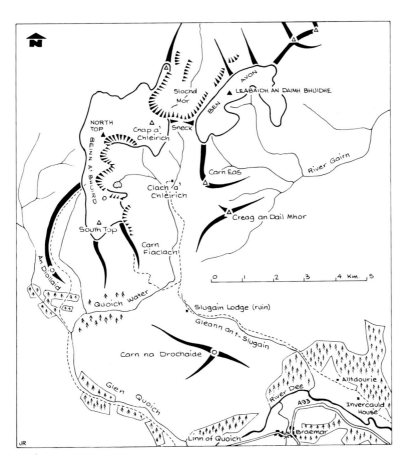

*The South Top of Beinn a' Bhuird above the pinewoods of Glen Quoich*     A. Watson

**Beinn a' Bhuird, North Top;** 1196m; (OS Sheets 36 and 43; 093006); M10; *hill of the table.*

This great mountain between Glen Quoich and Glen Avon has the biggest high tableland in the Cairngorms, and although it sweeps down gently on the west side to lower peaty glens and plateaux, on the east and north-east it plunges in spectacular cliffs to great wild corries.

One possible approach is from Invercauld Bridge a few kilometres E of Braemar, following the same route as described for Ben Avon as far as the entry to Glen Quoich 1km beyond the ruined Slugain Lodge. There a path breaks off to the W towards Quoich Water, crosses the stream and on the far bank the path continues high up past Carn Fiaclach, from where easy dry slopes of short grass and gravel lead up to the edge of the plateau of Beinn a' Bhuird. From there it is a short distance W to the South Top (1179m). The walking on the plateau is excellent, on dry ground, with grand views at times into the corries. In misty weather in summer the cliff edge on the right can be useful for navigating, but remember that snow wreaths and unstable cornices sometimes persist at the edge far into the summer. The cliffs lead to the North Top, where a small cairn stands in the midst of the featureless plateau. (16km; 980m; 5h 10min).

The grassy Top of Cnap a' Chleirich (1172m) rises from the plateau to the NE, and the return journey can be varied by crossing this Top, descending E to the saddle called The Sneck, and then turning S to reach Clach a' Chleirich and the path which leads down Glen Quoich to Gleann an t-Slugain.

A quite different route to Beinn a' Bhuird starts at the Linn of Quoich which can be reached by car from Braemar via Mar Lodge. Walk up the track on the SW side of the Quoich Water through fine stands of Old Caledonian pines, and after 6km cross the W tributary of the Quoich Water. Keep N, following the bulldozed track through the highest trees and then by a few zig-zags onto the ridge of An Diollaid. The track leads high onto Beinn a' Bhuird, ending only about 1½km SSW of the summit, which is reached easily along the plateau. (14km; 870m; 4h 40min). Although shorter than the alternative route, this one is aesthetically spoiled by the bulldozed track high onto the mountain.

Map on page 119.

*Looking south from Bynack More to Beinn a' Chaorainn (left) and the Lairig an Laoigh pass*    A. Watson

**Beinn Bhreac**; 931m; (OS Sheets 36 and 43; 058971); M245; *speckled hill.*
**Beinn a' Chaorainn**; 1082m; (OS Sheet 36; 045013); M58; *hill of the rowan.*

These two hills occupy a large area of high ground on the east side of upper Glen Derry with, between them, the vast expanse of the Moine Bhealaidh, a flat featureless plateau at about 850m altitude. From Derry Lodge or Luibeg, Beinn Bhreac stands out prominently above the Old Caledonian pine forest of Derry, a broad heathery hill speckled with grey screes that obviously give its Gaelic name. Beinn a' Chaorainn is a conical stony hill rising at the head of Glen Derry, just above the Lairig an Laoigh pass, towards which its western slopes drop steeply in broken crags.

The car park near the Linn of Dee is the starting point for this expedition, as well as for others to the mountains round Glen Derry and at the southern end of the Lairig Ghru. As an alterntaive to walking, a bicycle can be used along the private road as far as Derry Lodge. From there take the bulldozed track up the E side of Glen Derry for about 2km to its highest point at 500m. Then strike uphill NE through trees and over heather slopes to the 673m col between Meall an Lundain and Beinn Bhreac, and finally climb NNE on wind-clipped heath up the broad ridge to the summit of Beinn Bhreac (10km; 570m; 3h 10min).

Continue NW then N across the grassy, peaty plateau of the Moine Bhealaidh, dropping only to 850m. Stay near the watershed as this gives the driest ground. The route offers spacious views towards Ben Macdui and Beinn a' Bhuird. After 4km the ground becomes firmer and the going is easy on wind-clipped heath, gravel and stones up the broad ridge to Beinn a' Chaorainn. (15km; 810m; 4h 50min).

The easiest return to Derry Lodge lies SW for 1½km, then steeply down W to the summit of the Lairig an Laoigh pass at 740m. There is a fine view N through the pass to the distant tors on Bynack More, the Barns of Bynack. Follow the path S down Glen Derry until it becomes a bulldozed track, and continue along this track for a further 1km until it begins to climb uphill to the left. At that point diverge to the right along a footpath, cross the Derry Burn by a footbridge and go down the W side of the burn, a more pleasant way to return to Derry Lodge than along the bulldozed track.

Map on page 123.

*Carn a' Mhaim and Ben Macdui from the south*                    *A. Watson*

**Ben Macdui**; 1309m; (OS Sheets 36 and 43; 988989); M2; *hill of the black pig, or perhaps hill of the sons of Dubh (the black one).*

**Carn a' Mhaim**; 1037m; (OS Sheets 36 and 43; 994952); M93; *cairn of the large rounded hill.*

**Derry Cairngorm**; 1155m; (OS Sheets 36 and 43; 017980); M20; *blue hill of Derry (from doire, a thicket).*

The central group of the Cairngorms, lying between the north-south defiles of the Lairig Ghru and the Lairig an Laoigh, has as its highest point the great dome of Ben Macdui. From it two long high ridges thrust southward, separated by Glen Luibeg. The eastern ridge includes Derry Cairngorm and ends above the woods of Glen Derry; the western ridge is Carn a' Mhaim, whose crest, one of the narrowest of Cairngorm ridges, is joined to Ben Macdui by a high col. These three mountains can all be climbed from Derry Lodge, either together or singly, and the following description is for the complete traverse, a long day's hill-walking which can be shortened by starting or ending the circuit at intermediate points.

Start at the Linn of Dee as described on the preceding page along the private road to Derry Lodge and cross the Derry Burn by the footbridge W of the lodge. Go W along the N side of the Lui, following the wide path through splendid scattered native pines for 3km to the Robbers' Copse where the Lairig Ghru and Glen Luibeg paths diverge. At this point the direct route to Ben Macdui goes up the path along the Luibeg Burn and the Sron Riach ridge. (15km; 950m; 5h).

The route to Carn a' Mhaim crosses the Luibeg Bridge, below which the boulder debris is evidence of the power of the flood which carried away the earlier bridge after a cloud-burst. Leave the Lairig Ghru path to climb the SE ridge of Carn a' Mhaim. There is a grassy col between its two boulder clad tops, of which the NW one is the summit. (11½km; 700m; 3h 50min).

Continuing to Ben Macdui, go NNW down the narrow ridge, passing several rocky knobs and small tors until after 2km a wide col is reached at 800m. Beyond it climb the steep side of Ben Macdui up the Allt Clach nan Taillear (the Tailors' Burn), or the slopes to its SE, to reach the flatter plateau and the nearby summit. (16km; 1210m; 5h 40min).

Descend 1km E to the edge of Coire Sputan Dearg and turn NE down the ridge along the edge of the corrie to the col which is the watershed between the Luibeg Burn and Loch Etchachan. This is an excellent point from which to appreciate the grandeur of the central Cairngorms, with their deep glaciated hollows, granite slabs, snow beds, streams and lochs. From the col contour SSE round the side of Creagan a' Choire Etchachan (1108m) and descend a little to reach the saddle on its S side. Then go SE up the boulder strewn elongated cone of Derry Cairngorm. (21km; 1350m; 7h).

Continue SSE along the long broad ridge, keeping to the E side above Glen Derry, and climb 50m to the minor top of Carn Crom. From there descend SE to the Derry woods and the road back to Linn of Dee.

Ben Macdui can also be climbed from the N with Cairn Gorm, and this route is described on p124-5.

*Derry Cairngorm from Beinn Mheadhoin*                                    *D. Scott*

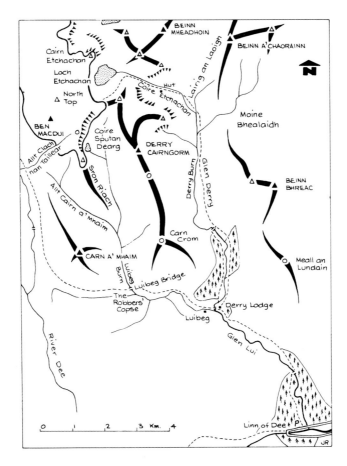

*Cairn Gorm from the snow beds at the head of the Garbh Uisge on Ben Macdui*    H.M. Brown

**Cairn Gorm;** 1245m; (OS Sheet 36; 005041); M5; *blue hill.*

Standing at the highest point of the northern edge of the central Cairngorm massif, Cairn Gorm itself is prominently visible from Aviemore and is easily identified by the lines of its ski pistes in winter, and the summer scars of these developments. Its rounded summit rises above the bowl of Coire Cas, with the narrow Coire na Ciste to the north-east, and the fine rocky cirques of Coire an t-Sneachda and Coire an Lochain, the Northern Corries, to the south-west.

The easy access provided by the ski road into Coire Cas makes Cairn Gorm one of the easiest and most climbed of all Munros. It is possible to go by car and chairlift to within 160m of the summit, but no self-respecting Munroist would do this. However, most climbers use the access road and start their climb from the car park at a height of 640m. To avoid the unsightly pylons and snow-fences of Coire Cas, climb steeply NE for a short distance to join the path up the broad ridge of Sron an Aonaich. Follow this much trodden path SE to the hemispherical dome of the Ptarmigan restaurant, and for a further 1km S to the summit of Cairn Gorm. (3km; 610m; 1h 50min). Various structures for weather recording and radio relay are sited on the boulder clad summit area, and once every half hour the weather instruments emerge automatically from their housing to sample the elements for a few minutes.

Several possiblities exist for continuing the day's walk rather than returning directly by the ascent route. Descend ½km W by stony slopes to the broad col at the head of Coire Cas. From there a quick return to the car park may be made down the Fiacaill a' Choire Chais in little more than half an hour. Alternatively, continue S then SW following a worn path across the stony plateau, along the rim of Coire an t-Sneachda and over the Top of Stob Coire an t-Sneachda (1176m) to the next col. From there a path drops steeply in zig-zags N into Coire an t-Sneachda, and a pleasant walk down the corrie leads back to the car park.

To extend the walk further, one can climb W from the col for ½km to Cairn Lochan (1215m), a fine summit right on the edge of the vertical cliffs of Coire an Lochain. The high-level circuit of the Northern Corries is completed by going W along the edge of the corrie past spectacular cliff scenery, and descending NW then N to a wide grassy saddle known as the Miadan. Continue N down the ridge bounding Coire an Lochain until it is possible to join the path which crosses NE below the corries back to the car park.

Ben Macdui can also be climbed from the direction of Cairn Gorm, and this is probably the most popular route. Certainly the Coire Cas car park is a good deal nearer to Ben Macdui than the Linn of Dee. However, this route goes for several kilometres across a high and exposed plateau, and cannot be recommended in bad weather. From the col at the head of Coire an t-Sneachda bear SSW along a path which climbs slightly and then descends to Lochan Buidhe which lies at the lowest point of the plateau and is the only landmark in this wide expanse of stony tundra. At 1125m it is the highest body of water in the British Isles. Continue SSE for another 2km, keeping just W of the rounded spine of the plateau to the summit of Ben Macdui. (By Cairn Gorm, 9½km; 990m; 3h 50min. Direct by Coire an t-Sneachda, 8km; 700m; 3h). Return by the same route to the col at the head of Coire an t-Sneachda, down this corrie and so back to the car park.

No restrictions on access by these routes in the stalking season.

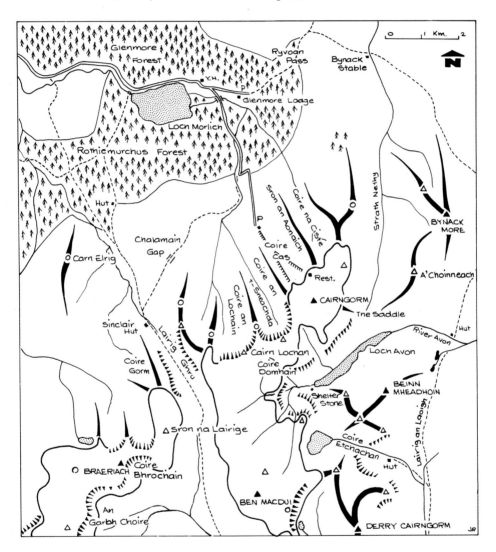

*Looking across Loch Avon towards Beinn Mheadhoin*                    *J.E.S. Bennet*

**Beinn Mheadhoin;** 1182m; (OS Sheet 36; 024017); M12; *middle hill.*

Beinn Mheadhoin is on the east side of the central Cairngorms, separated from Ben Macdui by the hollow of Loch Etchachan, and from Cairn Gorm by the deep trough holding Loch Avon. It is rather an inaccessible mountain, in the centre of the massif as its name implies, and not easily seen from either the Dee or Spey valleys, although it is just visible from the latter through the defile of Strath Nethy. It is well seen from Glen Derry, and also from the Cairn Gorm plateau across Loch Avon, and the granite tors along its summit ridge give it a distinctive appearance.

The nearest approach is from the car park at the foot of Coire Cas on Cairn Gorm, and the route from there involves first crossing the plateau SW of Cairn Gorm and descending to Loch Avon before climbing Beinn Mheadhoin itself. There is thus a good deal of up and downhill effort both on the way there and back, and particularly in winter the route is a serious one, calling for mountaineering experience. From the Coire Cas car park either (a) ascend the Fiacaill a' Choire Chais ridge on the SW side of the corrie to reach the plateau ½km W of Cairn Gorm and descend SSE down Coire Raibeirt, following a rough path down the E side of the stream in the lower corrie to Loch Avon, or (b) take the path SW from the car park into Coire an t-Sneachda, going right up to the innermost SW corner of the corrie, climbing the zig-zag path to the col on the plateau and descending SSE down Coire Domhain where there is a faint path down a steep slope between the cliffs.

Thus one enters the place which well merits its description as the 'heart of the Cairngorms'. The Loch Avon basin is ringed by precipitous slopes and high crags, and at its upper end the streams from the plateau above cascade down granite slabs in a profusion of white torrents. Continue round the head of Loch Avon where the crossing of the Feith Buidhe may cause a problem, particularly if it is swollen by melt water in spring, pass below the Shelter Stone and the great cliffs of the Sticil and Cairn Etchachan and climb SE up a slanting path towards Loch Etchachan. Before reaching the loch bear E up to the SW Top of Beinn Mheadhoin (1163m) and finally go NE along the crest past several granite tors or barns to the largest of these, which forms the summit. (8½km; 980m; 3h 40min).

On the return to Coire Cas by either of the alternative routes described above, there is a further 410m of ascent from Loch Avon to the Cairn Gorm plateau.

No restrictions on access by the routes described during the stalking season.

Map on page 125.

*The Barns of Bynack More, looking towards the plateau of Ben Avon*                    *A. Watson*

**Bynack More**; 1090m; (OS Sheet 36, 042063); M52; *possibly from Gaelic beannag meaning a kerchief or cap.*

Ben Bynack or Caiplich as it was once known forms the north-eastern outpost of the central Cairngorms, separated from Cairn Gorm itself by the low col of The Saddle and the deep trench of Strath Nethy. When seen from Nethybridge and other nearby viewpoints in the Spey Valley it appears as a shapely pointed mountain rising above the dark Forest of Abernethy.

The traditional approach to Bynack More is from Loch Morlich through the Ryvoan Pass, and it is possible to drive to Glenmore Lodge, park a few metres beyond, and start from there. Continue on foot through the picturesque Ryvoan Pass with its beautiful Lochan Uaine, the aptly named green lochan, and ½km further on take the track going E to cross the River Nethy at Bynack Stable. Beyond this point the track becomes a path, climbing SE over the lower shoulder of Bynack More towards the distant Lairig an Laoigh. Follow this path for 3km to its highest point at around (043083) and then bear S up the N ridge to the summit. (9½km; 750m; 3h 30min).

Since the construction of the access road to the ski slopes on Cairn Gorm, two other routes to Bynack More have become popular, being shorter and more interesting, though crossing rougher, pathless and more demanding terrain. Both start from the car park at the foot of Coire na Ciste.

The lower level route heads ENE across the heather clad hillside, above a small conifer plantation, for 2km to the col just S of Pt. 737m. Descend steeply E down heather and gravelly scree to Strath Nethy, cross the river and climb the NW ridge of Bynack Beg (964m). Continue SE across boulders and granite outcrops to the upper slopes of Bynack More. (6km; 790m; 2h 40min).

The higher route goes up the ridge flanking Coire na Ciste on its E side to reach the flat col 1km NNE of Cairn Gorm where the hollow of Ciste Mearaid is a summer snow pocket. Descend diagonally SE down steep slopes to reach The Saddle at the head of Strath Nethy. From there a broad ridge leads NE over the whaleback Top of A' Choinneach (1017m) to a grassy plateau from which rise the upper slopes of Bynack More. On the ridge crest above are the tors of the Little Barns, and beyond them, 40m down on the E side at (045058), are the Barns of Bynack proper; huge and impressive granite castles well worth the short diversion required to visit them before going on to the summit. (9½km; 960m; 3h 50min). These two routes from the Coire na Ciste car park can be combined to give a very interesting circular traverse.

Map on page 125.

*Braeriach from Ben Macdui*                                    *D.J. Bennet*

**Braeriach;** 1296m; (OS Sheets 36 and 43; 953999); M3; *brindled greyish upper part.*

Mighty Braeriach forms a high peninsula of the great Western Cairngorm plateau, joined to Cairn Toul around the rim of An Garbh Choire. When seen from the vicinity of Aviemore, it appears as the western part of the Cairngorm scarp, lying to the right of the deep cleft of the Lairig Ghru, its northern slopes scalloped by three graceful corries. The hidden south-east face of the mountain is even more impressive, for on that side the precipices of Coire Bhrochain drop from the summit sheer into the depths of An Garbh Choire.

Although the mountain can be climbed from Whitewell in Gleann Einich, or even more distantly from Achlean in Glen Feshie, the usual route today is from the car park at the end of the road to the ski slopes in Coire Cas on the north-west side of Cairn Gorm.

Leave the car park going W along the path towards Coire an t-Sneachda, but soon diverge right and continue W across the heather clad slopes, losing a little height and crossing two streams coming down from the northern corries. In about 1½km reach the path which leads SW into the prominent notch of the Chalamain Gap, and follow the path through this little gorge, cut out by glacial melt water. Continue SW downhill to reach the Lairig Ghru path, where on the opposite side of the stream the Sinclair Hut stands on a little knoll and gives simple shelter from the elements within its stark walls. Behind the hut a path leads up the hillside to the broad base of the Sron na Lairige ridge, which is climbed for 400m, steeply at first, then less so. A line along the E edge of this ridge gives some striking views down into the Lairig Ghru. Traverse the gravelly tundra of the crest over the Top of Sron na Lairige (1184m), descend SSW to a wide col and finally climb 140m, SW at first to reach the edge of Coire Bhrochain, and then round the edge of the corrie to the summit. (10½km; 840m; 3h 50min).

The cairn stands on the brink of the 200m granite cliffs of Coire Bhrochain, and looks out across An Garbh Choire to Cairn Toul and Sgor an Lochain Uaine, and the high hanging corrie between them which holds the Lochan Uaine. To the SW the plateau stretches for many kilometres, gradually dropping towards the Moine Mhor. The return may be by the same route, or to give a little variation by the Coire Gorm just W of the Sron na Lairige ridge to rejoin the uphill route at the Sinclair Hut.

No restrictions on access by this route in the stalking season.

Map on page 125.

*Cairn Toul and The Angel's Peak above the Lairig Ghru*                                        *D.J. Bennet*

**Cairn Toul;** 1293m; (OS Sheets 36 and 43; 964972); M4; *from Gaelic carn an t-sabhail, hill of the barn.*
**The Devil's Point;** 1004m; (OS Sheets 36 and 43; 976951); M127; *from Bod an Deamhain, penis of the devil.*

The west side of the deep valley of the Lairig Ghru is dominated by the plateau of Braeriach which curves round the huge embayment of An Garbh Choire before continuing over the shapely peaks of Sgor an Lochain Uaine (The Angel's Peak) and Cairn Toul, whose corries hang high above the valley floor. Southwards from Cairn Toul the crest, now forming a broad ridge, drops to the col at the head of Coire Odhar before thrusting outward to The Devil's Point. This remarkable feature is a spur truncated by the streams of ice which once flowed down Glen Dee and Glen Geusachan, and it now forms a prominent landmark with its great headland of granite slabs.

The approach to Cairn Toul and The Devil's Point starts at the Linn of Dee and follows the same route as that for Ben Macdui and its neighbours. namely the private road up Glen Derry to Derry Lodge, followed by the track up Glen Luibeg to the Luibeg Bridge. From there the way to Cairn Toul continues W, rising slightly round the southern base of Carn a' Mhaim along a well worn path which in a few more kilometres drops to join the path in Glen Dee leading N to the Lairig Ghru.

Continue only about 200 metres N from the path junction, and diverge W to cross the River Dee by a cable bridge and reach Corrour Bothy. This one-time stalker's bothy is now the best known Cairngorm refuge for climbers and walkers. A well worn path leads W behind the bothy up the grassy banks of the Allt a' Choire Odhair, and reaches the col at the head of this corrie by steep zig-zags. Any potentially dangerous snow slope is probably best avoided on the S side of the corrie. From the col an easy walk heading S then bearing round E leads to the tip of The Devil's Point. (15½km; 700m; 4h 40m). A splendid viewpoint above the River Dee.

Return to the col. From there a broad grassy ridge rises N around the shallow bowl of Coire Odhar, then swings NW, becoming stonier, to Stob Coire an t-Saighdeir (1213m). Beyond this Top the ridge curves round the Soldiers' Corrie, dropping slightly and then climbing more steeply up the last 120m to the summit of Cairn Toul. (18½km; 1120m; 6h). Return to the Linn of Dee by the outward route.

Sgor an Lochain Uaine is less than 1km NW of Cairn Toul, and is a fine point from which to appreciate the grandeur of An Garbh Choire and its wild recesses. Returning from this peak to the head of Coire Odhar, it is not necessary to re-ascend Cairn Toul as a traverse across its SW side at about the 1150m level leads to the lowest point of the ridge at the head of Coire an t-Saighdeir.

Map on page 130.

*The Devil's Point*                                                H.M. Brown

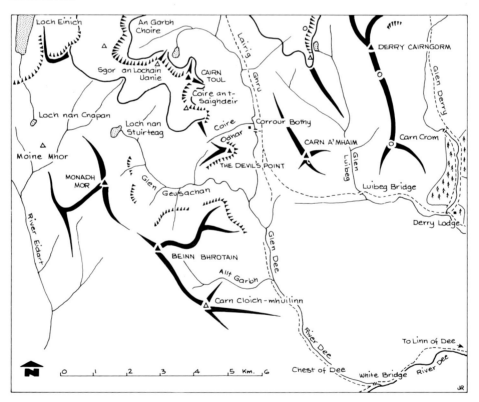

*The view south-west from Ben Macdui over the summits of The Devil's Point,*          A. Watson
*Beinn Bhrotain, and Monadh Mor.*

**Monadh Mor;** 1113m; (OS Sheet 43; 938942); M39; *big hill.*
**Beinn Bhrotain;** 1157m; (OS Sheet 43; 954923); M18; *hill of the mastiff.*

These two rounded mountains are the southern extension of the great Braeriach - Cairn Toul plateau, separated from it by Glen Geusachan, and separated by the River Eidart from the Glen Feshie hills. The grandest features of these two mountains are their steep faces overlooking Glen Geusachan which form a discontinuous line of slabby buttresses and gullies for several kilometres. At its north end Monadh Mor merges gradually into the undulating expanse of the Moine Mhor, the great moss, a vast lonely basin of peat and tundra which sweeps across from the crests of Braeriach and Cairn Toul to the edge of Glen Feshie.

From the Linn of Dee take the private road W up the River Dee to reach White Bridge, and continue on the other side past the Chest of Dee, where the river plunges over granite slabs, to a conifer plantation and some ruined shielings. Thus far the road is rough and stony, but the use of a bicycle might be justified. Beyond, the road deteriorates and ends ½km N of the crossing of the Allt Garbh. Continue up the pathless W bank of the River Dee, choosing the best line possible over rough ground, and enter Glen Geusachan. This remote and enchanting glen is flanked by the imposing slabs of Beinn Bhrotain and The Devil's Point, and directly ahead rises Monadh Mor with a prominent plaque of slabs below and to the right of the summit. These may be outflanked on the right by following the stream up to the outflow from Loch nan Stuirteag, and then heading back SW to the summit of Monadh Mor. (18km; 750m; 5h 20min). A more direct ascent of the E face can be made through a wide gap in the slabs on that side, but it is steep and should be avoided if there is snow to be climbed.

The elongated whaleback summit of Monadh Mor is almost completely flat, dipping gradually NNW towards the Moine Mhor. Continue S for ¾km to a slightly lower cairn, and then SE by grassy tundra for another 1km, descending quite steeply at the end to reach a narrow col at 975m. From there climb SE up a boulder strewn slope for about 800 metres to reach the summit of Beinn Bhrotain. (21km; 930m; 6h 20min).

Descend SE over (or round) the Top of Carn Cloich-mhuilinn (942m) and down its E ridge. Before the glen is reached, drop down on the S flank of this ridge to avoid slabs and boulders at its foot, and reach the road back to the Linn of Dee at the conifer plantation.

These two mountains may also be climbed from Glen Feshie by a shorter, although less interesting route. From Achlean at the end of the public road on the E side of the glen take the path over Carn Ban Mor to Loch nan Cnapan at the centre of the Moine Mhor. Go E for 1km, then bear SE to gain the N ridge of Monadh mor, and up to the summit. (11km; 950m; 4h 10min). Continue to Beinn Bhrotain as above (14km; 1130m; 5h 10min), and return by the same route.

To the west of the main Cairngorm mountains which enclose the Lairig Ghru, the Moine Mhor or great moss extends for several kilometres forming a wide and shallow basin whose western edge is the long broad ridge of the Glen Feshie hills. This range rises in the north above the pine woods of Loch an Eilein and Inshriach, and extends eighteen kilometres south to end above the desolate upper reaches of Glen Feshie. At its north end the ridge is quite well defined, particularly on its east side which falls steeply into upper Gleann Einich in a long series of buttresses and gullies above Loch Einich. Further south the crest broadens out to form a plateau between Coire Garbhlach and the River Eidart in the south-west corner of the Moine Mhor. From the west and south-west the range looks like a long level plateau, the dips between its summits being almost imperceptible, and on that side the deep gash of Coire Garbhlach is the most prominent feature. Despite its length and height, there are only two Munros in this group, Sgor Gaoith and Mullach Clach a' Bhlair. They are both usually climbed from Glen Feshie, where a narrow public road goes south from Feshiebridge up the east side of the glen to end at Achlean farm.

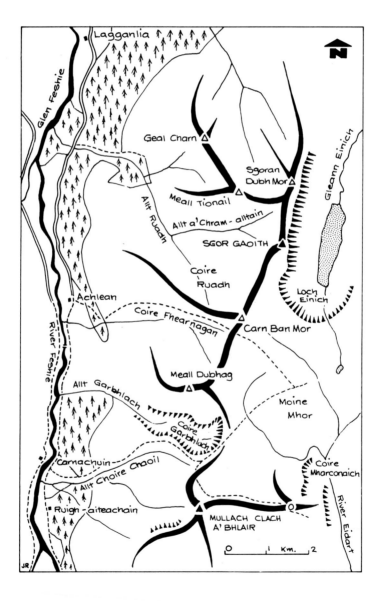

*On the Glen Feshie hills near Carn Ban Mor*                                             *J.S. Stewart*

**Mullach Clach a' Bhlair;** 1019m; (OS Sheets 35, 36 and 43; 883927); M111; *summit of the stone of the plain.*

Between the indentations of Coire Mharconaich on the east and Coire Garbhlach on the west the high plateau extends south in a featureless tableland of grassy tundras. At its south-west corner it swells upward slightly to reach its highest point at the summit of Mullach Clach a' Bhlair, seen from Glen Feshie as a wide, gentle dome.

The end of the public road on the E side of Glen Feshie just N of Achlean farm is the nearest starting point for the ascent of Mullach Clach a' Bhlair, and for other expeditions onto the Moine Mhor. Go past the farm and follow paths along the E bank of the River Feshie for 4km. The only possible problem might be the crossing of the Allt Garbhlach in spate conditions, in which case it would be better to cross the Feshie 1km S of Achlean and walk up the private road on the W side. At the Carnachuin bridge a track leads SE across the level floor of the glen among stately scattered pines, and swings E upwards along the N bank of the Allt Coire Chaoil. Follow this track high on the steep side of the narrow glen to gain the ridge on the brink of Coire Garbhlach at which point there is a fine view into this unusual V-shaped corrie, largely cut in schistose rocks instead of granite. The track continues upward until it reaches the plateau and forks, its right branch making a sweeping curve across the tundra and passing within 300 metres of the small summit cairn of Mullach Clach a' Bhlair. (9½km; 700m; 3h 20min). Although undistinguished in itself, there are a few better places than this from which to appreciate the scale and character of the vast tract of hill and moorland which extends SE across the wide trough of the upper Feshie beyond the An Sgarsoch ridge to the Tarf, and NE over the Moine Mhor to the uptilted rim of Braeriach and Cairn Toul.

Return along the track to its junction, from where the descent may be made by the route of ascent, or by the following alternative which is little longer. Continue NE along the left fork of the track for 1½km to its high point near Pt 953m, then head due N along the broad expanse of ridge for 2½km almost to the summit of Carn Ban Mor (1052m), one of the Tops of Sgor Gaoith. About 300 metres before reaching the summit, turn NW along the path which crosses the ridge from the Moine Mhor to Glen Feshie and follow this path by either of its two branches down the N flank of Coire Fhearnagan to reach Achlean.

*The cliffs of Sgor Gaoith and Sgoran Dubh from Gleann Einich*                    *W.B. Young*

**Sgor Gaoith;** 1118m; (OS Sheets 36 and 43; 903989); M34; *peak of the wind.*

This is the highest point of the ridge which extends north from Carn Ban Mor to Sgoran Dubh forming the west side of the Einich glacial trough. The east side of the ridge between Sgor Gaoith and Sgoran Dubh Mor forms a magnificent series of ridges, buttresses and gullies above Loch Einich in a wild and remote setting, but the approach to that side of the mountain is long and there are no easy routes up the steep slopes above the loch. The usual routes of ascent are from Glen Feshie, either starting from Achlean and traversing Carn Ban Mor or by an alternative and more attractive route up Coire Ruadh which is described below.

Leave the road on the E side of Glen Feshie at (853013) near the bridge over the Allt Ruadh and go E along a forest track for ½km. Cross the deer fence and continue uphill along the track through pine trees high on the N side of the narrow valley of the Allt Ruadh. After crossing a small side stream and passing through the last scattered pine trees the path continues across the open hillside to a deer fence. Beyond this point it becomes faint and intermittent across heather and boggy ground, but its line can be followed SE round the lower slopes of the Meall Tionail spur until it finally disappears. Cross the shallow bowl of the Allt a' Chrom-alltain and ascend E for 400m up broad slopes of grass and heath to reach the ridge. The summit of Sgor Gaoith is on a little promontory, right on the brink of the crags which plunge for 500m to Loch Einich far below. (7km; 830m; 3h). On the far side of the loch rises the massive bulk of Braeriach.

The descent may be varied by going N for 1½km along the broad ridge, crossing a dip of 60m and climbing to the Top of Sgoran Dubh Mor (1111m). From the rocks of its summit tor descend SW for ½km to reach the start of the spur which projects NW towards Geal-charn (920m), once classified as a Munro in its own right but now just a Top. Follow the undulating crest of this spur over Meall Buidhe (976m) for 2½km to the stony summit of Geal-charn. Descend WSW down slopes of boulders, grass and heather to rejoin the Coire Ruadh track near the tree-line.

Map on page 132.

*On the ridge of Stob Poite Coire Ardair*                    D.J. Bennet

# SECTION 9

The Monadh Liath and Creag Meagaidh

*The approach to the Monadh Liath up Glen Banchor*                    *D.J. Bennet*

**Carn Dearg**; 945m; (OS Sheet 35; 635024); M219; *red hill.*
**A'Chailleach**; 930m; (OS Sheet 35; 681042); M247; *the old woman.*
**Carn Sgulain**; 920m; (OS Sheet 35; 684059); M263; *hill of the basket, or of the old man.*

The Monadh Liath range is an extensive undulating plateau on the north-west side of the Spey Valley above Newtonmore and Kingussie. This great desolate high moorland extends a long way north and west across the headwaters of the River Findhorn towards Loch Ness, but it is mainly the south-east corner near Glen Banchor that holds any interest for the hill-walker, for it is there that the only four Munros of the Monadh Liath are situated. Of the four, Geal Charn on the west side of Glen Markie is separated from the others, and will be described separately.

From a viewpoint on the A9 road opposite Newtonmore, Carn Dearg and A'Chailleach show up well, for they have well defined summits and prominent east-facing corries; but Carn Sgulain is rather inconspicuous, little more than a high point on the horizon almost hidden by A'Chailleach. The starting point for all three is 2km from Newtonmore where the road up Glen Banchor changes from being public to private at the foot of the Allt a' Chaorainn.

The route to Carn Dearg continues up Glen Banchor for 1km and then takes the rough track NW up the Allt Fionndrigh. Continue beyond the end of the track for a short distance, then cross the stream by a footbridge and follow a faint path SW through a gap onto the broad ridge above Gleann Ballach. Now go NW up rough heathery ground on the NE side of the glen for 2km towards its head. Cross the stream and climb an easy grassy slope above broken rocks (appearing from below to be a slanting shelf) in a SW direction to reach the ridge of Carn Dearg ½km N of the top. A short climb up this ridge leads to the summit cairn perched right on the edge of the E corrie. (9km; 650m; 3h 10min). This corrie is mostly steep grass, with a few small crags, and a shorter route could be made directly up its face from Gleann Ballach, but it could not be regarded as an easy route.

The way to A'Chailleach and Carn Sgulain goes up the rough track on the E side of the Allt a' Chaorainn. Continue up the glen for a short distance following the scar in the heather worn by tracked vehicles, cross the stream and climb NW to a tiny stalker's bothy on the slopes of A'Chailleach. Keep on uphill in the same direction to reach the broad SW ridge of the hill, and climb this easy-angled ridge to the big cairn at the edge of the E corrie of A'Chailleach (6km; 630m; 2h 30min). Descend N into the deep little glen of the Allt Cuil na Caillich, and climb rough tussocky grass and peat to Carn Sgulain. A line of fence posts across the flat summit makes finding the cairn easy, even in thick weather. (8km; 750m; 3h 10min).

The direct return to the day's starting point goes down the Allt Cuil na Caillich, on its right (S) bank at the point where it cascades down through crags to join the Allt a' Chaorainn. Cross this stream to its E side where there is a sheep track for a long way down the glen.

It is quite possible to traverse the three hills in a single expedition. The plateau between Carn Dearg and Carn Sgulain is an undulating featureless expanse of grass, moss and boulders, giving fairly easy

*Carn Dearg in the Monadh Liath*                                    *D.J. Bennet*

walking past a series of minor tops and cairns, and at least one tiny lochan. (Others may appear in wet weather). Even in the thickest of weather there are no route finding problems for a line of fence posts goes all the way from Carn Ban, ¾ km NNW of Carn Dearg, to Carn Sgulain. The distance for the circuit is about 24km.

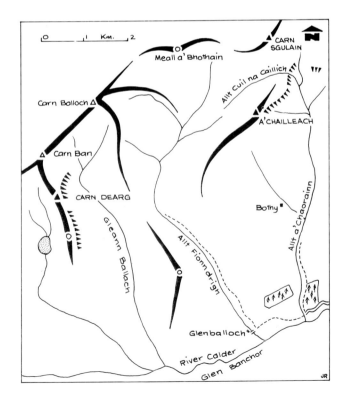

*The approach to Geal Charn at the foot of Glen Markie*                    D.J. Bennet

**Geal Charn**; 926m; (OS Sheet 35; 561988); M256; *white hill.*

Geal Charn is the westernmost of the Monadh Liath Munros, and it has many of the characteristics of these hills. Its most interesting feature is the eastern corrie, with its high lochan above Glen Markie and the ice-carved window in the innermost corner of the corrie forming a steep-sided col between Geal Charn and its near neighbour Beinn Sgiath.

The approach to the hill is along the minor road west from Laggan Bridge on the north side of the River Spey. This leads west towards the Corrieyairack Pass, one of the military roads constructed by General Wade in the eighteenth century.

One route to Geal Charn is up Glen Markie from the Spey Dam, there being a track for 3½km on the E side of the Markie Burn. Follow this track and the path beyond it to the foot of the Piper's Burn, the stream flowing down from Lochan a' Choire. Cross the Markie Burn and climb NW into the corrie, keeping well to the NE of the lochan until above the level of the crags. Then go SW across the featureless grassy plateau to the huge finely built cairn which marks the summit. (7½km; 650m; 2h 50min).

If the Markie Burn is in spate, the preceding route may not be practicable. In this case go further W up the Spey to Sherramore or Garva Bridge. The ascent from the latter is easy and involves no awkward stream crossings. The path marked on the OS map on the SE side of the Feith Talagain is hard to find at first, but it improves 1km up the glen. At its end cross the Allt Coire nan Dearcag and climb the heathery SW ridge of Geal Charn directly to the top. (7½km; 630m; 2h 50min).

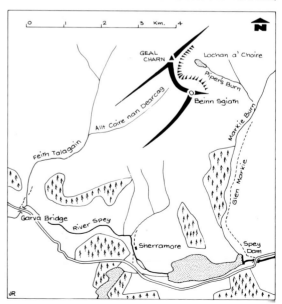

*Beinn a' Chaorainn from Glen Spean*                    A. Thrippleton

**Beinn a' Chaorainn**; 1052m; (OS Sheets 34 and 41; 386851); M76; *hill of the rowan.*
**Beinn Teallach**; 915m; (OS Sheets 34 and 41; 361860); M276; *forge hill.*

These two mountains lie north of the Laggan Dam on either side of the north-south glen of the Allt a' Chaorainn. Beinn a' Chaorainn has three tops on a north-south spine, the highest being the middle one which does not have its height shown on the OS 1:50000 map. The western slope is uniformly steep but not rocky, while the eastern side of the mountain is very steep and rocky, forming the fine Coire na h-Uamha. The eastern and northern corries of Beinn Teallach are steep, but to the south and west there are long easy-angled slopes which give the mountain an undistinguished appearance. Both are excellent viewpoints for the hills to the south round Loch Treig.

Start the traverse from the A86 road at Roughburn, ½km E of the Laggan Dam, and follow a forestry road NW for ¾km to the slopes below Meall Clachaig. As the road then runs across the hillside it is necessary to follow a firebreak N to reach the upper deer fence where there is a gate above a point 200 metres W of the road junction. Climb N, turning Meall Clachaig on the W, and then bear NE up easy slopes to the South Top (1050m) and thence ½km along the broad ridge to the summit of Beinn a' Chaorainn. (4½km; 800m; 2h 20min).

Continue along the ridge to the North Top (1045m) and descend NNW for 1km, then W to the col at the head of the Allt a' Chaorainn which is marked by a large cairn. Climb the slopes immediately to the W to reach the NE ridge of Beinn Teallach, which is followed to the summit. (9km; 1100m; 3h 50min).

The descent from Beinn Teallach goes S down the long shoulder of the mountain, but as there is no bridge across the Allt a' Chaorainn, and this stream may be difficult to cross when in spate, it is advisable if such conditions do exist to descend E into the glen to cross the stream high up and continue down its E bank.

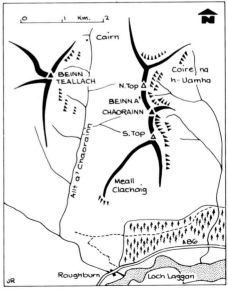

*Looking up Coire Ardair to Creag Meagaidh*                                    *W.D. Brooker*

**Creag Meagaidh**; 1130m; (OS Sheets 34 and 42; 418875); M26; *bogland rock.*

This is a massive and magnificent mountain with a rather complicated topography. From its high central plateau several steep-sided ridges radiate outwards enclosing exceedingly fine corries, of which Coire Ardair to the north-east is the finest, providing a superb approach to the mountain and some of the best winter climbing in Scotland. It is quite difficult to get a good impression of the mountain from the A86 road which goes along its south side by Loch Laggan, and one has to walk up towards Coire Ardair to fully appreciate the grandeur of Creag Meagaidh.

There are two very fine walking routes to the summit which if combined into a traverse make a magnificent mountain expedition, but the finishing point is 8km along the A86 road from the start. Two cars would be useful for this trip.

The first route starts at Aberarder, half way along Loch Laggan. Walk up the road to Aberarder farm and continue along the path behind the farm, heading W at first then NW and climbing high above the Allt Coire Ardair through scattered birches. In about 3km the corrie and the path bear round towards the W and the great cliffs of Coire Ardair come into view. The path continues on the N of the burn to the outlet of Lochan a' Choire in a superb situation under the cliffs. Bear WNW, climbing across grassy slopes, then up scree and boulders into the steepening, narrowing corrie leading to the obvious col, The Window, on the N side of Creag Meagaidh. From there climb steep slopes S to reach the grassy plateau, which is followed SW then W to the summit of Creag Meagaidh. (9km; 880m; 3h 30min).

The return to Aberarder may be by the same route, or more directly by going E across the plateau, over the flat Top of Puist Coire Ardair (1070m) and along the narrower ridge E then NE to the Top of Sron a' Choire. (1001m) From there a descent E leads to Aberarder; there is a footbridge across the Allt Coire Ardair near the farm.

The second route starts at Moy, 2km W of the W end of Loch Laggan. Leave the road on the W side of the Moy Burn and cross gently rising moorland to the steep craggy ground below Creag na Cailliche. Climb through the broken rocks to the top and reach the crest of the ridge on which there is a substantial wall. This ridge is followed all the way to the summit. (6km; 880m; 2h 50min).

**Carn Liath**; 1006m; (OS Sheet 34; 472904); M123; *grey hill.*
**Stob Poite Coire Ardair**; 1053m; (OS Sheet 34; 429889); M75; *peak of the pot of the high corrie.*

These two mountains lie on a long, fairly level ridge which forms the north bounding wall of Coire Ardair. They are best combined in an east to west traverse which gives a fine high level walk with excellent views of the impressive cliffs at the head of Coire Ardair. This traverse can in fact be combined with the ascent of Creag Meagaidh, which is described separately.

Start from the A86 road about half way along Loch Laggan at Aberarder. Walk up the private road past the farm, and once on open ground beyond the farm leave the path to Coire Ardair and climb N towards Na Cnapanan which appears from below as an obvious shoulder. Above, the slopes rise steadily for almost 400m over grass, heather and occasional patches of boulders to the flat stony summit of Carn Liath. (3½km; 750m; 2h).

Turn W and follow the broad mossy ridge, descending gradually to a col and climbing again to the Top of Meall an t-Snaim (969m). Continuing WSW, the ridge narrows and drops to a well defined notch followed by a short steep rise to the next Top, Sron Coire a' Chriochairein (991m). Thereafter the ridge continues around the edge of this corrie to the level crest of Stob Poite Coire Ardair, the summit cairn being at the W end. (8km; 980m; 3h 30min).

Continue WSW down the smooth ridge for barely ½km, then turn S and drop steeply down to the narrow pass called The Window. From this point Creag Meagaidh can be climbed in about 1 hour as described separately; however, the return to Aberarder goes E down steep slopes of boulder and scree, then easier grass towards the outlet of Lochan a' Choire and the start of the path down Coire Ardair.

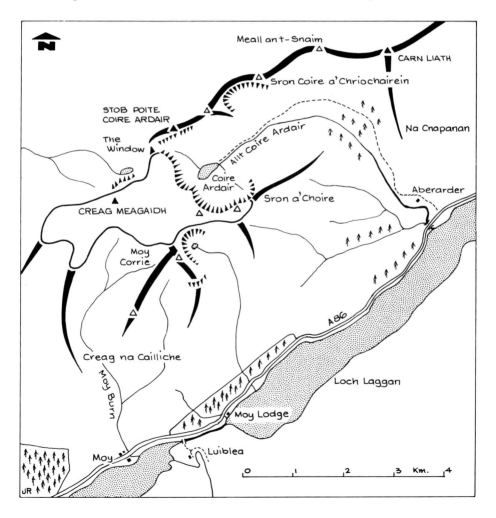

*Beinn Sgritheall from the north-east*                    H.M. Brown

# SECTION 10

## Loch Eil to Glen Shiel

*The approach to Gulvain up Gleann Fionnlighe*                                      *D.J. Bennet*

**Gulvain**; 987m; (OS Sheets 40 and 41; 003876); M156; *from Gaelic, either gaorr, filth or gaoir, noise.*

Gulvain, or Gaor Bheinn, is a secretive mountain hidden in the jumble of hills between Loch Eil and Loch Arkaig. Apart from the route described below, it is a rather remote and complicated Munro to reach. The highest point (987m) is on OS Sheet 41, so beware of mistaking the OS trig point (961m) on Sheet 40 for the summit. Gleann Fionnlighe gives a pleasant approach, with the route of ascent in view ahead for many miles. Being a solitary peak, the summit is a rewarding panoramic viewpoint.

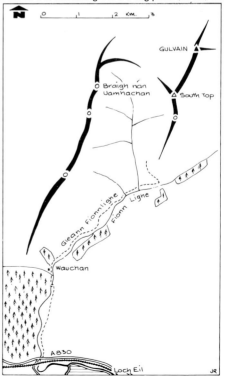

Start from the A830 Fort William to Mallaig road 1km W of the W end of Loch Eil, and follow the rough road up the E side of the large Fionn Lighe river. After 2km it crosses to the W bank, passes Wauchan cottage and continues (becoming a path) for another 4½km to end at about 200m on the SSE Ridge of Gulvain. The ascent of this ridge is unrelentingly and uniformly steep, but as long as the crags to the W are avoided, it is straightforward on grass. A craggy knoll (855m) is reached, and beyond it the South Top (961m), the trig point, lies just over ½km N. Continue NNE, dropping 60m to a saddle, and climb the narrowing ridge to the summit, which has a substantial cairn. (10½km; 1050m; 4h 10min). Coire Screamhach to the NE is worth looking at from above, but it is best to return by the route of ascent.

*Sgurr Thuilm from Strathan at the head of Loch Arkaig*                              *D.J. Bennet*

**Sgurr Thuilm**; 963m; (OS Sheet 40; 939879); M189; *peak of the rounded hillock.*
**Sgurr nan Coireachan**; 956m; (OS Sheet 40; 903880); M202; *peak of the corries.*

These Munros are just two of many peaks in an area of unusually rough and steep complexity, belonging in nature if not in name to the Rough Bounds of Knoydart further north-west. For the sake of the wild scenery the summits are best traversed from east to west, but the route is as easy in reverse. The approach from Glenfinnan has been rather tamed by afforestation and road-making, but it is still the easiest and most popular route.

The National Trust for Scotland's Visitor Centre at Glenfinnan is worth a visit, and it is interesting to recall that after his defeat at Culloden the fugitive Prince Charles spent a night out on Sgurr Thuilm - an unlikely Munroist. Park ¼km NW of the Centre, and walk up the private road on the W side of the River Finnan; this road passes under the spectacular railway viaduct and continues well up the glen which is now extensively tree-planted. 3½km up the glen Corryhully Lodge is extraordinarily out of character with its surroundings, and below it by the river is a spartan bothy. There are recently built bridges over all the potentially dangerous streams. Follow the road to its crossing of the stream that drains the deep-set Coire Thollaidh and Coire a' Bheithe, and a few hundred metres beyond aim for the spur that leads to the long Druim Coire a' Bheithe ridge and Sgurr Thuilm. (9km; 960m; 3h 40min).

The summit is slightly N of the main ridge leading to Sgurr nan Coireachan, so it is necessary to return S for a short distance before continuing the traverse W. There are many ups and downs over Beinn Gharbh and Meall an Tarmachain; much bare rock is exposed, but the easiest line is along the crest. It is a grand highway. Sgurr nan Coireachan, though lower, has the trig point and is a grand viewpoint. (13km; 1360m; 5h 10min).

Descend SE and climb again to Sgurr a' Choire Riabhaich. The ridge over this point is steep-sided and rocky, and care is needed on the descent in thick weather. Keep to the crest to minimise difficulties. Lower down the ridge becomes broader and grassy; aim to reach the stalker's path on its E side at (917859) and follow it down to the road in Glen Finnan.

An alternative and equally fine traverse of these two mountains can be made from Strathan at the head of Loch Arkaig, and this route takes one into the extraordinarily wild corries on the N side of the ridge. The road along the N side of Loch Arkaig is public to within 1km of Strathan, and there seems to be no objection to cars being taken along this last kilometre of rough road and parked near the bridge over the River Dessarry. Going to Sgurr Thuilm, continue SW along the road up Glen Pean for 1km, cross the River Pean and climb directly up the long NE ridge of Sgurr Thuilm. (5km; 960m; 2h 50min). Coming back from Sgurr nan Coireachan, return to Meall an Tarmachain and descend very steeply NE down the wild Coire nan Gall to Glen Pean. In spate conditions the crossing of the River Pean to the track on its N side may be difficult or impossible, as also may be the crossing of the Allt a' Chaorainn at the foot of Sgurr Thuilm's NE ridge, so this traverse should not be attempted when the streams are in spate.

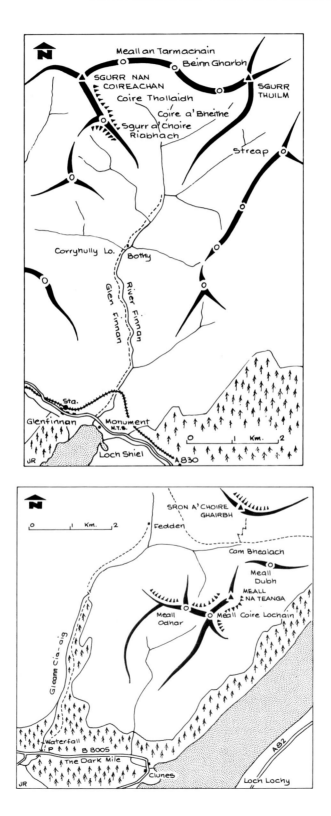

*Sron a' Choire Ghairbh from the head of Gleann Cia-aig*                    *J. Renny*

**Sron a' Choire Ghairbh**; 935m; (OS Sheet 34; 223945); M237; *nose of the rough corrie.*
**Meall na Teanga**; 917m; (OS Sheet 34; 220924); M271; *hill of the tongue.*

These two summits are elusively situated west of Loch Lochy in the Great Glen, and dominate the view across that loch from the A82 road north of Spean Bridge. They are bold, deeply-corried hills, and their lower slopes above Loch Lochy are heavily forested. These forests, now mature, are being felled. The hills are usually climbed together, and the traverse can be started either at Kilfinnan near Laggan Locks at the north-east end of Loch Lochy, or at the foot of Gleann Cia-aig near the east end of Loch Arkaig, and this route is described first. The times and distances for both routes are approximately the same.

The start is from the narrow B8005 road just before it reaches the E end of Loch Arkaig. From the car park at the Eas Chia-aig waterfalls follow the signposted 'Forest Walk' footpath up through the trees until it reaches a forestry road (about 20 minutes). Turn N and follow this road, then a path up Gleann Cia-aig to Fedden, a sad ruin. Cross the glen to the E to reach the path between Loch Garry and Loch Lochy over the Cam Bhealach, and follow the path ESE to the pass (615m). From there climb the stalker's path which zig-zags N up the steep grassy hillside (further than the map shows) to end almost on the ridge. Finally an easy walk for a few hundred metres NW along this broad mossy ridge leads to Sron a' Choire Ghairbh. (9½km; 880m; 3h 40min).

Having returned down the stalker's path to the Cam Bhealach, climb S below the screes of Meall Dubh to gain the col between that hill and Meall na Teanga. A steep, slippery climb up mossy boulders leads to the crest of Meall nan Teanga at a small cairn, and the larger summit cairn is a few hundred metres further S. (11½km; 1200m; 4h 40min). It is a commanding viewpoint.

To return to Gleann Cia-aig, descend SW from Meall na Teanga and climb a narrow rocky ridge to Meall Coire Lochain, whose top is reached suddenly at the edge of a broad grassy ridge. Go W along the crest of the Meall Odhar crags and descend easy grassy slopes to reach the path in Gleann Cia-aig 3½km N of the day's starting point.

For the northern approach, drive along the narrow public road from Laggan Swing Bridge on the A82 road to Kilfinnan. Continue on foot along the upper Forestry Commission road through an area of forest which has recently been clear-felled. After 3km take a good path which climbs W through the cleared forest and emerges into a steep-sided glen leading to the Cam Bhealach, where the preceding route is joined. Unless a complete traverse to Gleann Cia-aig is intended, it is necessary to return from Meall na Teanga to the Cam Bhealach on the way back to Kilfinnan.

Map on page 145.

*Gairich from the Loch Quoich dam*                                              *J. Renny*

**Gairich**; 919m; (OS Sheet 33; 025995); M265; *roaring.*

Gairich is the isolated peak which looks well in the view westwards along Loch Garry. It stands boldly on the south side of Loch Quoich, with lonely Glen Kingie to its south, and gives an easier day's climb than most peaks in the wild westland.

The starting point for the ascent is the dam at the E end of Loch Quoich, which is reached along the unclassified road which branches off the A87 beside Loch Garry and goes W to Kinloch Hourn. From the S end of the dam a path is evolving which after 600 metres joins the old stalker's path which is now submerged by the raised water level of Loch Quoich. Take this path S over the boggy moors, dropping a little to the upper limit of the Glen Kingie plantations where another stalker's path leads W up the Druim na Geid Salaich. This path peters out on the broad, easy crest leading to Bac nam Foid. The lochan shown on the map does not exist. At the foot of the final steep rise to Gairich the path reappears, but goes off left onto the S face, so abandon it and keep to the crest which gives one narrow place and some rockier steps. The spacious summit dome has a large cairn. (8km; 730m; 3h).

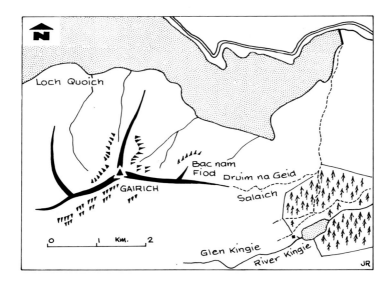

*Sgurr na Ciche from Loch Quoich*                                    H.M. Brown

**Sgurr nan Coireachan**; 953m; (OS Sheets 33 and 40; 933958); M207; *peak of the corries.*
**Garbh Chioch Mhor**; 1013m; (OS Sheet 33s and 40; 909961); M113; *big rough place of the breast.*
**Sgurr na Ciche**; 1040m; (OS Sheets 33 and 40; 902966); M89; *peak of the breast.*

These grand mountains are in the heart of the remote wilderness between Loch Arkaig, Loch Quoich and Loch Nevis, an area which fully lives up to the name and character of The Rough Bounds of Knoydart. The day spent traversing them will be a memorable one, and one calling for Munro experience, for it is a serious expedition in rugged terrain. It is worth waiting for a clear day, if that is not expecting too much in a corner of Scotland that has the reputation for the country's highest rainfall.

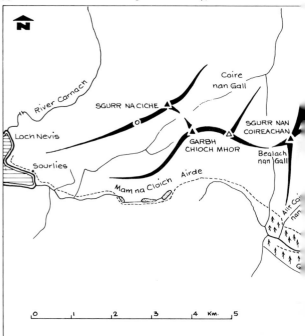

The approach is from Strathan at the W end of Loch Arkaig, as described for Sgurr Mor. An early start is advised, for it is a long day and rough walking will make for a slower pace than usual. Walk up the private road on the N side of Glen Dessarry, which has been extensively planted with trees, to the house at Upper Glendessary. Continue along a path which climbs the hillside behind the house for a short way, then contours along the glen just above the forest plantings. There is a footbridge across the Allt Coire nan Uth, well hidden from sight and not shown on the OS map, which is essential if the burn is in spate.

Once across the Allt Coire nan Uth leave the path to climb N up the steep grassy ridge to Sgurr nan Coireachan, an unrelenting 750m grind. The ridge narrows and is edged with crags near the top, but there is no difficulty if the crest is followed. (8km; 900m; 3h 20min).

The continuation of the traverse goes

*Looking west from Sgurr nan Coireachan to Garbh Chioch Bheag*       H.M. Brown

WSW steeply down to the Bealach nan Gall (c. 735m), and W from there the Garbh Chiochs live up to their name. The ridge is a succession of rocky outcrops, and Coire nan Gall on its N side is one of the roughest corries outside Skye. The fugitive Prince Charles travelled through it on his flight after Culloden. Navigation along the ridge is simplified by there being a sturdy wall to follow. Garbh Chioch Bheag (968m) is passed on the way to the summit of Garbh Chioch Mhor. (10½km; 1200m; 4h 20min).

Keep following the wall W then NW to drop to the col below Sgurr na Ciche. This pass is called Feadan na Ciche, the 'whistle' or 'chanter' of the peak; an apt description on a windy day. Sgurr na Ciche is craggy, but by skirting up towards the W the crags can be turned to reach the summit cairn (11½km; 1400m; 5h).

To return to Strathan, retrace the route to the Feadan na Ciche col and descend the bouldery gully SW towards Coire na Ciche. At a height of about 650m turn SE and traverse along a grassy terrace under Garbh Chioch Mhor to descend steep grassy slopes by a little stream down to the pass at the head of Glen Dessarry. Follow the path down this glen; at first it is wet and disappears from time to time, but it improves and the outward route is rejoined at the Allt Coire nan Uth.

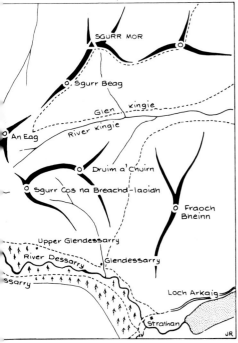

*Looking across Loch Quoich to Sgurr Mor*                                    *J.S. Stewart*

**Sgurr Mor;** 1003m; (OS Sheets 33 and 40, 965980); M128; *big peak.*

This mountain is situated in very remote country, part of the long ridge from Gairich to Sgurr na Ciche which runs from east to west on the south side of Loch Quoich, and which is barred by the loch from easy access on the north. South of Sgurr Mor is desolate but delightful Glen Kingie, and one has to pass through the hills on the south side of this glen to find the nearest point of access, at the western end of Loch Arkaig.

The public road along the N side of Loch Arkaig ends between Murlaggan and Strathan, but there seems to be no objection to driving along the last kilometre or two, and parking near Strathan. This is the nearest point of access by car to all the mountains west and north-west from Loch Arkaig towards Loch Nevis and Knoydart.

Walk up the private road to Glendessarry, and from there take the stalker's path which heads N up to the pass at about 360m between Druim a' Chuirn and Fraoch Bheinn. This path is not so clear on the Glen Kingie side, and at the point where it turns NE towards Kinbreak bothy descend NW to cross the river and gain another stalker's path on its N side. In spate conditions it may be necessary to go up the glen for some distance to find a possible crossing place. The path rises steadily, then dog-legs back up to the col between An Eag and Sgurr Beag. This is one of the country's most dramatic man-made paths; continue along it over Sgurr Beag, down steeply to the col at 750m and steeply up again to Sgurr Mor. (10km; 1200m; 4h 20min).

The route described above can be used for the return. However, it is quicker, if there are not problems crossing the River Kingie, to continue about 350 metres E along the level summit ridge to Sgurr Mor and go down the SE ridge, still on the stalker's path, to the col below Sgurr an Fhuarain. Descend S down 500m of steep grassy slopes to cross the Kingie and return over the pass to Glendessarry and Strathan.

Map on page 149.

*Mountains of Knoydart from Ladhar Bheinn*                                      *W. Forbes*

The next three mountains to be described are in the Knoydart peninsula, one of the wildest and most inaccessible parts of the Scottish Highlands. No roads penetrate into this area, and access is either by boat or on foot along one of the rights-of-way which go west from the nearest road-ends. Because of the remoteness of Knoydart, the climbing of its mountains entails finding overnight accommodation in the area. Wild camping is possible almost anywhere except near the habitations at Inverie and Barrisdale.

The following routes of access to Knoydart are possible:-

1. By mail boat from Mallaig to Inverie three days a week. Contact Bruce Watt Cruises, The Pier, Mallaig, Inverness-shire. Tel. 0687 2233.

2. From the road-end at the west end of Loch Arkaig by the right-of-way through Glen Dessarry to the head of Loch Nevis, and then over the Mam Meadail pass to Inverie.

3. From the road-end at Kinloch Hourn by the right-of-way along Loch Hourn to Barrisdale, and then over the Mam Barrisdale pass to Inverie.

4. By private arrangement a boat may be hired at Arnisdale or Corran on the north side of Loch Hourn to cross the loch at Barrisdale.

Accommodation may be available at the following places:-

1. Inverie, where an estate hostel and bed and breakfast are sometimes available. Contact the Factor, Knoydart Estate, Inverie, by Mallaig, Inverness-shire. Tel. 0687 2331.

2. Barrisdale, where there is a bothy beside the keeper's house. Contact the Keeper, Barrisdale, by Glenelg, Inverness-shire.

3. Sourlies bothy, at the head of Loch Nevis. A small open bothy, often crowded.

Climbing routes are described starting at Inverie, as this is the most easily accessible place in Knoydart using public transport. Deer stalking is economically vital for the local community, and the hills should not be climbed in the stalking season without permission from the local factor or keepers.

*Meall Buidhe from Luinne Bheinn*                                                    *H.M. Brown*

**Meall Buidhe**; 946m; (OS Sheets 33 and 40; 849990); M215; *yellow hill.*
**Luinne Bheinn**; 939m; (OS Sheet 33; 868008); M230; *perhaps hill of anger, or hill of mirth or melody.*

These two fine and complex mountains are in the heart of Knoydart, and their traverse is one of the roughest hill walks in Scotland. From Inverie take the estate road up the glen of the Inverie River for 3½km until just beyond the knoll on which stands the Brocket Memorial. Follow the right hand track across the river and continue along this right-of-way up Gleann Meadail to the pass at its head, the Mam Meadail (c. 550m). The slopes on the N side of the pass are craggy, but any difficulties can be avoided by keeping slightly to the E, aiming for the little col W of Sgurr Sgeithe. From there climb the SE ridge of Meall Buidhe, which is narrow and rocky in places and leads in ½km to the South-east Top (c. 940m). ½km further NW along a broad grassy ridge is the summit of Meall Buidhe. (10½km; 960m; 4h). If only climbing this mountain, return by the same route, or descend the long W ridge.

To continue to Luinne Bheinn return to the South-east Top, descend the narrow NE ridge to the Bealach Ile Coire, and climb 90m to the rocky knoll of Druim Leac a' Shith. (This up and down section of the ridge can be avoided by traversing grassy rakes on the W side). Continue over another rocky knoll and drop to the Bealach a' Choire Odhair (c. 675m), the lowest point between the two Munros. Climb NE to reach the E ridge of Luinne Bheinn a short distance SE of its East Top (937m) which is sometimes wrongly taken for the summit. This lies about 450 metres W, and only 2m higher, at a small cairn. (15km; 1400m; 5h 40min).

Follow the ridge NW past another larger cairn, and when it steepens descend W to about 550m and make a descending traverse NNW to join the Mam Barrisdale path; in this way the traverse over the top of Bachd Mhic an Tosaich can be avoided. A good path leads down to Gleann an Dubh-Lochain and joins the estate road back to Inverie.

*Luinne Bheinn from Lochan nam Breac*                    J.S. Stewart

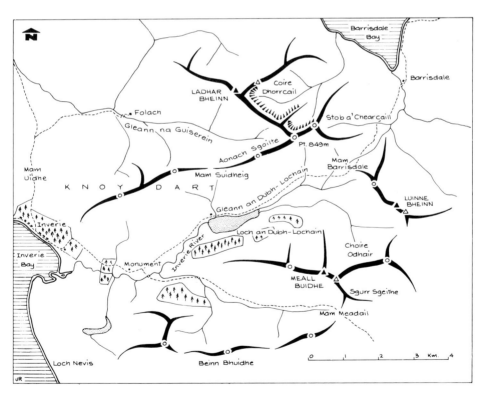

*Ladhar Bheinn from Stob a' Chearcaill*                    D.J. Bennet

**Ladhar Bheinn;** 1020m; (OS Sheet 33; 824040); M108; *hoof or claw hill.*

Ladhar Bheinn (pronounced Larven) rises in the northern part of the Knoydart peninsula, overlooking Loch Hourn. It is one of the finest mountains in Scotland, with narrow rocky ridges, spectacular corries and a seascape setting which makes the views from it, or towards it, among the best in the land. The circuit of Coire Dhorrcail is the finest traverse of the mountain, but it is rather difficult of access from Inverie, being on the Loch Hourn side of Ladhar Bheinn. The direct approach from Inverie by Gleann na Guiserein is easier, but less interesting; however, it is possible to continue this route along the ridge above Coire Dhorrcail, as described below. The magnetic compass is unreliable on the northern flank of the mountain.

From Inverie take the road N through the forest to the Mam Uidhe pass. This road continues over the pass, beyond the point shown on the OS map, but at (766027) turn off on the footpath down to Folach in lonely Gleann na Guiserein. This sad, peaceful spot is dominated by the huge, steep flank of Ladhar Bheinn. Climb NE to the tiny lochan on top of the precipitous WNW ridge of the mountain, and follow this ridge, turning occasional crags, to reach the final tent-like crest at the 1010m trig point. The summit, 1020m, is ½km further on and feels like the top of the world. (10km; 1080m; 4h).

The return may be made by the same route, but it is better to carry on to make a fine traverse. Continue along the level summit ridge for a further hundred metres to the junction of the NE and SE ridges. Go down the SE ridge, steeply at first, then over a succession of rocky crests, the tops of the great buttresses of Coire Dhorrcail. The Bealach Coire Dhorrcail is reached and is followed by a climb up the broad grassy ridge to Pt. 849m. Turn SW at this point and traverse the long narrow Aonach Sgoilte ridge, a route of constant interest, typical of the Rough Bounds of Knoydart. In 3km reach the Mam Suidheig and drop steeply down S to the outflow of Loch an Dubh-Lochain, finally returning to Inverie along the estate road down the Inverie River.

The classic traverse of Ladhar Bheinn, namely the circuit of Coire Dhorrcail, is best done from Barrisdale, and it is even possible for very fit walkers to do the traverse starting from and returning to Kinloch Hourn in a day. Take the stalker's path WNW from Barrisdale for 1½km to the shoulder of Creag Bheithe, and then strike SW up this ridge, gaining superb views of Ladhar Bheinn across Coire Dhorrcail. Beyond a level section of the ridge the steep buttress of Stob a' Chearcaill rears up and for 100m there is a steep scramble up broken rock and grassy ledges, traversing to and fro to find the easiest line. From Stob a' Chearcaill continue SW along the narrow ridge to Pt. 849m, and then go NW to Ladhar Bheinn, thus reversing the route described in the preceding paragraph. (From Barrisdale: 6½km; 1180m; 3h 30min. 10km further from Kinloch Hourn). Descend the NE ridge over the Top of Stob a' Choire Odhair (960m) and continue down to a more level part of the ridge at about 400m where one should turn SE and drop down into Coire Dhorrcail to reach the stalker's path which leads back to Barrisdale.

Map on page 153.

*Looking across Loch Hourn to Beinn Sgritheall*                                    W. Forbes

**Beinn Sgritheall**; 974m; (OS Sheet 33; 836126); M180; *probably scree or gravel hill.*

This grand peak dominates the Glenelg peninsula and gives fine views over Loch Hourn to Knoydart, and down the Sound of Sleat to Rum and Eigg. Its best features, the northern ridges and corries, tend to be hidden, and the southern flanks above Loch Hourn present a steep mass of rotten crags and scree slopes that would deter the bravest. On closer acquaintance, however, Beinn Sgritheall proves to be one of the best of the solitary Munros.

The approach by road from the A87 at the foot of Glen Shiel goes over the spectacular Bealach Ratagain and through Glenelg village to Arnisdale on the N shore of Loch Hourn, where the ascent begins. Climb NE behind the village up the steep stream to the Bealach Arnisdail (c. 600m) which separates Beinn Sgritheall from its rocky lower neighbour, Beinn na h-Eaglaise. From the col climb NW up steep scree to gain the East Top (903m). Continue along the ridge for 1km, a delightful traverse with one short exposed section, to reach the summit trig point. (3½km; 1050m; 2h 40min).

Return the same way, or perhaps, transport allowing, continue down the rockier W ridge to the lochan at its foot, (816126), and then S by a steep path through the woods of Coille Mhialairigh to the road 3km from Arnisdale.

Other interesting approaches to Beinn Sgritheall can be made from the N, up either Glen More or Gleann Beag of the famous brochs. From the wood at Strath a' Chomair in Gleann Beag there are routes by the northern ridges and corries which give rewarding days in wild country, but the burns may be difficult to cross when in spate.

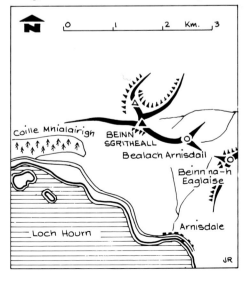

*Spidean Mialach and Gleouraich from the north, with Sgurr Mor appearing between them*    *H.M. Brown*

**Gleouraich**; 1035m; (OS Sheet 33; 039054); M94; *possibly uproar or noise.*
**Spidean Mialach**; 996m; (OS Sheet 33; 066043); M143; *peak of deer, or other wild animals.*

The road westwards along the north side of Loch Quoich passes close below three fine peaks whose ascents are among the easiest in the Western Highlands. Not only are the distances from road to summits short, but stalker's paths give fast and easy walking onto the high ridges, and in some places along them. Gleouraich and Spidean Mialach, the eastern pair, are joined by just such a ridge and are separated from Sgurr a' Mhaoraich to the west by the deep trough of Glen Quoich into which the raised waters of Loch Quoich thrust a narrow arm.

Gleouraich and Spidean Mialach make a fine pair of hills with two quite distinct aspects, dark rocky corries and steep spurs on their north side, and more gentle grassy slopes to the south. Their traverse is a delightful expedition combining good stalker's paths and a splendid undulating high-level ridge.

The start is from the road on the N side of Loch Quoich at a point about 4½km W of the Loch Quoich dam. There is a small wood just E of the Allt Coire Peitireach, and a cairn on the W side of the stream marks the rhododendron-overgrown start of a superb stalker's path which climbs to 850m on Gleouraich. This is one of the most impressive of all such paths, particularly high up where it traverses along the edge of the steep-sided SW ridge, almost giving a feeling of exposure as one looks straight down to Loch Quoich hundreds of metres below. Beyond the end of the path continue up the ridge to its junction with the N ridge, then turn SE up the crest to the summit trig point of Gleouraich. (3½km; 830m; 2h 10min).

A descent of ½km and 70m follows in the same direction, then there is a rise to Craig Coire na Fiar Bhealaich (1006m). Beyond this Top a stalker's path zig-zags down to the Fiar Bhealaich (c. 740m), and from this col the ascent of Spidean Mialach is straightforward, following the scalloped cliff-edge of three successive corries. (7km; 1150m; 3h 30min).

Descend easy slopes to the SW, aiming for Loch Fearna, and when half way to it bear off to the W towards Coire Mheil. Reach the end of the stalker's path in this corrie and follow it down to the road 400 metres E of the start.

*Sgurr a' Mhaoraich from Loch Quoich*                                      J. Renny

**Sgurr a' Mhaoraich**; 1027m; (OS Sheet 33; 984065); M101; *peak of the shellfish.*

Sgurr a' Mhaoraich is an isolated mountain which bulks large in any view up Loch Hourn, although to Loch Quoich it shows only its grassy side. Its hidden northern aspects hold vast flanks of black rock and a complex of ridges and steep corries. The traverse described below does justice to the mountain.

Leave the road to Kinloch Hourn at the start of a stalker's path 1km SW of the bridge which spans the northern extension of Loch Quoich into Glen Quoich. Follow this path N up the Bac nan Canaichean ridge to Sgurr Coire nan Eiricheallach (891m), and a short distance further across a slight dip to its NW top. There is another drop and then a rather contorted ridge leads to the summit of Sgurr a' Mhaoraich. There are outcrops of rock to either turn or scramble over, and one crag is pegged, a dramatic part of the old path. (5km; 910m; 2h 40 min).

While easy descents can be made southwards or by the ascent route, it is more interesting to complete the circuit of Coire a' Chaorainn. Head NNW for 300 metres to a finger of rock, then descend steeply NNE to the col (c. 790m) at the head of this long narrow corrie. The traverse of Am Bathaich (910m) is rocky and narrow in places, and beyond it another stalker's path is found zig-zagging steeply down the grassy E ridge to Glen Quoich. The private road in this glen is reached and followed S back to the Kinloch Hourn road.

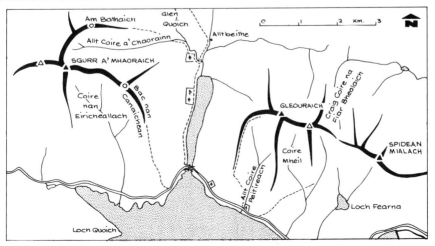

*Aonach air Chrith from the west*                                    H.M. Brown

**Creag a' Mhaim**; 947m; (OS Sheet 33; 088078); M214; *rock of the large rounded hill.*
**Druim Shionnach**; 987m; (OS Sheet 33; 074085); M155; *ridge of the fox.*
**Aonach air Chrith**; 1021m; (OS Sheet 33; 051083); M107; *trembling hill.*
**Maol Chinn-dearg**; 981m; (OS Sheet 33; 032088); M166; *bald red head.*

The South Glen Shiel Ridge, or the South Cluanie Ridge as it is sometimes known, is deservedly regarded as being in the top handful of Scottish mountain ranges. It extends for 14km and has seven Munros in its length. Only once does the ridge drop below 800m, so it is a lofty walkway indeed. Strong walkers can cull all seven Munros in a single day, but to savour the ridge more and possibly double the pleasure it may be better to take two days to it, and it is here described in this way. The north flank of the ridge is well seen from the A87 road through Glen Shiel; it is a succession of fine rocky corries carved along the hillside. The south side of the ridge is a long uniform grassy slope dropping to Glen Quoich.

The first part of the ridge to be described is the eastern half, which is not far to the S of Cluanie Inn across the headwaters of the River Cluanie. Start just E of the Inn at the junction of the old road from Cluanie to Tomdoun, and walk up this road for 3km to the bridge over the Allt Giubhais. From there climb S to the easternmost peak of the ridge, Creag a' Mhaim. The going is pathless, but not particularly rough, and the crags shown on the OS map near the summit present no problems. (5½km; 730m; 2h 30min).

A broad grassy ridge leads down to the first col, and on the way up to Druim Shionnach there is one surprisingly narrow section of ridge before the flat summit is reached. (7km; 850m; 3h). Navigation all along the ridge is simplified by having cliff-bitten corries on the N side, and bare grass slopes on the S. The next 3km section to Aonach air Chrith is defined by the slabby crags of Coire an t-Slugain. (10km; 1020m; 4h). Beyond, the crest of the ridge is narrower, but the traverse to Maol Chinn-dearg is perfectly easy. (12km; 1180m; 4h 40min).

The descent is down the NE ridge, steep at first, but becoming a very pleasant grassy crest with lower down a stalker's path leading back to the road in Glen Shiel 4km W of the day's starting point.

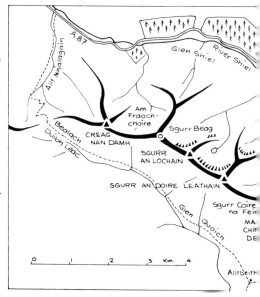

*Sgurr an Lochain from the east*                                              *D.J. Bennet*

**Sgurr an Doire Leathain**; 1010m; (OS Sheet 33; 015099); M116; *peak of the broad thicket.*
**Sgurr an Lochain**; 1004m; (OS Sheet 33; 005104); M126; *peak of the little loch.*
**Creag nan Damh**; 918m; (OS Sheet 33; 983112); M268; *rock of the stags.*

The western half of the South Glen Shiel Ridge has two slightly lower summits to cross as well as its three Munros, so this traverse is just as long as the eastern section. The views are better, particularly to the south and west where great mountains such as Ladhar Bheinn and Beinn Sgritheall dominate the horizon.

The start is at the point where the eastern half traverse ended, a few hundred metres E of the summit of the A87 road on the watershed between the Shiel and Cluanie rivers. Take the stalker's path S across the Allt Coire a' Chuil Droma Bhig, and follow its W branch onto the Druim Thollaidh. Climb up this ridge to reach the romantically named peak of Sgurr Coire na Feinne (the Feinne were the mythical warrior-heroes of early legends). The first Munro, Sgurr an Doire Leathain, is 1½km NW along the main ridge with its summit on a grassy spur about 100 metres N of the ridge. (4½km; 800m; 2h 20min).

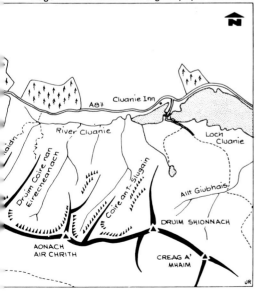

The next corrie is the only northern one on the ridge to hold a lochan, hence the name of the shapely Sgurr an Lochain, not the highest peak on the ridge, but the most distinctive. (6km; 910m; 3h). Sgurr Beag is the next peak, a smaller one as the name implies, not a Munro and for this reason often traversed on its S side where a tiny stream high up on the grass slopes is a welcome source of water on a hot day. Drop to the next col, the lowest on the ridge at 726m and climb the last Munro, Creag nan Damh. (9km; 1210m; 4h 10min).

To return to Glen Shiel, two routes are possible. The first descends NE, very steeply in places, to Am Fraoch-choire where a stalker's path is reached at about 400m, and is followed down to the plantation in Glen Shiel near the site of the 1719 battle. The other longer route is to continue W along the main ridge to the Bealach Duibh Leac (c. 725m) from where a path goes down by the Allt Mhalagain to Glen Shiel. Both descent routes end in Glen Shiel a long way W of the starting point.

*The Saddle from Sgurr na Forcan*                                      *W.B. Young*

**The Saddle;** 1010m; (OS Sheet 33; 936131); M118.
**Sgurr na Sgine;** 945m; (OS Sheet 33; 946113); M220; *peak of the knife.*

The peaks to the north and south of Glen Shiel are certainly well known but The Saddle is even more so for it combines in one mountain a complex of narrow ridges and deep corries that makes it one of the great Highland hills. With its neighbouring sharp peak Faochag (meaning the whelk), it forms the classic view down Glen Shiel from the site of the 1719 battle. Many visits are needed to explore The Saddle fully, and here the description is restricted to the traverse of it and Sgurr na Sgine.

Start in Glen Shiel from the A87 road ¾km SE of the quarry at Achnangart. A good stalker's path is followed W to the col between Biod an Fhithich and Meallan Odhar. Continue S then SW to the foot of the narrow E ridge of The Saddle, the Forcan Ridge. This superb rock ridge involves some exposed scrambling, and a short tricky pitch to descend on the far side of Sgurr na Forcan, but it is not technically difficult. (However, nervous or inexperienced walkers may prefer the alternative route described below). The crest of the Forcan Ridge sweeps up, narrowing to a knife edge above the slabs of Coire Mhalagain before reaching Sgurr na Forcan (c. 960m). Continue W, descending a short steep pitch with good holds and traversing the narrow ridge over the East Top (958m) to the summit cairn on top of a rocky crag. (5km; 1080m; 3h). The OS trig point is about 100 metres W along a level grassy ridge, and apparently slightly lower than the cairn.

The alternative route bypassing the Forcan Ridge is to traverse below its S flank, following a dry stone dyke across the rough hillside to the Bealach Coire Mhalagain. From there climb WNW in a rising traverse to reach the trig point.

To continue to Sgurr na Sgine, descend this easy route from the trig point to Bealach Coire Mhalagain, and climb S to the NW Top of Sgurr na Sgine (944m). Continue SE along the rocky ridge to the summit cairn perched right at the edge of the steep SE face of the mountain. (7½km; 1330m; 4h).

Return past the NW Top and continue W to Faochag along a fine narrow crest. Descend the NE ridge, a continuously steep but otherwise easy route which leads to Glen Shiel ½km up the road from the day's starting point.

*The east face of Sgurr na Sgine*                                    *H.M. Brown*

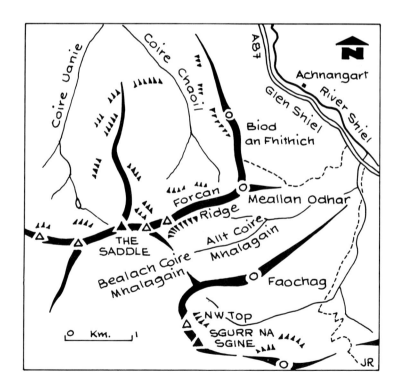

*Mullach Fraoch-choire from Glen Affric*                                    R. Robb

# SECTION 11

## Glen Affric and Kintail

*Toll Creagach from Tom a' Choinich*                                      H.M. Brown

**Toll Creagach;** 1054m; (OS Sheet 25; 194283); M73; *rocky hollow.*
**Tom a' Choinich;** 1111m; (OS Sheet 25; 163273); M40; *hill of the moss*

These two hills are at the eastern end of the long range of mountains on the north side of Glen Affric, a range which stretches 25km from the forested lower reaches of Glen Affric and Cannich westwards to the Glomach chasm above Glen Elchaig. Toll Creagach is a hill of rounded outlines and a fairly level summit ridge 2km long with the highest point at the east end. Tom a' Choinich has a more distinctive shape with a crescent-shaped ridge enclosing its east corrie. Between the two hills is the Bealach Toll Easa, across which goes the stalker's path which in former days led from Affric Lodge to Benula Lodge, the latter now submerged below the raised waters of Loch Mullardoch.

Although it is possible to climb these hills from Glen Cannich, this route is not recommended as the going along the S side of Loch Mullardoch through the pinewoods is trackless and very rough. It is better to approach from Glen Affric, leaving the road at the foot of Gleann nam Fiadh near the W end of Loch Beinn a' Mheadhoin. Walk up the track in this glen for 3km and then climb N up Toll Creagach, at first up steep and in places bouldery slopes, then more easily over grass and heath to the summit cairn a few metres W of the OS trig point. (5½km; 830m; 2h 40min).

Go WSW along a broad ridge of grass and stones to the West Top (952m), then descend more steeply down a narrowing crest to the Bealach Toll Easa (873m). Continue due W up the spur which rises in the centre of Tom a' Choinich's E corrie, grassy at first, then steepening, becoming rockier and leading directly to the summit. (9km; 1070m; 3h 50min).

Return to Gleann nam Fiadh either down the SE ridge, easy at first but becoming steeper and rocky lower down, or by descending the ascent route to the Bealach Toll Easa and following the stalker's path SE down the Allt Toll Easa.

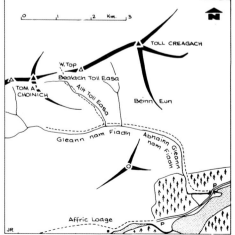

*Mam Sodhail and Carn Eighe from Sgurr na Lapaich*                                    *G.S. Johnstone*

**Mam Sodhail**; 1180m; (OS Sheet 25; 120253); M13; *hill of the barns.*
**Carn Eighe**; 1183m; (OS Sheet 25; 123262); M11; *file hill.*
**Beinn Fhionnlaidh**; 1005m; (OS Sheet 25; 115282); M125; *Finlay's hill.*

Carn Eighe and Mam Sodhail, almost identical twins in height and appearance, are the highest mountains north of the Great Glen and dominate the high ground between Glen Affric and Loch Mullardoch. They form a great horseshoe around Gleann nam Fiadh, both throwing out long ridges to the east to enclose this glen. From Carn Eighe another important ridge goes north to end at Beinn Fhionnlaidh, a very remote mountain overlooking the head of Loch Mullardoch. The most familiar view of this group is from Glen Affric, from where Sgurr na Lapaich (one of the Tops of Mam Sodhail) is the most prominent peak, projecting far in front of its two higher neighbours. These are not particularly rocky mountains, but their ridges are steep sided and their corries wild and craggy enough to make this a fine group whose traverse gives a long and serious mountain expedition. Beinn Fhionnlaidh is included as it is difficult to reach from any other glen, only Glen Elchaig offering a feasible but long approach, unless one has a canoe on Loch Mullardoch.

The closest starting point is at the end of the public road in Glen Affric, 1½km E of Affric Lodge, and from the lodge two alternatives exist for the ascent of Mam Sodhail. The quicker is along the right-of-way on the N side of Loch Affric to Coire Leachavie and up the stalker's path in this corrie. It ends on the SW ridge of Mam Sodhail at 1086m, and the final ½km up the final slope is easy, past the remains of a stone shelter used by the men of the Ordnance Survey many years ago. The summit has a huge circular cairn which was an important point in the Ordnance Survey's primary triangulation of Scotland in the 1840's. (10km; 940m; 3h 50min). Alternatively, a route for good weather goes N then W from Affric Lodge by a stalker's path for 2km. Continue W across rising moor for 1½km to the foot of the SE ridge of Sgurr na Lapaich and so directly to this Top (1036m). Continue W along a splendid 3½km ridge, following a well worn path along the grassy crest. The ridge narrows and crosses Mullach Cadha Rainich (993m) before rising to Mam Sodhail.

Descend N for 140m to the col at 1044m and climb the opposite slope to Carn Eighe. (11km; 1070m; 4h 20min). At this point a long diversion is needed to include Beinn Fhionnlaidh, going N along the grassy ridge over Stob Coire Lochan (917m) for 2½km to its summit (13½km; 1260m; 5h 10min), and returning the same way to Carn Eighe. (16km; 1640m; 6h 20min).

Now embark on the long E ridge of Carn Eighe, first ENE to Stob a' Choire Dhomhain (1148m), then ESE along a narrow rocky ridge which gives an enjoyable scramble if the crest is followed to reach Sron Garbh (1132m). Descend NE quite steeply down the rocky ridge where at one point a stalker's path has been so well constructed as to form a flight of stone steps. From the Garbh-bhealach (963m) go SE past two tiny lochans to reach a path which leads down to Gleann nam Fiadh. Two km further down this glen the stalker's path S to Affric Lodge gives the shortest route back to the day's starting point.

If one prefers to climb Beinn Fhionnlaidh by itself, then Loch na Leitreach in Glen Elchaig is the best starting point and the route is the same as for Mullach na Dheiragain (see p166) as far as the W end of Loch Mullardoch. From there climb the W side of the hill directly. (12½km; 930m; 4h 20min). There are two streams to be crossed on this route that may be impossible in spate.

**An Socach**; 920m; (OS Sheets 25 and 33, 088230); M264; *the snout.*

This Munro is the lowest on the long chain of mountains on the north side of Glen Affric, and it is rather overshadowed by its big neighbours Mam Sodhail and Sgurr nan Ceathreamhnan. Its position is very isolated, 12 kilometres up Glen Affric from the end of the public road in that glen, nearly the same distance over the hills from Cluanie Inn, and 3km from the remote Alltbeithe youth hostel, the loneliest in Scotland. The effort required to climb An Socach is more in the approach march than in the ascent of the hill itself. In shape it has three broad ridges converging at a flattish, bouldery summit, and the east-facing Coire Ghadheil has some small crags around its rim, but lower down it is a maze of eroded peat bog.

The approach from the car park at the W end of Loch Beinn a' Mheadhoin in Glen Affric is either along the right-of-way past Affric Lodge and on the N side of Loch Affric, or along the Forestry Commission road which crosses from the car park to the S side of the loch. It is quite possible to cycle along this road for 7km to Athnamulloch, where the River Affric is recrossed to join the right-of-way on the N side. Whichever way one choses, the approach up Glen Affric is scenically the best part of the day.

Beyond Athnamulloch the glen becomes bare, but the track continues and in 2½km the footbridge over the Allt Coire Ghadheil is reached. On the W side of the stream bear NW up easy slopes of grass and heather leading to the broad flat ridge which leads round the edge of Coire Ghadheil. After a long level section a final short rise leads to the summit. (13½km; 680m; 4h 10min).

To vary the descent, go down the NE ridge to the Bealach Coire Ghadheil and follow the good stalker's path down the E side of the corrie to Glen Affric. From the bealach one can continue the traverse to Mam Sodhail up another stalker's path which climbs diagonally NE to reach the SW ridge of Mam Sodhail near a prominent cairn 1km SW of its summit.

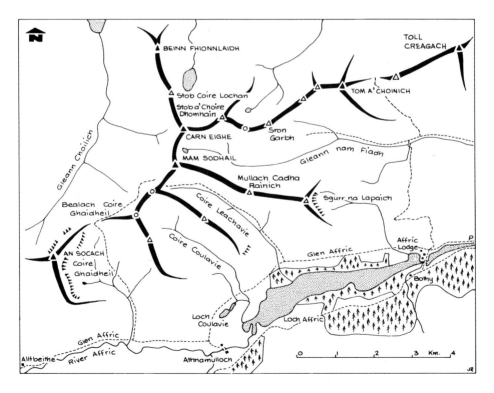

*Sgurr nan Ceathreamhnan from A' Chralaig*                                                                D.J. Bennet

**Sgurr nan Ceathreamhnan;** 1151m; (OS Sheets 25 and 33; 057228); M21; *peak of the quarters.*
**Mullach na Dheiragain;** 982m; (OS Sheets 25 and 33; 081259); M164; *perhaps summit of the hawk.*

The long hill-range on the north side of Glen Affric culminates at its western end in the great massif of Sgurr nan Ceathreamhnan, a superb and complex mountain of many ridges, peaks and corries. In size it is the equal of several normal peaks, and from its summit long ridges radiate out to the north and east. The longest of these goes for 7km towards the head of Loch Mullardoch, and rises near its mid-point to the subsidiary peak of Mullach na Dheiragain, classified as a separate Munro, though very much a part of its higher neighbour.

Sgurr nan Ceathreamhnan is in a very remote and wild situation, surrounded by other mountains and many kilometres from the nearest public road. This remoteness adds to its character and makes it one of the great prizes for the Scottish hill-walker, involving a long approach from any direction unless one happens to be staying at the youth hostel at Alltbeithe in Glen Affric. If Mullach na Dheiragain is included in the traverse, then Glen Elchaig is the logical starting and finishing point and the Falls of Glomach can be visited en route to give one of the great day's hill-walking in the north-west. The feasibility of this route depends on permission being given to drive up the private road in Glen Elchaig as far as Loch na Leitreach at the foot of the path up to the Falls of Glomach. At present this is normally possible, but the situation may change. One other factor must be borne in mind: the route described below involves two river crossings which may be hazardous or even impossible in spate conditions, which may include spring when snow in the high corries of Sgurr nan Ceathreamhnan is melting.

Drive up Glen Elchaig (with permission) to Loch na Leitreach and start walking there. Continue up the glen to Iron Lodge, and take the path E through the pass towards Loch Mullardoch until ½ km beyond Loch an Droma. There branch S along the path to Gleann Sithidh and cross the Abhainn Sithidh, possibly with difficulty if this stream is in spate with rain or melting snow. From the end of the path near the waterfalls climb steeply E up a grassy slope onto the NW ridge of Mullach Sithidh (973m) and continue up the broad shoulder to this Top. Drop 40m to a col and climb the ridge ahead to Mullach na Dheiragain. (10½km; 930m; 4h).

The long, and in places rough ridge is followed SW over Carn na Con Dhu (968m) to the Bealach na Daoine (840m), and from there a narrow rocky ridge with some easy scrambling leads to Sgurr nan Ceathreamhnan. (14½km; 1140m; 5h 10min). Traverse the narrow summit crest to the West Top (1143m) and descend W, then NW along the broad grassy ridge round the rim of Coire Lochan. Continue in a NW direction, descending to Gleann Gaorsaic, cross the Abhainn Gaorsaic and continue down its left bank to reach the path near the Falls of Glomach. The Falls may be visited by a short diversion, and the descent continues along the path which traverses across the precipitous SW flank of the Glomach chasm before dropping to the Allt a' Ghlomaich and Glen Elchaig. It is a fitting end to a great expedition.

*Looking towards Sgurr nan Ceathreamhnan from the Mullach na Dheiragain ridge*    *K.M. Andrew*

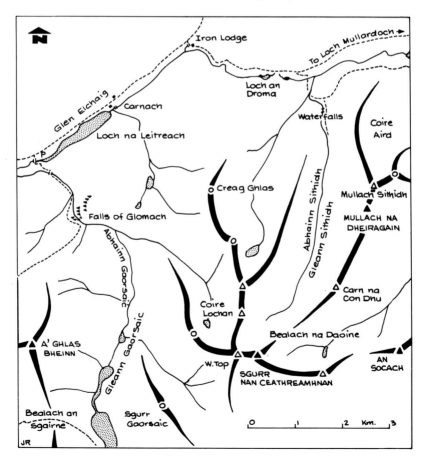

*Looking up Glen Affric to Beinn Fhada*                                    *R. Robb*

**Beinn Fhada**; 1032m; (OS Sheet 33; 018192); M97; *long hill.*
**A' Ghlas-bheinn**; 918m; (OS Sheet 33; 008231); M269; *the greenish-grey hill.*

To the north of the Five Sisters of Kintail a single great mountain, Beinn Fhada, extends from Glen Affric to the head of Loch Duich. It is well named the long mountain, for it extends from east to west for almost 9km, and occupies an area equal to all the Five Sisters. The only roadside view of the mountain is from Loch Duich, from where the knobbly ridge of Sgurr a' Choire Ghairbh is seen. The summit, however, is far beyond and above this ridge. The south and west sides of Beinn Fhada above Gleann Lichd are uniformly steep and in places craggy, and the north side of the mountain is a succession of wild corries. By contrast, A' Ghlas-bheinn is a rather small and insignificant hill rising above the forest in Strath Croe. Beinn Fhada is in National Trust for Scotland property, and is accessible at all times of the year; A' Ghlas-bheinn is in the Inverinate estate.

The simple traverse of these two mountains starts in Strath Croe where there is a Forestry Commission car park at the end of the public road a few hundred metres W of Dorusduain. Cross the Abhainn Chonaig by a footbridge at Dorusduain and follow the path E up Gleann Choinneachain below the steep and craggy NW end of Beinn Fhada. After crossing the stream which comes down from Coire an Sgairne take the stalker's path up this corrie onto the ridge of Meall a' Bhealaich at (011206). Go S along this ridge, which merges into the great summit plateau of Beinn Fhada, the Plaide Mhor, and continue SE along the edge of this plateau to the big summit cairn. (6km; 980m; 3h).

Return by the same route along the Meall a' Bhealaich ridge and go N to this outlying top. The descent N to the Bealach an Sgairne is steep and rocky, and the easiest descent is slightly E of the direct line to the pass, down the E side of a prominent gully. (An alternative which may be preferable in bad conditions of visibility or rain is to return down Coire an Sgairne by the stalker's path of the uphill route to the junction with the main path in Gleann Choinneachain, and then to climb 1km up this path to the pass. This is a longer, but absolutely certain route).

From the Bealach an Sgairne climb the knobbly SE ridge of A' Ghlas-bheinn past Loch a' Chleirich. (11km; 1380m; 4h 50min). Descend WNW along a broad grassy ridge which steepens lower down near the forest. Aim for the point where the path from Strath Croe to the Bealach na Sroine emerges from the forest, and from there continue S through the forest along a track to Dorusduain.

*The cliffs of Sgurr a' Choire Ghairbh at the west end of Beinn Fhada*                    D.J. Bennet

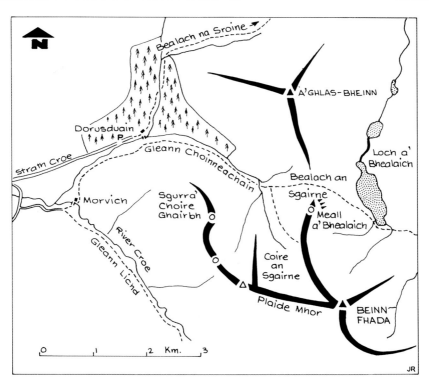

*Sgurr nan Conbhairean from the east*                                    R. Robb

**Carn Ghluasaid**; 957m; (OS Sheet 34; 146125); M201; *hill of movement.*
**Sgurr nan Conbhairean**; 1110m; (OS Sheet 34; 130139); M42; *peak of the keeper of the hounds.*
**Sail Chaorainn**; 1002m; (OS Sheet 34; 134155); M131; *hill (literally heel) of the rowan.*

These three mountains are on the north side of Loch Cluanie mid-way between Loch Ness and Loch Duich. From the A87 road they do not look very impressive, for their southern slopes and corries are undistinguished and their tops hidden. Only when one is on the summits can their true character be appreciated, in particular the great wild eastern corrie in which rise the headwaters of the River Doe. The southern slopes by which the ascent is made are for the most part grassy.

Start the traverse at Lundie, 4km W of the Loch Cluanie dam. Follow the old military road W for ½km, then turn N along a fine stalker's path which leads right up to the flat plateau of Carn Ghluasaid. The summit cairn may be hard to find in mist, it is about 50 metres back from the precipitous N face of the hill. (4km; 720m; 2h 10min).

Traverse W then NW along a broad ridge of moss and stones to Creag a' Chaorainn (999m), then W to the Glas Bhealach over a remarkably smooth expanse of grass, and finally climb NW to Sgurr nan Conbhairean. (7km; 990m; 3h 20min). Descend N along a curving ridge to the col at 910m and reach Sail Chaorainn by its easy-angled SSW ridge. (8½km; 1100m; 3h 50min).

Return by the same route towards Sgurr nan Conbhairean, whose summit can be by-passed on the W. Continue SW down a narrowing ridge to the col above Gorm Lochan, and climb a short distance further to Drochaid an Tuill Easaich (1000m), a Top not named on the OS 1:50000 map. Turn S and descend the easy grass ridge which leads to the shoulder of Meall Breac. When the descent steepens bear SE, cross the Allt Coire Lair to reach the path on its E side and go down it to the old military road which leads E back to Lundie.

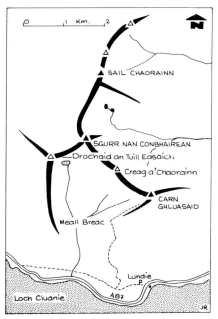

*A' Chralaig from Mullach Fraoch-choire*                                    *K.M. Andrew*

**A' Chralaig**; 1120m; (OS Sheets 33 and 34; 094148); M32; *the basket, or creel.*
**Mullach Fraoch-choire**; 1102m; (OS Sheets 33 and 34; 095171); M46; *heather-corrie peak.*

These two peaks are the high points of an 8km long ridge extending north from the west end of Loch Cluanie to Glen Affric. A' Chralaig is a massive mountain; certainly this is the impression gained when looking from the south-west at the long grassy slopes rising high above Loch Cluanie. Mullach Fraoch-choire is more elegant, its summit being the meeting point of three narrow ridges, and it looks particularly fine seen from the pine woods round Loch Affric. The east side of the high main ridge drops in a series of large grassy corries draining towards Glen Affric, while the west side is more uniformly steep above the deep glen of An Caorann Mor.

Start the traverse from the A87 road near the W end of Loch Cluanie where the track through An Caorann Mor leaves the road. Climb steeply NE up grassy slopes for 500m until the angle eases on the S ridge of A' Chralaig. Continue up this ridge, which becomes quite narrow and well defined, and leads easily to the summit, crowned by a huge cairn visible for miles around. (3½km; 900m; 2h 20min). Continue N along a grassy ridge to a col at 950m and climb the outlying Top, Stob Coire na Cralaig (1008m). The ridge becomes narrower, dropping NE across another col, then turning N to Mullach Fraoch-choire. The ascent to this peak is the best part of the traverse, along a narrow ridge broken into several rocky towers which give very pleasant and easy scrambling along their crests to the summit. (6km 1110m; 3h 20min).

The return to Loch Cluanie may well be best made by the outward route, over the summit of A' Chralaig. However, if circumstances dictate a quick descent to lower ground, the best route is back to the col ¼km NE of Stob Coire na Cralaig, then down NW (steeply at first) into Coire Odhar. Lower down this corrie bear round SW to reach the path near the pass at the head of An Caorann Mor, and follow this path SSE to the road at Loch Cluanie.

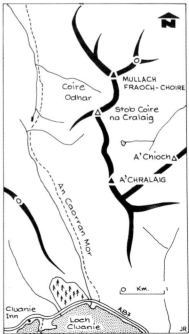

*Sgurr an Fhuarail from the east, with Aonach Meadhoin just visible behind*    *H.M. Brown*

**Ciste Dhubh**; 982m; (OS Sheet 33; 062166); M163; *black chest.*
**Aonach Meadhoin**; 1003m; (OS Sheet 33; 049137); M129; *middle hill.*

These two mountains lie to the north and north-west of Cluanie Inn at the west end of Loch Cluanie. They are separated by a low col, the Bealach a' Choinich which is 3km north-north-west of the Inn. Ciste Dhubh is a pointed peak at the north end of the ridge which rises north of the bealach. The flanks of this ridge are very steep, and its crest narrow, and the summit is also steep and rocky, presenting a fine appearance from the south. Aonach Meadhoin and its slightly lower Top, Sgurr an Fhuarail (988m), lie to the south-west of the Bealach a' Choinich, and form a fine horseshoe ridge above Coire na Cadha. All these peaks have narrow, but perfectly easy ridges and give exhilarating high-level walking. From Cluanie Inn they give a fairly easy round traverse, which can be extended westwards by energetic hill-walkers to include the next two Munros on the north side of Glen Shiel.

Leave the A87 road ½km E of Cluanie Inn and follow the path N along the E side of the Allt a' Chaorainn Bhig. In due course this path tends to disappear, but the going is easy up the grassy slopes on the E side of the stream, leading to the Bealach a' Choinich. A finer, but rather longer route to this col is along the narrow grassy ridge of Am Bathach. Start just E of the wood at the foot of the SSE ridge and follow an old stalker's path up the first few hundred metres, then continue along the delightful undulating crest. A bit of extra effort, but well worthwhile.

The Bealach a' Choinich is a wide flat col, rather wet and peaty, and the S ridge of Ciste Dhubh rises abruptly from its N side. Climb a very steep grass slope for 150m until the gradient eases and a little rocky rop is reached. From there the ridge goes N for 1km, level and very narrow, but perfectly easy and with a distinct path. There is a slight drop before the final rise to the summit of Ciste Dhubh. (5½km; 740m; 2h 30min).

Return to the Bealach a' Choinich and go SW up the NE ridge of Sgurr an Fhuarail. The first part is a broad grassy slope, but higher up the ridge becomes better defined and leads directly to the sharp summit. Continue W along the fine narrow ridge, dropping to about 910m, then climb more steeply to Aonach Meadhoin. (9½km; 1230m; 4h 10min).

The best return to Cluanie is back over Sgurr an Fhuarail and down its SE ridge. There is a little top at 800m which must be climbed as its flanks are very steep, and once past it an easy descent down grassy slopes leads to the road just W of the Inn.

*Aonach Meadhoin and Sgurr an Fhuarail from the west*                    D.J. Bennet

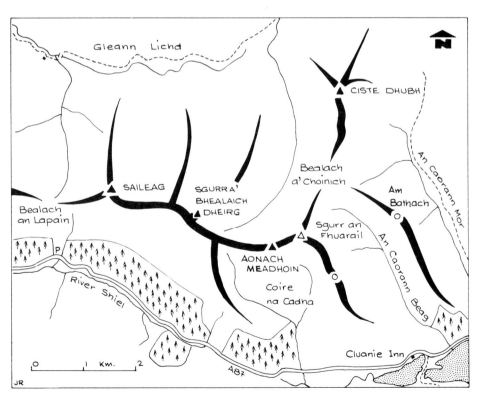

*Looking west from Sgurr a' Bhealaich Dheirg to Saileag with the Five Sisters of Kintail beyond*     *J. S. Stewart*

**Sgurr a' Bhealaich Dheirg**; 1038m; (OS Sheet 33; 035143); M92; *peak of the red pass.*
**Saileag**; 959m; (OS Sheet 33; 017148); M195; *little heel.*

Near its head Glen Shiel is densely forested along its north side, and above the forest rise the smooth grassy slopes of Sgurr a' Bhealaich Dheirg and Saileag, two mountains which form a continuation of the Five Sisters of Kintail eastward beyond the Bealach an Lapain. They have some of the same character as the Five Sisters, long uniform slopes above Glen Shiel, and grand wild corries to the north overlooking Gleann Lichd. The summit ridge and northern corries are in National Trust for Scotland territory.

Sgurr a' Bhealaich Dheirg has a level summit ridge ½km long, and at its south-east end a long spur projects north-east. The summit is a short distance along this spur. Saileag, 2km west, is mainly a grassy hill, 'a mere swelling in the ridge', but its north-west face is steep and craggy. The two give a short and easy traverse from Glen Shiel, and can be combined with Aonach Meadhoin and Ciste Dhubh to give an excellent, but not unduly long day.

Start the traverse from the A87 road at its highest point between Glen Shiel and Loch Cluanie where there is a clear gap on the forested hillside. Climb N onto Meall a' Charra, and NW along the grassy crest of this spur to reach the main ridge ½km SE of Sgurr a' Bhealaich Dheirg. Climb steeply up to the level ridge of this peak and go out for about 70 metres along the narrow NE spur, following a low dry-stone wall to reach the summit where a large, finely built cairn stands astride the crest. (3km; 770m; 2h).

Return to the level ridge and go NW along it for about 400 metres, then turn W down the narrower continuation of the ridge where there is a fairly good path all the way, over a little bump, down to the col and up a grassy rise to Saileag. (4½km; 900m; 2h 30min).

Go down an easy grassy slope WSW to the Bealach an Lapain, and from there descend steeply S to Glen Shiel, following traces of a path, to reach the road 4km NW of the day's starting point.

No restriction on climbing these hills by the Bealach an Lapain route during the stalking season.

Map on page 173.

*Sgurr nan Saighead and Sgurr Fhuaran from the north-west*                    *D.J. Bennet*

For most of its length Glen Shiel is enclosed on the north-east side by a mountain range of awe-inspiring height and steepness - the Five Sisters of Kintail. They rise from glen to summit crests in uninterrupted slopes of heather, grass, scree and crag, riven by great gullies. The best known view of the group is from the south side of Loch Duich, from where the mountains have a remarkable simplicityand symmetry of outline. Of the Five Sisters, four exceed the magic height, and of these two are Munros and two are Tops. The classic hill-walking expedition is the complete traverse, preferably from south-east to north-west; it is not an unduly strenuous day, but is does end at least 8km away from the starting point, so some suitable transport arrangement will be needed if a long walk through Glen Shiel is to avoided. Possibly the bus services through the glen might help. The Five Sisters are in National Trust for Scotland property, and access is possible all year.

**Sgurr Fhuaran**; 1068m; (OS Sheet 33; 978167); M66; *meaning obscure.*

The highest and finest peak of the Five Sisters, and the outstanding landmark in this part of the Western Highlands. The most striking feature of Sgurr Fhuaran seen from Glen Shiel is the long WNW ridge which rises from the River Shiel directly to the summit, bounded on both sides by great deep-cut ravines. The ascent starts from the A87 road near the foot of the glen, from where the full height of the mountain is all too obvious.

Cross the River Shiel by the suspension bridge just upstream of Loch Shiel. To make the shortest, most direct ascent, walk up the E bank of the river for 1½km to the Allt a' Bhuilg. On the S side of this stream start up the WNW ridge of the mountain, a long grassy slope narrowing to a ridge and leading at a steady angle right to the summit, a long unrelenting grind. (4km; 1060m; 2h 40min).

A more varied and interesting ascent traverses the peak of Sgurr nan Saighead (peak of the arrows) en route to Sgurr Fhuaran. After crossing the suspension bridge climb NE up a steep grassy slope which levels out at 450m on a flat col. Continue SE across level peaty ground to the foot of the WNW ridge of Sgurr nan Saighead, and climb this ridge direct to the NW peak, which is a superb viewpoint. The route continues along a fine narrow ridge, with a steep drop on the right, to the highest point of Sgurr nan Saighead (929m) and down across a grassy col, following a fairly well-defined path. Beyond the col, and below the steep final slope of Sgurr Fhuaran, the path bears right across the NW face to reach the WNW ridge, which is followed to the summit. (5km; 1230m; 3h 10min). The descent may be made by the same route, or down the WNW ridge.

Map on page 176.

*Sgurr na Carnach and Sgurr Fhuaran from Sgurr na Ciste Duibhe*    H.M. Brown

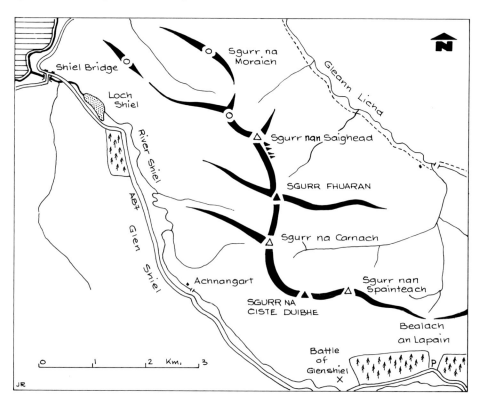

*Looking towards Sgurr na Ciste Duibhe from the east end of the Five Sisters ridge*                    *D.J. Bennet*

**Sgurr na Ciste Duibhe**; 1027m; (OS Sheet 33; 984149); M102; *peak of the black chest.*

This mountain near the south-east end of the Five Sisters range is less shapely than its neighbours, and it is difficult to get a good impression of it from Glen Shiel for it rises so abruptly in rough craggy slopes, presenting rather an unattractive appearance. Its south face is one of the highest and steepest mountainsides in Scotland, rising 1000m in a horizontal distance of 1½km, an average angle of 34 degrees.

The best starting point for the ascent of Sgurr na Ciste Duibhe is further up Glen Shiel, about 1¾km E of the bridge at the site of the 1719 Battle of Glenshiel. At that point there is a wide gap between the rows of spruce trees on the N side of the glen. Climb steeply due N up this gap onto the open hillside, following a path worn by many hill-walkers. The ascent is continuously steep until at about 720m the level grassy ridge is reached at the Bealach an Lapain. Turn W and follow a well marked path along the narrow grassy ridge, climbing gradually to Sgurr nan Spainteach (c. 990m). Beyond this Top (which is not counted as one of the Five Sisters) the ridge drops more abruptly, with a short rocky pitch down to the next col. At this point, below Sgurr na Ciste Duibhe, the ridge has a curious double crest, with a hollow in between the two crests. This may be confusing in misty weather, but if the path is carefully followed there is no problem in climbing the final steep stony slopes to Sgurr na Ciste Duibhe, where there is a large cairn. (3½km; 950m; 2h 30min). Descend by the same route.

If the traverse of the Five Sisters is intended, continue W, bearing round N along a broad ridge to Sgurr na Carnach (1002m), peak of the stony ground. Descend its rather steep N side, still following a broad, rather ill-defined ridge and reach the foot of the S face of Sgurr Fhuaran. This slope is steep and bouldery, but a path zig-zags up to the summit. (6km; 1300m; 3h 30min). The descent to Glen Shiel can be made by either of the two routes described for Sgurr Fhuaran.

*The approach to An Socach up Glen Elchaig*                    *D.J. Bennet*

# SECTION 12

## Glen Cannich to Glen Carron

*An Socach from the south*                                    *K. Rezin*

**An Socach;** 1069m; (OS Sheet 25; 100333); M64; *the projecting place, or snout.*

Situated in the remote hinterland of south-east Ross-shire at the head of Glen Cannich, An Socach is rather an inaccessible Munro, many kilometres from the nearest public road. It might be thought of as the westward extension of An Riabhachan, but the col between the two is low enough to give An Socach the character of a separate mountain. In plan its summit ridge is an east-facing crescent enclosing Coire Mhaim, whose lower level is an extensive area of eroded peat bog and upper rim a line of broken crags. Around its western perimeter An Socach is grassy, and a curving ridge goes out to enclose Coire Lungard.

The shortest approach is from Glen Elchaig in the south-west, and this way has the advantage of easy going on tracks and paths, but it does depend on one's being able to drive up Glen Elchaig as far as Loch na Leitreach. (Otherwise a bicycle would be needed). From the parking place ½km SW of the loch continue up the glen towards Iron Lodge along a good track, quite passable for bicycles. Stay on the NW side of the river, the Allt na Doire Gairbhe, following the path to Loch Mhoicean, then bear E up grassy slopes to reach the level ridge above Coire Lungard. Finally climb NE up the uniformly steep hillside to reach the summit ridge where the OS trig point is situated at the NE end. (11km; 980m; 4h 10min).

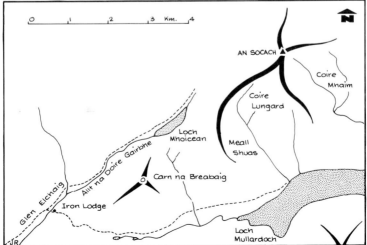

*Looking up the east ridge of An Riabhachan from the western slopes of Sgurr na Lapaich*          *A.J. Bennet*

**An Riabhachan**; 1129m; (OS Sheet 25; 134345); M28; *the brindled, greyish one.*
**Sgurr na Lapaich**; 1150m; (OS Sheet 25; 161351); M22; *peak of the bog.*
**Carn nan Gobhar**; 992m; (OS Sheet 25; 182344); M149; *hill of the goats.*

These three mountains, together with An Socach further west, form the main range between Glen Strathfarrar and Glen Cannich along the north side of Loch Mullardoch. An Riabhachan is a 4km long ridge with open grassy corries on all sides except at the north-east end where there is a steep rocky face above Loch Beag and Loch Mor. Sgurr na Lapaich is a more defined peak, visible from some distance down Strath Glass, and holding some steep rocky corries on its flanks. Carn nan Gobhar is a rounded and rather undistinguished hill with an outlying Top, Creag Dubh, 2km east along a fairly level ridge.

The closest access to these mountains by road is from Glen Strathfarrar, particularly if it is possible to drive to the little power station in Gleann Innis an Loichel. However, if this approach is impractible (e.g. on Tuesdays under the present arrangements, see page 183) the alternative starting point from the road end in Glen Cannich at the Loch Mullardoch dam may be used.

From the power station in Gleann Innis an Loichel continue W along the track for 1km and then up the stalker's path WSW for a further 1½km before branching off left. Cross the stream (possibly difficult if in spate) and climb SW up a grassy path which ends at the lip of An Riabhachan's NE corrie, the Toll an Lochain, a grand wild place with dark crags overlooking two high lochans. Beyond the path the best way lies along the level ridge between the two lochans, then SE on a gradually rising traverse among huge fallen boulders towards the col, the Bealach Toll an Lochain, at the head of the corrie.

From this col the ridge to An Riabhachan rises at a fairly easy angle, with one short narrow section to the North-east Top (1117m), and then over level mossy ground to the summit. (8½km; 950m; 3h 30min. 3km and 40min more if the start is from the Loch Monar dam).

Return to the col and climb the steep grassy SW shoulder of Sgurr na Lapaich to the large circular cairn enclosing the trig point. (11½km; 1300m; 4h 50min). Descending E it is best to keep just on the S side of the true E ridge, which forms a narrow rocky crest involving some scrambling. On its S side a slope of grass and boulders leads down easily to the next col. The first part of the broad ridge leading to Carn nan Gobhar is littered with huge boulders, and higher up the ridge steepens to the small cairn on the summit. (14km; 1500m; 5h 40min). The top of Carn nan Gobhar is a fairly wide level ridge running N-S, with a big cairn about 200 metres SSE of and slightly lower than the small summit cairn.

To return to the day's starting point, descend more or less due N, at first down steep grassy slopes, then across several streams in the very rough and peaty Garbh-choire and finally over a little col to drop down through scattered birches on the steep hillside above the power station.

*Sgurr na Lapaich from Glen Strathfarrar*                                    D.J. Bennet

The alternative route from the Loch Mullardoch dam involves the ascent of the SSE ridge of Carn nan Gobhar over Mullach na Maoile. From Sgurr na Lapaich the best return route is probably along the S ridge for 3½ km to Mullach a' Ghlas-thuill, then E to the lochside. The inclusion of An Riabhachan in this traverse makes a very long day indeed, much of it over rough and pathless terrain on the N side of Loch Mullardoch.

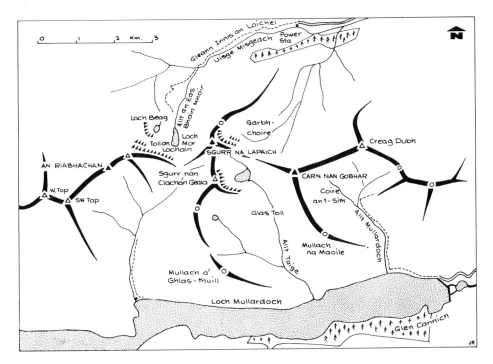

*Looking W from Carn nan Gobhar to Sgurr a' Choire Ghlais*          D.J. Bennet

**Sgurr na Ruaidhe;** 993m; (OS Sheet 25; 289426); M148; *peak of the redness.*
**Carn nan Gobhar;** 992m; (OS Sheet 25; 273439); M150; *hill of the goats.*
**Sgurr a' Choire Ghlais;** 1083m; (OS Sheet 25; 259430); M56; *peak of the greenish-grey corrie.*
**Sgurr Fuar-thuill;** 1049m; (OS Sheet 25; 235437); M79; *peak of the cold hollow.*

The four Munros on the north side of Glen Strathfarrar form a well-defined ridge several kilometres long which can be traversed in a single day, the only drawback being that the starting and finishing points on the road are about 6km apart. The two eastern hills, Sgurr na Ruaidhe and Carn nan Gobhar, are smooth and rounded and of no distinction. Sgurr a' Choire Ghlais at the centre of the ridge is distinctly higher, steeper and more impressive, and at the west end Sgurr Fuar-thuill and its two adjacent Tops form an undulating crest with steep faces to the north. South-west of these, Sgurr na Muice (891m) can justifiably be regarded as the finest peak in the group by virtue of its great slabby face above the dark waters of Loch Toll a' Mhuic. It alone among these hills has any significant exposure of rock, elsewhere grass and heather prevail. Aesthetically the east to west traverse is preferable, leaving the best of the ridge and the scenery to the end of the day.

Leave the Strathfarrar road at the foot of the Allt Coire Mhuillidh and climb the zig-zag track, followed by a stalker's path on the E side of the stream for 2km. Beyond the first side stream climb NE up the grassy shoulder of Sgurr na Ruaidhe, easy going all the way to the summit. (5km; 850m; 2h 40min). The upper slopes of this hill on its N and W sides are remarkably smooth and mossy. Descend these slopes WNW to a col at 780m and go NNW then W to Carn nan Gobhar which has a boulder strewn summit area with the cairn at its N edge. (7½km; 970m; 3h 20min).

Continue SW along a level mossy ridge, then W down to the next col at 860m. From there climb Sgurr a' Choire Ghlais along the steep ridge on the edge of the N corrie. The summit is crowned by two large cairns and a trig point. (8½km; 1120m; 3h 50min). The ridge drops again to 900m before rising over Creag Ghorm a' Bhealaich (1030m), and continuing, now with a steep drop on the N side, to Sgurr Fuar-thuill. (11km; 1350m; 4h 50min).

At the next col, before Sgurr na Fearstaig (1015m), the top of a stalker's path is reached and it may be followed downhill. However, it is worth continuing along the ridge to the last Top for the westward view, and then going S along the ridge towards Sgurr na Muice for a few hundred metres until a short easy descent can be made E to join the stalker's path lower down. This path tends to disappear here and there, for it is rather overgrown, but it reappears near Loch Toll a' Mhuic and thereafter gives a good fast descent to the glen.

Access to Glen Strathfarrar.

The road up Glen Strathfarrar is private, and a gate near its junction with the main Strath Glass road at Struy is kept locked. An arrangement between the landowners concerned and the Nature Conservancy Council (who administer a small Nature Reserve in the glen) allows access by car up this road, the key of the gate being kept by the local representative of the Nature Conservancy Council who lives in the cottage beside the gate. The hours when permission is normally granted to drive up the glen are at present:-

Weekdays (except Tuesdays), 9.00 a.m. to 6.00 p.m.

Sundays, 1.30 p.m. to 6.00 p.m.

Tuesdays, no access.

(Please do not call at the cottage between 1.00 p.m. and 1.30 p.m.).

The above information applies between Easter and the end of October. In winter the Nature Conservancy Council representative may not always be at home, and it is therefore advisable to telephone beforehand, (046 376 260).

At the present time cars can be driven up to the Loch Monar dam, and there appears to be no restriction to continuing across the dam for a further 3km to the small power station in Gleann Innis an Loichel, thus giving close access to the north side of Sgurr na Lapaich.

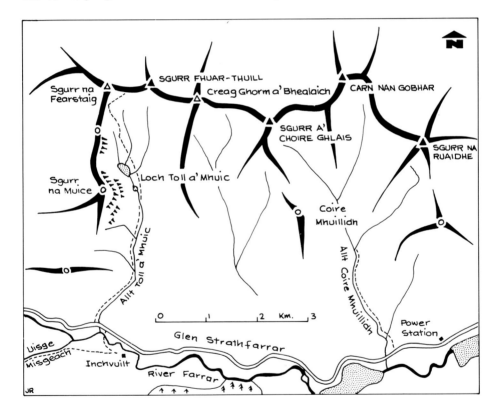

*Bidein a' Choire Sheasgaich from the north*                                    *H.M. Brown*

Five grand mountains lie to the south-east of Glen Carron in a fairly remote setting round the head of Loch Monar. Two of them, Lurg Mhor and Bidein a' Choire Sheasgaich are among the least accessible, and hence the most highly prized, of all the Munros. The easiest approach to all five is from the A890 road at Craig in Glen Carron, 3½km east of Achnashellach. A Forestry Commission road crosses the railway and goes east from there along the north side of the Allt a' Chonais through the Achnashellach Forest, and it may be possible to get permission to drive a car for 3km up this road as far as the locked gate at the upper edge of the trees. (Quite a help in view of the long distance to some of these mountains). From there the track continues beneath the steep face of Sgurr nan Ceannaichean, and in a

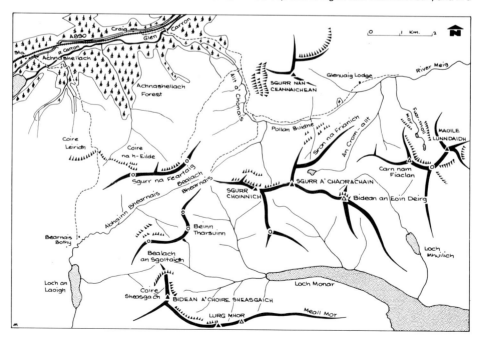

*Lurg Mhor from the south*                                                                 *H.M. Brown*

further 2½km, at the point where the glen turns east towards distant Strathconon, the climber reaches the parting of the ways: east to Maoile Lunndaidh, south to Sgurr Choinnich and Sgurr a' Chaorachain and south-west to Bidein a' Choire Sheasgaich and Lurg Mhor.

**Bidein a' Choire Sheasgaich**; 945m; (OS Sheet 25; 049413); M218; *peak of the corrie of the barren (or milkless) cattle.*
**Lurg Mhor**; 986m; (OS Sheet 25; 165405); M158; *big ridge stretching into the plain.*

These two mountains are the remotest of the group on the south-east side of Glen Carron, and there is very much the feeling of a real expedition to climb them. Some might prefer to take two days and stay at the remote and lonely Bearnais bothy (021430). Bidein a' Choire Sheasgaich is a very fine peak indeed, its sharp pointed summit being a landmark visible and easily recognisable from many distant hills. Lurg Mhor is a long, rather level ridge, steep on the north side and narrow to the east where it joins the Top, Meall Mor (947m). This east ridge runs out for quite a long way above the west end of Loch Monar to lonely Pait Lodge. One of the best views of these two mountains is had from the east, looking along Loch Monar from the west end of the North Strathfarrar Ridge.

The start from Craig follows the route already described up the Allt a' Chonais. Cross the footbridge at (074467) and follow the stalker's path to the Bealach Bhearnais. Continue SW, climbing to the ridge of Beinn Tharsuinn and traversing its undulating crest to the summit (863m). Descend SW to a small lochan on the ridge, then WSW along a grassy ridge to the col between the summit and the W top, and finally lose a lot of height down to the 550m Bealach an Sgoltaidh, the pass at the foot of the N ridge of Bidein a' Choire Sheasgaich. This ridge rises steeply, encircled by crags, but a way up can be found bearing towards the right, scrambling up a steep 'path' and emerging suddenly on the nearly level ridge above. Continue over a slight bump, down to a little lochan and up again steeply to the pointed summit of Bidein a' Choire Sheasgaich. (From Craig, 12½km; 1300m; 5h).

Descend S at first, then SE to the next col at 740m. The ridge is now much broader, though bounded on its N side by steep craggy slopes, and it leads directly to Lurg Mhor. (From Craig, 14½km 1550m; 5h 50min). Only the most dedicated of 'Top-baggers' are likely to continue the extra ¾km E to Meall Mor; the intervening ridge is narrow and rocky, and at one point there is some airy scrambling which cannot be easily avoided.

The return from Lurg Mhor to Craig is hardly less strenuous or time-consuming than the outward journey, for it involves retracing one's steps over Bidein a' Choire Sheasgaich and Beinn Tharsuinn. Altogether a hard day's hill-walking that would be helped by driving from Craig up to the edge of the forest.

For those spending two days on these mountains and staying at Bearnais bothy, the best starting point is Achnashellach, and there is a good path all the way to the bothy, initially up through the forest on the E side of Coire Leiridh. The crossing of the Abhainn Bhearnais may be difficult in spate conditions. Once across the river, the ascent goes SE up Coire Seasgach to reach the N ridge of Bidein.

*On the ridge from Bidean an Eoin Deirg towards Sgurr a' Chaorachain*          *G.S. Johnstone*

**Sgurr Choinnich**; 999m; (OS Sheet 25; 076446); M136; *moss peak.*
**Sgurr a' Chaorachain**; 1053m; (OS Sheet 25; 087447); M74; *peak of the little field of the berries.*

These two peaks are clearly seen as one approaches up the track along the Allt a' Chonais, and they are the most accessible of the five in this group. Sgurr Choinnich presents a steep rocky front, and it has a level summit ridge, while Sgurr a' Chaorachain appears as a more rounded hill. Between them is a fine little corrie, very rocky on its west side below the cliffs of Sgurr Choinnich, less so on the east side of the stream, and at the head of this corrie the col between the two peaks is about 860m.

To reach this pair, cross the Allt a' Chonais by the footbridge at (074467) and take the stalker's path leading to the Bealach Bhearnais. A good traverse of Sgurr Choinnich (although not the shortest ascent) can be made by continuing up this path to the bealach, and then heading back E up the W ridge of the peak. This is a pleasant grassy ridge, with little rocky steps, and it leads to the narrow level crest where the summit cairn is perched on the edge of the steep NE face. (From Craig, 9½km; 950m; 3h 50min). Continue SE along the nearly level ridge for about 200 metres, then turn NE down the steep ridge, quite rocky at first, to the 860m col. Climb ENE up the broad ridge to the stony summit of Sgurr a' Chaorachain. (From Craig, 11km; 1050m; 4h 20min).

At this point three posibilities exist for the return. The quickest descent is back to the 860m col and from there N down the corrie to return to the Allt a' Chonais. A longer descent goes N down a broad ridge, but the lower part of this ridge is steep and craggy and one should bear NE towards the watershed between the Allt a' Chonais and the River Meig to avoid any difficulties. The third possiblity is to go ESE from Sgurr a' Chaorachain along a broad, level and rather stony ridge to the outlying Top of Bidean an Eoin Deirg (1046m), a fine looking peak, particularly when seen from the E along Loch Monar. The descent N is too steep and rocky to be recommended as a good way down, so the best return is back along the ridge over Sgurr a' Chaorachain.

*Maoile Lunndaidh from the east end of Loch Monar*                                              *D.J. Bennet*

**Maoile Lunndaidh;** 1007m; (OS Sheet 25; 135458); M122; *bare hill of the wet place.*

Another very remote Munro, Maoile Lunndaidh rises to the north of Loch Monar in the wild hinterland between Glen Carron, Glen Strathfarrar and Strathconon, and it is roughly equidistant from starting points in these three glens. In appearance it is a flat-topped hill, almost Cairngorm-like in its character with a level plateau ending abruptly in deep corries. This appearance is particularly evident looking along Loch Monar from the dam at its east end. From Glen Carron the hill is invisible, and one has to walk several kilometres up the Allt a' Chonais before seeing it and reaching the foot of its north face, cleft by the deep Fuar-tholl Mor.

Of the three approaches, that from Glen Carron is described, being slightly shorter than the other two if one starts at Craig, and very much shorter if one drives up to the tree line by the Allt a' Chonais. The Glen Carron route has the further advantage of no river crossing problems, which might complicate other ways in spate conditions.

Walk up the track along the Allt a' Chonais to the watershed and continue for barely 1km more towards Glenuaig Lodge before breaking off to the E over the foot of Sron na Frianich to cross An Crom-allt. Climb steeply up the NNW ridge of Carn nam Fiaclan (996m), and from this Top continue ESE then NE along the level plateau, with the Fuar-tholl Mor on the left and the other corrie, the Toll a' Choin, biting deeply into the plateau on the right, to reach Maoile Lunndaidh. (From Craig, 13km; 980m; 4h 40min).

The descent may be varied by going N down to a col at 750m, then turning W to descend across the foot of the Fuar-tholl Mor and, still heading W, return to the track leading back to the Allt a' Chonais.

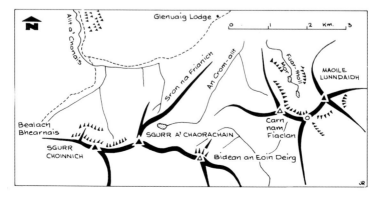

*Looking south-west from Moruisg to Sgurr nan Ceannaichean*                    H.M. Brown

**Moruisg**; 928m; (OS Sheet 25; 101499); M252; *big water.*
**Sgurr nan Ceannaichean**; 915m; (OS Sheet 25; 087481); M275; *peak of the merchants or pedlars.*

These two mountains are on the south side of Glen Carron near the bleak upper reaches of that glen. Moruisg is long and flat-topped; its northern corries look out over featureless moorland towards Achnasheen, and its west flank drops in concave grassy slopes to the River Carron. Not a very exciting mountain. Sgurr nan Ceannaichean is a more interesting, though smaller peak; its west face is remarkably steep and craggy, and looks impressive when seen from Craig in Glen Carron. Between the two the Coire Toll nam Bian is a deep set hollow with a steep headwall of grass and broken crags.

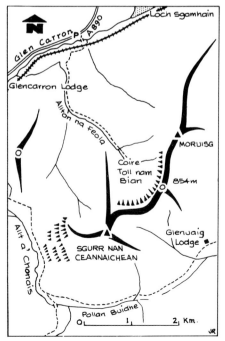

The traverse of the two mountains is most easily done from Glen Carron, leaving the A890 road at a car park 1¼km W of the outflow of Loch Sgamhain. Cross the River Carron by a footbridge and follow the stalker's path up the E bank of the Alltan na Feola towards Coire Toll nam Bian. After about 2½km leave the path and climb E up the ever-steepening grass slopes of Moruisg, keeping N of an area of crags and selecting an easy line between the gullies which seam this side of the hill. Higher up, as the slope becomes slightly less steep, bear SE and reach the flat mossy summit of Moruisg. (4½km; 780m; 2h 20min).

Go SW then S along the broad mossy ridge to Pt 854m, then descend more steeply SW to the col at 730m. Climb W up a broad grassy ridge for ½km, then SW to reach the flat summit of Sgurr nan Ceannaichean. The summit cairn is a short distance S, overlooking the E corrie. (7½km; 980m; 3h 20min).

Retrace the last part of the ascent route for ½km down the NE ridge, then bear N down a steep broad ridge to the Alltan na Feola which should be crossed at the first convenient place to rejoin the stalker's path. Follow this back to the day's starting point.

*Looking south-east from Beinn Alligin to Mullach an Rathain (left) and Sgorr Ruadh*      *P. Hodgkiss*

# SECTION 13

The Torridon Mountains

*Sgorr Ruadh from the Coire Lair path*                                    *D.J. Bennet*

**Beinn Liath Mhor;** 925m; (OS Sheet 25; 964520); M258; *big grey hill.*
**Sgorr Ruadh;** c. 960m; (OS Sheet 25; 959504); M191; *red peak.*

The mountainous country between Glen Torridon and Strath Carron tends to be neglected, perhaps because it is overshadowed by the giant Torridonian mountains to the north. This is a pity for its peaks, Munros and Corbetts alike, are full of interest with many fine rock features, splendid corries with a network of good stalker's paths, and grand summit views.

Coire Lair above Achnashellach is a splendid place surrounded by three mountains of character; Fuar Tholl, though only 907m, is the most impressive, very much a rock climbers' peak with its great Mainreachan Buttress; Sgorr Ruadh is the shapely highest summit of the group, and what Beinn Liath Mhor lacks in height it makes up for in the length of its summit ridge on the north side of Coire Lair. The traverse of the mountains round this corrie is a rewarding walk.

Park at the side of the A890 near the telephone box at the end of the private road leading to Achnashellach station. Walk up to the station and SW for about 100 metres past a cottage to a gate on the NW side of the railway where a wet overgrown path starts up towards Coire Lair. The path improves, and the woods and waterfalls make this a fine approach to the mountains. At a height of 370m, with the corrie opening out ahead, there is a junction of paths. Before going on it is worth walking a short distance down to the River Lair, particularly if it is in spate, to inspect the crossing which has to be made at the end of the day. There is no better crossing place lower down.

Continue along the path which branches off NNE as far as its summit, ½km further on. The hardest part of the day's climbing comes next, the long steep slope of heather and boulders to the 876m east top of Beinn Liath Mhor. Traverse WNW along the undulating ridge of quartzite scree and moss to the summit. (7km; 1030m; 3h 20min). Some care is needed on the descent SW to the Bealach Coire Lair as the rock becomes red sandstone with big steps and some crags to bypass. There is a knoll to cross, and the two lochans are useful landmarks in thick weather.

From the pass (c. 650m) climb SW to the tiny lochan on the NW ridge of Sgorr Ruadh and follow this steep ridge over scree to the summit. (9½km; 1380m; 4h 30min). The descent SE is down a rough slope of grass and boulders, and leads to the broad col where there are several lochans, Loch a' Bhealaich Mhoir being the largest one. A few hundred metres S of this loch a fine stalker's path is found below the great crags of Fuar Tholl, and this path is followed down to the River Lair and the path of the uphill route. If the river is likely to be difficult to cross, it is better to descend NW from the col beside the stream flowing to Loch Coire Lair, and go round the W side of this loch to rejoin the path in Coire Lair.

*Maol Chean-dearg from the north-west*                                              *K.M. Andrew*

## Maol Chean-dearg; 933m; (OS Sheet 25; 924498); M241; *bald red head.*

Maol Chean-dearg, one of the three Munros in the area, can just be glimpsed from the A890 road in Strath Carron near Coulags, from where it is usually climbed. It is rather an isolated mountain whose summit is a great dome of bare rock and sandstone boulders, making its name, bald red head, particularly apt.

From Coulags follow the path, which is a right-of-way, on the E side of the Fionn-abhainn, crossing a bridge to the W side after 2½km, and continue past a derelict cottage to the Clach nan Con-fionn, the stone to which the legendary Fionn tethered his hunting dogs. In a further ½km take the path which bears off to the W and climbs more steeply up to the col between Maol Chean-dearg and Meall nan Ceapairean at about 590m. Turn NW and climb the broad ridge over a succession of steps to the large cairn of Maol Chean-dearg. (7½km; 900m; 3h 10min). The going up this final ridge is rough as it is covered with scree and boulders of sandstone and angular quartzite.

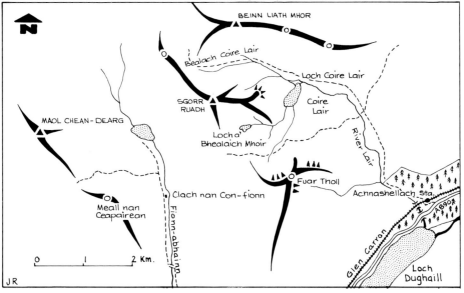

*Looking across Loch Torridon to Beinn Alligin*                                    *D. Scott*

**Beinn Alligin**; 985m; (OS Sheets 19 and 24; 866613); M160; *possibly jewelled hill.*

The Torridon tryptych of Beinn Alligin, Liathach and Beinn Eighe is regarded as one of the finest mountain groups in Scotland, and their fame is well deserved. They rise in castellated tiers and battlements of red Torridonian Sandstone, in places crowned by grey quartzite screes, with massive corries and cliffs for the climber, and long demanding ridges for the walker who enjoys airy crests with some scrambling. Beinn Alligin rises above the north side of Upper Loch Torridon in land owned by the National Trust for Scotland, and is best seen from the road high on the south side of the loch. It is the least complex of the three mountains, possibly the one which should be tackled first by the visiting hill-walker.

The narrow road from the head of Loch Torridon to Inveralligin passes below Beinn Alligin. Start at the car park on the W side of the bridge over the Abhainn Coire Mhic Nobuil. On the N side of the road a climbers' path crosses the moor, steadily gaining height N then W into Coir' nan Laoigh. Continue N up to the head of this corrie and climb Tom na Gruagaich (922m), the hill of the maiden. This is a fine peak in its own right, with a tremendously steep NE face plunging into the Toll a' Mhadaidh. Descend N down a narrow rocky ridge to the col at 766m, beyond which the crest becomes broader, its W side being bald open slopes although the E side is steep and rocky. Climb NNE over a knoll (858m), and drop a little to a col before the final climb NE to Sgurr Mhor, the summit of Beinn Alligin. Just below the top, the ridge is interrupted in startling fashion by the Eag Dhuibh, the black cleft, a sheer-sided gash in the steep hillside which should be avoided as a route of ascent or descent. (5km; 1130m; 3h).

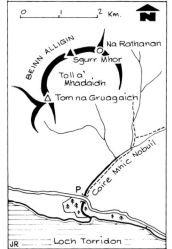

The fastest and easiest return is by the same route. However, the great pleasure of the Torridonian mountains is to traverse their castellated ridges, and on Beinn Alligin this means the crossing of Na Rathanan, the horns of Alligin. Descend from the summit steeply ENE then E down a narrow ridge to the col at 757m and traverse the horns; there is a well marked path over these three rocky tops giving some exposed, but perfectly easy scrambling. From the third continue the descent SE, keeping on the crest until the moor is reached and the stalker's path is joined and followed down Coire Mhic Nobuil to the road.

No restriction on climbing in the stalking season.

*Beinn Eighe from Loch Coulin*                                              *D.J. Bennet*

**Beinn Eighe (Ruadh-stac Mor);** 1010m; (OS Sheets 19 and 25; 951611); M117; *file hill (big red peak).*

Beinn Eighe is the easternmost of the Torridonian mountains. Unlike its two neighbours, it is characterised by the pale quartzite screes and rock of the long ridge which links its several Tops on the north side of Glen Torridon. The great corries of Beinn Eighe all face north into country which is totally desolate and seldom penetrated by hill-walkers, while the long scree flanks facing Glen Torridon give the mountain a disheartening appearance, possibly suggesting a giant treadmill. The finest feature of the mountain is Coire Mhic Fhearchair, with its dark loch mirroring the Triple Buttress that forms the headwall of the corrie. Any ascent of Beinn Eighe should include this, the finest corrie in Scotland as it has been described. The highest point of the mountain is Ruadh-stac Mor, which lies on a spur off the main ridge overlooking Coire Mhic Fhearchair.

The starting point is at the car park on the A896 road W of th Allt a' Choire Dhuibh Mhoir. Follow the footpath (signposted) up the Coire Dubh Mor round the E end of Liathach to the watershed. At (934594), above a small elongated lochan, take a branch path N round the prow of Sail Mor, split by a great gully, to reach Loch Coire Mhic Fhearchair at c. 580m. Cross the outflow and go round the E side of the loch. The corrie floor is rough and the flanks of Ruadh-stac Mor pour down screes from broken crags above. Continue upwards by the pools draining into the loch to gain the col at c. 910m that separates the peak from the main ridge of Beinn Eighe. The final walk up to the summit presents no problems. (9km; 930m; 3h 40min).

The return may be made by the same route. Alternatively, return to the 910m col and climb its opposite side SW to the cairn at the E end of the grassy dome of Coinneach Mhor. Turn SE to follow the main ridge across a col (821m) to the trig point on Spidean Coire nan Clach (972m), the peak of the stony corrie. Descend a spur SSE off the main ridge for a short distance and turn down E into Coire an Laoigh. Follow the burn for 1km to reach a stalker's path which leads to the A896 road in Glen Torridon 2km E of the car park.

The traverse of Beinn Eighe may be continued E from Spidean Coire nan Clach along the main ridge to Sgurr Ban (971m) and Sgurr nan Fhir Duibhe (963m) from which the easiest descent to Glen Torridon is down the E ridge for 1½km and then S down easy scree-free slopes.

No restriction on climbing the SW side of Beinn Eighe in the stalking season. See OS map for boundary of NTS property.

Map on page 194.

The OS 1:25000 Outdoor Leisure Map 'The Cuillin and Torridon Hills' is recommended for the additional detail that it shows for the Torridon mountains.

*Spidean a' Choire Leith, the highest peak of Liathach*                    D.J. Bennet

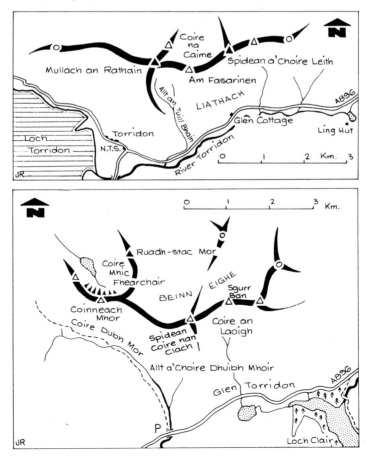

Beinn
Eighe
see
page 193

*Looking west along the ridge of Liathach to Mullach an Rathain*                    R. Robb

**Spidean a' Choire Leith**; 1054m; (OS Sheet 25; 929580); M72; *peak of the grey corrie.*
**Mullach an Rathain**; 1023m; (OS Sheet 25; 912577); M105; *summit of the row of pinnacles.*

The central, highest and most awsome of the Torridonian tryptych is Liathach, the grey one. Its great terraced wall rising above Glen Torridon is unique among Scottish mountains in conveying an impression of impregnability, an impression which is quite real for there are few chinks in Liathach's armour. The mountain is a huge 7km long ridge with two principal summits, both Munros, Spidean a' Choire Leith near the eastern end, and Mullach an Rathain towards the west. The 2km ridge between these summits is narrow, and for almost half its length it is riven into a succession of pinnacles, Am Fasarinen. The traverse of these pinnacles is an exposed and in places difficult scramble, particularly in wet weather, so the complete traverse of Liathach, one of the great mountain expeditions in Scotland, is reserved for hill-walkers with experience of scrambling and a good head for heights. However, the two main summits can be climbed quite easily by routes which are described below.

The route to Spidean a' Choire Leith starts from the A896 road in Glen Torridon about ¾km E of Glen Cottage. The path begins at a cairn 50 metres W of the Allt an Doire Ghairbh, crosses this stream and climbs steeply on its E bank into the Toll a' Meitheach. Heather, steep grass, scree and rocky steps are all encountered. High up in the corrie, where the stream forks, work up to the right (NE) over steep ground to the col on the main ridge at 833m. From this col follow the quite well defined path up the ridge on quartzite scree and rocks, NW at first, then W over two small tops to the final bouldery summit cone of Spidean a' Choire Leith. (2½km; 1040m; 2h 20min). Return by the same route, as the terraced nature of Liathach's steep sides conceal many vertical steps, invisible from above.

Mullach an Rathain is also best climbed from the Glen Torridon road, starting near the pinewoods 1km E of the National Trust for Scotland's Information Centre at the Torridon road junction. Basically the route follows the Allt an Tuill Bhain, first on its W side over many slabby sandstone terraces, then up grassier slopes in the corrie. There are traces of a path here and there. High up, the headwall of the corrie steepens, and the best route bears left to emerge onto an easier-angled ridge which leads NNE to the summit. (2½km; 1000m; 2h 20min). Return by the same route. The hillside to the W of this route, in particular the great scree gullies above Torridon village, are not recommended as routes of ascent or descent. They are steep, craggy and in the lower slopes heathery, a combination which makes for purgatorial progress.

The ridge between the two main summits of Liathach is easy in its W half from Mullach an Rathain down to the col. The traverse along the pinnacles of Am Fasarinen is exposed, but the rock is generally sound and the route fairly obvious. The alternative is to follow a path on the S side of the ridge below the crest which avoids the pinnacles, but is nevertheless exposed. At the end of the pinnacles a slope of quartzite boulders leads up to Spidean a' Choire Leith.

No restriction on climbing in the stalking season.

*Slioch from Loch Maree*                                                    *D.J. Bennet*

# SECTION 14

Loch Maree to the Fannaichs

*On the ridge from Slioch to Sgurr an Tuill Bhain*                    D.J. Bennet

**Slioch**; 980m; (OS Sheet 19; 005688); M169; *from Gaelic sleagh, a spear.*

The south-eastern end of Loch Maree is dominated by Slioch, a magnificent Torridonian sandstone mountain rising like a huge castle above its foundation of Lewisian gneiss. It is one of the great sights of the Northern Highlands, well seen and much photographed from the A832 road on the opposite side of the loch, and its summit commands fine views of the surrounding mountains, some of them in the wildest part of Scotland. Around three quarters of its perimeter Slioch is defended by towering sandstone buttresses and steep crags and scree. Only on its south-east side, above Gleann Bianasdail, are there any easy routes to the summit.

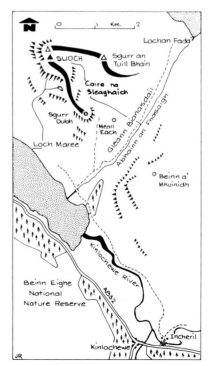

Start from Incheril, a group of cottages and crofts 1km E of Kinlochewe, where cars can be parked at the roadside. Take the road, degenerating to a track and then a footpath, which goes NW through some fields and then along the beautifully wooded bank on the NE side of the Kinlochewe River. This path reaches the shore of Loch Maree, and 1km further crosses the Abhainn an Fhasaigh by a footbridge. Once across the bridge turn right (NE) up the path which leads through Gleann Bianasdail to Lochan Fada.

In less than 1km (before reaching the steepening of the path at a rocky bluff) bear due N, following a less distinct path to the col between the rocky point of Sgurr Dubh and the knoll of Meall Each. At this col one enters the main east-facing corrie of Slioch, the Coire na Sleaghaich. Continue up the corrie on the S side of the stream for 1km and then climb a short steep grassy slope to reach a tiny lochan nestling on the SE ridge of Slioch. Continue up this ridge over a false summit and across a wide col to the true summit. (10km; 940m; 3h 50min). The N top at (004691) is the same height, but is a much finer viewpoint, being perched at the top of the great NW buttresses of the mountain.

The return route can be varied by going E along a narrowing ridge to Sgurr an Tuill Bhain (933m), and from there a descent due S leads down across Coire na Sleaghaich to the col between Sgurr Dubh and Meall Each where the uphill route is rejoined.

North of Slioch and Loch Maree there is a wild and uninhabited tract of mountainous country, with no road access, containing six Munros which are collectively the remotest in Scotland. Only Seana Bhraigh and Lurg Mhor can rival them for inaccessibility. The routes to these mountains from points on the perimeter of this great wilderness area are very long, and hill-walkers have to be fit to walk in, climb their peaks and walk out again in a single day. The three points of access are Kinlochewe in the south-east, Poolewe in the west and Corrie Hallie near Dundonnell in the north, and routes from these places are described below.

The alternative approach to these mountains involves either camping in the interior of the area, or staying in bothies, of which there are two - Shenavall in Strath na Sealga, and the stable at Carnmore, for which permission to use should be sought from the estate factor or the keeper at Kernsary. Many hill-walkers will find this a preferable way to visit these mountains. Shenavall, in particular, is a fine bothy from which all six Munros are accessible and can in fact be climbed in a single day by fit climbers. This traverse is also briefly described.

There is a good network of well-engineered stalker's paths throughout the area, but also an absence of footbridges at several crucial river crossings, so during and after heavy rain some of these crossings may be impossible. The old Ordnance Survey 'One Inch to the Mile' map is very inadequate in this area, lacking detail of the great cliffs and seriously inaccurate in its showing of contour lines and heights. The Letterewe and Fisherfield forests are jealously guarded deer stalking country, and should not be visited by hill-walkers during the stalking season.

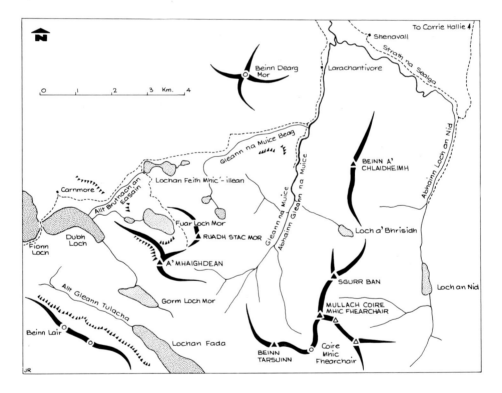

*A' Mhaighdean from Carnmore Lodge*                                    *W. Forbes*

**A' Mhaighdean;** 967m; (OS Sheet 19; 008749); M184; *the maiden.*
**Ruadh Stac Mor;** 918m; (OS Sheet 19; 018756); M267; *big red peak.*

A' Mhaighdean and Ruadh Stac Mor stand in the centre of the Letterewe wilderness, the former a cliff-girt bastion which is one of the most spectacular viewpoints in Britain. These two are among the most highly prized Munros for hill-walkers by virtue of their remoteness and the beauty of their setting. It is worth saving them for a fine day. The approach from Poolewe is described.

With permission a car can be taken from Poolewe for about 3km up the E side of the River Ewe to Inveran, a small but possibly important help at the beginning (and end) of a very long day. Continue 2½km along the road to the stalker's house at Kernsary, and then E and SE through the forest to gain the path on the N bank of the Allt na Creige. This path peters out, but after descending to pass Loch an Doire Chrionaich it becomes clear again, makes a short diversion S to cross Strathan Buidhe, and then descends gradually to the SE end of the Fionn Loch. Now the heart of the wilderness area is reached, and A' Mhaighdean soars up beyond the Dubh Loch. Cross the causeway between these two lochs and continue along the good stalker's path towards Carnmore, then E, climbing into the valley of the Allt Bruthach an Easain. Cross this stream and traverse SE across the hillside to the little stream flowing out of the Fuar Loch Beag, and reach the long stepped crest of A' Mhaighdean's NW ridge. This has plenty of crags, but any difficulties can be avoided, and the scenery is impressive. The ridge ends on a domed plateau with the summit perched above the cliffs at its S edge. (19km; 1090m; 6h 10min).

Descend NE from A' Mhaighdean by easy, mainly grassy slopes to the col at c. 750m, where there is a good 'shelter stone' howff. From there Ruadh Stac Mor seems well defended by a ring of sandstone crags, but by going N these can be climbed easily to the trig point of this mountain. (20½km; 1260m; 6h 50min). Return by the route of ascent to the col and take the stalker's path, not completely shown on the OS map, which starts there and descends above Fuar Loch Mor to the outflow of Lochan Feith Mhic'illean. Go SW along the path which leads down the Allt Bruthach an Easain to Carnmore and the long return journey towards the sunset and Poolewe.

*Beinn a' Chlaidheimh, Sgurr Ban and Mullach Coire Mhic Fhearchair from Beinn Tarsuinn*     H.M. Brown

**Beinn Tarsuinn**; 936m; (OS Sheet 19; 039727); M234; *transverse hill.*
**Mullach Coire Mhic Fhearchair**; 1019m; (OS Sheet 19; 052735); M109; *summit of the corrie of Farquhar's son.*
**Sgurr Ban**; 989m; (OS Sheet 19; 055745); M153; *light-coloured peak.*

This is another hard to reach group, but while A' Mhaighdean is a peak that collects superlatives, the Mullach and its neighbours fail to inspire such enthusiasm. The scenery is less majestic, the quartzite capping gives some tedious walking and the paths all end many rough, boggy kilometres from the summits. However, the traverse of these Munros gives a long, hard day of considerable character. The approach from Kinlochewe is described.

From Incheril, 1km E of Kinlochewe, there are two possible approaches to the SE end of Lochan Fada, where the actual climbing begins. The first is the same as the route described to Slioch, continuing up Gleann Bianasdail along a fine path high above the deep gorge of the glen and then dropping down to the outflow of Lochan Fada. The crossing of this stream may be impossible in bad weather, in which case the alternative route from Incheril by the private road to the Heights of Kinlochewe and up Gleann na Muice is advised. The latter way is slightly longer and less fine scenically.

From the SE end of Lochan Fada the going is rough and boggy at first, but improves as height is gained. Head N until the craggy hillside at about 500m is passed, then bear NW towards the summit of Beinn Tarsuinn along a gently rising ridge, then a steeper slope of stepped sandstone. (14km; 910m; 4h 40min). Beinn Tarsuinn has a narrow crest running in the direction of A' Mhaighdean, and fills the head of Gleann na Muice as a grand bastion.

Descend ESE to the col (c. 730m) below Meall Garbh and follow a well-worn deer track across the NW face of this little peak to the next col (c. 760m) below Mullach Coire Mhic Fhearchair. The final climb to the summit of this mountain goes up shattered quartzite boulders. (16km; 1200m; 5h 40min).

Sgurr Ban lies about 1½km NNE across a col at c. 820m. As the name hints, it is a quartzite peak, and while the traverse presents no technical difficulty, the unstable slippery rocks and boulders require constant care. The summit is well to the NE on the flat quartzite plateau. (17½km; 1390m; 6h 20min).

The simplest return route is back over Mullach Coire Mhic Fhearchair to the Meall Garbh - Beinn Tarsuinn col, and then S to retrace the ascent route. Descents to the E lead down huge areas of bare quartzite slabs above Loch an Nid and a long re-ascent over the Bealach na Croise, not recommended.

Map on page 198.

*Beinn a' Chlaidheimh from the north*                                              *P. Hodgkiss*

**Beinn a' Chlaidheimh;** 914m; (OS Sheet 19; 061775); M277; *hill of the sword.*

This mountain, which just reaches Munro height and no more, lies 3km north of Sgurr Ban and is the northern outlier of the group just described. It overlooks the beautiful Strath na Sealga, and is most easily climbed from Dundonnell. Beinn a' Chlaidheimh is much more a sandstone mountain than its southern neighbours, with the characteristic terracing of this rock. The summit ridge is quite narrow, and the western slopes drop very steeply into Gleann na Muice.

Start from the A832 road in the strath of the Dundonnell River 3½km above the head of Little Loch Broom where there is a car park at Corrie Hallie. Take the track S up the beautifully wooded Gleann Chaorachain, and follow it over the featureless pass to Strath na Sealga. The crossing of the Abhainn Loch an Nid may present a problem if it is in spate, for there is no bridge between Loch an Nid and Loch na Sealga. In such conditions it would be better not to attempt Beinn a' Chlaidheimh.

Once across the river, climb SW up fairly rough ground, getting steeper as the rockier upper slopes are reached. The final climb is up the ridge just E of the summit. (11km; 1130m; 4h 20min). Return by the same way, with 270m more climbing up the track from Strath na Sealga over to Corrie Hallie.

The complete traverse of the 'Big Six' Fisherfield and Letterewe Munros is a magnificent hill-walking expedition, quite possible for fit hill-walkers in a single day. Shenavall bothy is the ideal base for this trip and is justifiably popular, but it should not be visited in the stalking season. The earlier remarks about river crossings are particularly apt, as the Abhainn Strath na Sealga has to be crossed both at the beginning and the end of the day, and it is a sizeable river in normal conditions. In spate it is quite impassable.

From Shenavall cross this river and climb directly up the NW shoulder of Beinn a' Chlaidheimh, a steep ascent with rough heather and minor crags, most of which can be avoided. At the top a fine narrow ridge leads to the summit. Continue S over a knoll, then SSE to the col (c. 600m) E of Loch a' Bhrisidh. Now the quartzite slopes of Sgurr Ban are reached, a long climb SW to its summit and on to Mullach Coire Mhic Fhearchair and Beinn Tarsuinn as already described.

From Beinn Tarsuinn descend the fine narrow ridge W then NW, and drop down W to the low boggy col at c. 520m between Gleann na Muice and Lochan Fada. The long ascent to A' Mhaighdean is up a broad grassy ridge, and the route continues to Ruadh Stac Mor as already described. The easiest, though not the shortest descent is back to the Ruadh Stac Mor - A' Mhaighdean col, then down the stalker's path past Fuar Loch Mor to the outflow of Lochan Feith Mhic'illean where the path E to Gleann na Muice Beag is followed. This path leads down to Gleann na Muice 1½km upstream from Larachantivore. The bridge shown on the map near there is in total disrepair and unsafe, so wade across the Abhainn Gleann na Muice and finally cross the level boggy Strath na Sealga to cross its river opposite Shenavall.

Map on page 198.

*The pinnacled ridge of Corrag Bhuidhe and Sgurr Fiona above Toll an Lochain*                    *G. Nicoll*

**Bidein a' Ghlas Thuill**; 1062m; (OS Sheet 19; 069844); M69; *peak of the greenish-grey hollow.*
**Sgurr Fiona**; 1059m; (OS Sheet 19; 064837); M70; *light coloured peak, or perhaps peak of wine.*

An Teallach, the Forge, is deservedly regarded as one of the finest of Scottish mountains. Forming a high massif between the heads of Little Loch Broom and Loch na Sealga, it is seen to best advantage from the A832 road crossing the divide from Braemore to Dundonnell. This aspect is dominated by three eastward projecting ridges, Glas Mheall Mor, Glas Mheall Liath and Sail Liath, and the two great corries which they enclose, Glas Tholl and Toll an Lochain. The highest summit lies at the head of the central ridge, and the other Munro, Sgurr Fiona, is at the upper end of the pinnacled crest which bends round the southern corrie to end at Sail Liath. An Teallach is largely of Torridonian sandstone, but its dramatic rocky outline is enhanced by the Cambrian quartzites which cap its eastern spurs and form distinctive light grey screes.

Two routes of ascent are widely used, the shorter one starts near Dundonnell Hotel. Leave the A832 road ½km SE of the hotel and follow a path zig-zagging up the steep and in places rocky shoulder of Meall Garbh until the angle falls back. After the path peters out at about 750m follow the broad, stony ridge S over a knoll to a second knoll from where a short ascent ESE leads to a top (not named on the OS 1:50000 map) at the edge of Glas Tholl, the northern corrie. Descend 30m S to a col and climb the imposing but easy ridge to the summit of Bidein a' Ghlas Thuill. (6km; 1120m; 3h 20min). Sgurr Fiona lies 1km away SSW, reached by descending easily to a col and climbing the steep and in places rocky ridge for 140m. (7km; 1260m; 3h 40min).

A much more interesting route begins at the Corrie Hallie car park on the A832 road at (114850). Follow the track SSW through the birches of Gleann Chaorachain for 1km, then cross the stream to ascend W by pale slabs and heather patches to gain the crest of a prominent quartzite escarpment. This provides a highway to the foot of Sail Liath, curving high above the slabby sandstone pavements below the Toll an Lochain. Alternatively, the track may be followed for 3km to the point where the Shenavall path strikes off WSW, and from there a rough walk of 1½km W leads to the lochan at the foot of Sail Liath.

Climbing W from this lochan, 500m of broken slabs, grass and scree lead to Sail Liath (954m), the first peak on the ridge. Continue across a dip and traverse a rocky knob before dropping to the Cadha Gobhlach, the forked pass. From there a small peak is traversed to the foot of the Corrag Bhuidhe Buttress. The imposing terraced nose which rises ahead and the continuation to the top of the Corrag Bhuidhe is the steepest part of the An Teallach traverse; the direct line is clearly worn and includes a 10m slab high up. The crest of Corrag Bhuidhe (1020m) gives excellent scrambling over four airy rock towers, followed by the leaning spire of Lord Berkeley's Seat. All difficulties on Corrag Bhuidhe can be avoided by following paths which traverse along the SW side of the ridge below the rocky crest, but much of the excitement of the climb is lost by going this way. The spectacular part of the ridge ends with a climb up sandstone steps to the shapely peak of Sgurr Fiona. (7½km; 1300m; 3h 50min).

*Corrag Bhuidhe and Sgurr Fiona*                                                    *D.J. Bennet*

The descent NNE to the col is steep and rocky in places, but there is no difficulty, and the last 140m pull up to Bidein a' Ghlas Thuill crowns one of the best days to be had in the Highlands. (8½km; 1440m; 4h 20min).

The return to Dundonnell can be made by the first route described above, or to Corrie Hallie as follows:- From the col ½km N of Bidein descend E into the Glas Tholl by a steep slope, taking special care if there is any snow. Continue directly down the corrie on the N side of the stream; there is a faint path through heather clad slopes and sandstone slabs to the Garbh Allt waterfalls where a better path is joined. This leads down the NW bank of the stream to the road ¾km N of the Corrie Hallie car park.

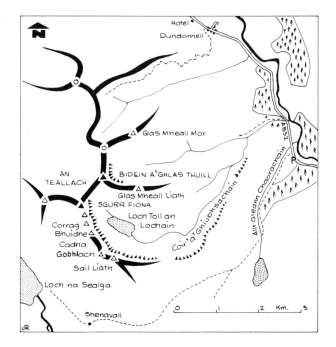

*Sgurr nan Clach Geala and Sgurr Mor from Meall Gorm*                                    *R. Robb*

This range of mountains, nine Munros in all, lies between Loch Fannich and the A835 road from Garve to Ullapool. Seven of the Munros form a fairly continuous chain, with short side ridges. The last two are western outliers, separated from the rest by a low bealach at about 550m height. The northern side of the Fannaichs, between the A835 road and the main mountain massif, has a lot of very rough ground - vast expanses of tussocky heather, rough grass, peat and boulders, which make for tiring walking if paths are not followed. By contrast, the upper parts of the mountains are much less rough, and most of the peaks give good easy going along broad smooth ridges of moss and short grass. On the south side of the main ridge the approaches from Loch Fannich are shorter and easier, but the loch can only be approached along a private road. The gate near the lower end of this road near Grudie Power Station is sometimes locked. Permission to drive up to the loch may be sought from the keeper at Fannich Lodge (Tel. Garve 227), and will normally be given outwith the stalking season. This road is often blocked by snow for long periods in winter.

**Beinn Liath Mhor Fannaich;** 954m; (OS Sheet 20; 219724); M204; *big grey hill of Fannich.*
**Sgurr Mor;** 1110m; (OS Sheet 20; 203718); M41; *big peak.*
**Meall Gorm;** 949m; (OS Sheet 20; 221696); M210; *blue hill.*
**An Coileachan;** 923m; (OS Sheet 20; 241680); M261; *the little cock.*

These hills lie on the main ridge of the Fannaichs which extends north-west from the east end of Loch Fannich to terminate at Meall a' Chrasgaidh, with the exception of Beinn Liath Mhor Fannaich which is on a spur projecting eastward from Sgurr Mor. The main ridge has a number of small corries scooped out of its north-east side; most are rocky and contain little lochans, and all but those of An Coileachan drain toward the A835 by two long shallow valleys. The route described below allows all four peaks to be climbed in a long horseshoe traverse, approaching along one of these valleys.

Start at the bridge over the Abhainn an Torrain Duibh just W of Loch Glascarnoch and follow the river upstream by a rough path on its W side. After crossing the Allt an Loch Sgeirich, leave the main river and follow this stream W trending gradually up the slope leading to Creag Dhubh Fannaich. Cross the top of this minor summit to the col beyond and climb Beinn Liath Mhor Fannaich by the easy slope of its SE ridge. (8½km; 710m; 3h 10min).

Sgurr Mor lies 2km SW around the upper bowl of Coir a' Mhaidaidh. Reach the connecting ridge by descending steeply for 100m to the col. The ridge is sharply defined on its NW side by the edge of the corrie, and dips more gradually on the other side, and there is a stalker's path along it which further on diverges across the SE face of Sgurr Mor. The last part of the climb is up a steep grassy slope eroded into big steps, and leads to the big summit cairn of Sgurr Mor perched close to the brink of the N cliff. (10 ½km; 990m; 4h).

Return down the SSE ridge over the flat rock slabs of Meall nam Peithirean (974m) and continue along the broad crest as it turns ESE round the corrie of the Fuar Tholl Mor to join the stalker's path which comes up from Fannich Lodge. This path leads to the flat bouldery summit of Meall Gorm. (13km; 1130m; 4h 50min). A few hundred metres E of the summit, where the path leaves the ridge to descend S, there is a small stalker's shelter made of rock slabs. The wide ridge continues E then SE, increasingly stony, but still easy walking ground. It descends to the Bealach Ban (775m) and then rises up broad, boulder patched and grass banded slopes to the top of An Coileachan, which is a conspicuous little crag. (15 ½km; 1300m; 5h 40min).

It is best to return towards the Bealach Ban and descend N, taking a line which keeps slightly E to gain the saddle below Meallan Buidhe. From there pass above the outlet of Loch Gorm and descend the gentle slope to the Abhainn a' Ghiubhais Li. Follow this stream by one of the rough paths which appear on both sides further downstream, and eventually return to the day's starting point.

From Fannich Lodge the ascent of these hills is greatly simplified by the splendid stalker's path from the lodge up the S ridge of Meall Gorm which gives quick access to the main Fannaich ridge on both sides of this peak. Sgurr Mor and An Coileachan are both within easy reach, and even Beinn Liath Mhor Fannaich is not beyond the range of a reasonably fit hill-walker.

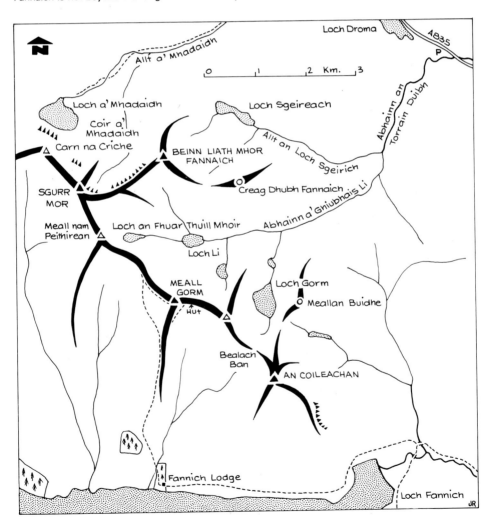

*Sgurr Mor*                                                           *W.D. Brooker*

**Meall a' Chrasgaidh**; 934m; (OS Sheet 20; 184733); M239; *hill of the crossing.*
**Sgurr nan Clach Geala**; 1093m; (OS Sheet 20; 184715); M51; *peak of the white stones.*
**Sgurr nan Each**; 923m; (OS Sheet 20; 184697); M262; *peak of the horses.*

These three central peaks of the Fannaichs lie just east of the path which crosses the pass from Loch a' Bhraoin to the head of Loch Fannich. They are on a ridge extending from Sgurr nan Each in the south, over Sgurr nan Clach Geala to Meall a' Chrasgaidh which also lies at the north-west end of the main Fannaich spine which stretches for many kilometres south-east towards the Loch Fannich dam. Sgurr nan Clach Geala may well be considered to be the finest of the Fannaichs, its tapering buttresses, soaring ridges and high hanging corrie combining in classic mountain architecture.

The start of the traverse from the A832 road near Loch a' Bhraoin is the same as that for Sgurr Breac (p208) for 2½km to the crossing of the Allt Breabaig. Continue along the stalker's path for ¾km as it climbs the hillside on the E of the stream, then strike due E uphill, easily selecting a way through steep mossy grass, heather and boulders. Higher up trend left towards the NW ridge of Meall a' Chrasgaidh until the slope lessens and leads to the top over patches of grass and weathered rock. (6km; 690m; 2h 30min).

From the summit a smooth slope dips SE to a wide mossy saddle at 819m, from which it is easy to traverse in the same direction to the foot of the NE ridge of Sgurr nan Clach Geala. However, the Top of Carn na Criche (961m) lies barely 1km to the E and is worth including en route. From it the shapely cones of Beinn Liath Mhor Fannaich and Sgurr Mor can be seen to advantage, so too can the Coire Mhoir face of Sgurr nan Clach Geala. The impressive profiles of its fine buttresses of mica-schist indicate the main climbing ground of the Fannaichs, at its best under winter conditions.

Descend SW from Carn na Criche to the wide col whose lush grass in summer provides ample feeding for the deer, hence the name Am Biachdaich, the place of fattening. A lochan lies on this col at the start of the ridge which sweeps above the great cliffs to the trig point on Sgurr nan Clach Geala. It rises in two sections, the upper one being narrow but offering an easy and enjoyable passage along the brink of the crags which plunge into the corrie below. The summit is an excellent viewpoint from which to appreciate the layout and character of the Fannaichs, all but one of which can be seen from there in clear conditions. (9km; 1080m; 3h 50min).

There is an easy descent S by grass slopes to the 807m col of the Cadha na Guite. The ridge crest beyond rises gently to the summit of Sgurr nan Each in an elegant asymmetric double curve with steep crags falling into Coire Mhoir on the E. (11km; 1200m; 4h 30min).

Return N along the ridge to the Cadha na Guite and descend W down grassy slopes to the pass at the head of the Allt Breabaig. From there follow the stalker's path N back to the E end of Loch a' Bhraoin to rejoin the road leading to the day's starting point at the A832.

*Sgurr nan Each and Sgurr nan Clach Geala*                    W.D. Brooker

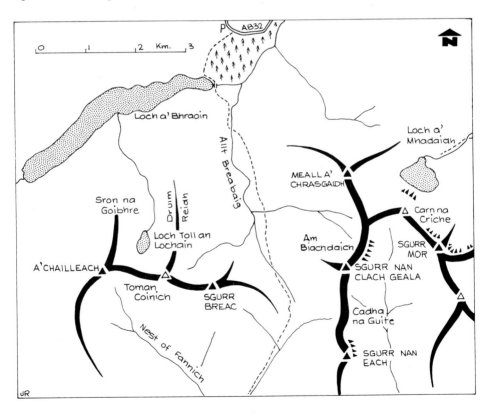

*The approach to the Fannaichs at the north end of Loch a' Bhraoin*          *D.J. Bennet*

**Sgurr Breac**; 1000m; (OS Sheet 20; 158711); M135; *speckled peak.*
**A' Chailleach**; 999m; (OS Sheets 19 and 20; 136714); M137; *the old woman.*

These two peaks are the most westerly of the Fannaichs, and lie south of the A832 road from Braemore Junction to Dundonnell. They are connected to the main group by a narrow col at the head of the Allt Breabaig at a height of 550m from which a ridge extends west over Sgurr Breac and the Top of Toman Coinich to A' Chailleach. Northward from this summit ridge the two spurs of Sron na Goibhre and Druim Reidh enfold the corrie of Toll an Lochain. There are no recognised climbing crags on these hills, but they have a generally steep and rocky northern aspect.

From the A832 road at (162761), several kilometres SW of Braemore Junction, take the private road to Loch a' Bhraoin and cross its outlet by a footbridge. Go S on the stalker's path which crosses the Allt Breabaig at the rocky linn or the ford some 200 metres upstream. Take care if the burn is in spate. The path continues higher on the E side of the glen until it reaches the pass leading over to Loch Fannich. From the pass climb the E ridge of Sgurr Breac, quite steeply through little rock outcrops at first, then up an easy-angled ridge. (9km; 750m; 3h 20min).

Continue by traversing Toman Coinich (937m), or skirting its summit on the S side, and descending to the bealach at 810m. Ascend the ridge along the rim of the Toll an Lochain to its junction with the Sron na Goibhre spur, then bear SW along the gently rising crest to the summit of A' Chailleach. (11km; 1020m; 4h 10min).

Return NE to the junction of ridges above the Toll an Lochain and descend, steeply at first, the spur of Sron na Goibhre, well marked by fence posts. Avoid the rock outcrops at the N end of this ridge by descending E towards the stream in the Toll an Lochain down steep and boulder strewn grassy slopes. Follow this stream for some distance along the W bank, then cross to the E and go diagonally down the grassy hillside NE towards Loch a' Bhraoin to regain the road back to the starting point.

Map on page 207.

*On the summit ridge of Fionn Bheinn*                                    *H.M. Brown*

**Fionn Bheinn**; 933m; (OS Sheets 20 and 25; 147621); M240; *pale-coloured hill.*

The only Munro of the Fannaichs to lie south of Loch Fannich, Fionn Bheinn rises directly on the north side of the A832 road at Achnasheen. With its smooth grassy slopes and subdued contours, it presents an undistinguished appearance to the south and keeps its more interesting north side concealed from most visitors.

The easiest approach is directly from Achnasheen, by following the Allt Achadh na Sine, keeping on its NE side and gaining the nose of Creagan nan Laogh (crag of the calf). From there ascend NW by gentle slopes of mossy grass to reach the summit in just over 1km. (5km; 780m; 2h 30min).

A different descent route which adds variety and allows the mountain to be traversed is as follows:- Go E, skirting the edge of the steep slabby face which plunges into the Toll Mor and follow the ridge E, then SE down a steeper slope close to the rim of another slabby corrie, the Toll Beag. Where the slope levels out, a prominent drystone wall leads E and can be followed, with a few gaps, until it intersects an old grass-grown path crossing the hill from N to S. Turn right down this path until it approaches a plantation, diverge to the right to avoid this obstacle and descend to Achnasheen.

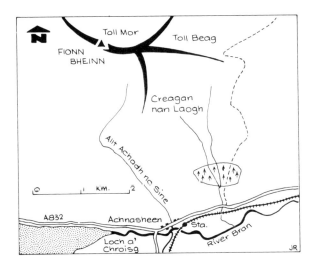

*Looking west from Ben Wyvis to the Fannaichs and An Teallach*  R. Robb

# SECTION 15 and 16

Ben Wyvis to Ben Hope

*Ben Wyvis from the Glascarnoch River*                                    H.M. Brown

**Ben Wyvis, Glas Leathad Mor**; 1046m; (OS Sheet 20; 463684); M83; *Ben Wyvis is from the Gaelic fuathas, meaning perhaps hill of terror. Glas Leathad Mor means big greenish-grey slope.*

Ben Wyvis (the name applies to the whole range) is a solitary hulk of a mountain shipwrecked far to the east of other northern hills. The highest summit, Glas Leathad Mor, is a high level ridge with two impressive corries on its eastern face, and long uniform grass slopes sweeping up from the dark forests on the west. Its isolated position makes it a good viewpoint. Despite the vast plantings of the Garbat Forest, the approach from the west is still the one most used.

Park off the A835 road from Garve to Ullapool just S of the Allt a' Bhealaich Mhoir, ½km S of Garbat, and follow the good footpath on the N bank of that stream. There is a gap between trees and river. A forestry road crosses the route at about the 200m contour, but the path continues heading up towards the Bealach Mor. There are additional plantings not shown on the OS 1:50000 map, but above these simply turn uphill to ascend An Cabar (946m), the end prow of the Wyvis ridge. The summit lies 2km NE along a soft, mossy ridge of delightful walking. (6½km; 920m; 3h).

The quickest descent is to return by the route of ascent. Alternatively, a traverse of the mountain can be made by continuing down the NNE ridge and climbing Tom a'Choinnich (955m). Descend its grassy WSW ridge to the Allt a'Gharbh Bhaid and follow this stream downhill to the point where it flows into the Garbat Forest. Go S along the fence for about ½km to a gate, then descend W down a break in the trees to a track leading to Garbat.

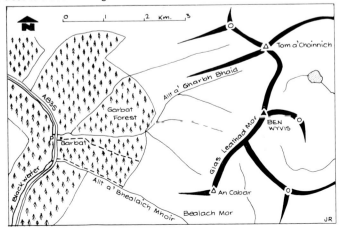

*Am Faochagach from Cona'Mheall*                                    D. Snadden

**Am Faochagach**; 954m; (OS Sheet 20, 304794); M206; *the place of the shells.*

   The great range of rounded hills which forms the heart of the Strathvaich Forest between Loch Glascarnoch and Strath Vaich culminates in Am Faochagach. Like its lower outliers, it is a massive rounded hill, well seen from the NW end of Loch Glascarnoch from which it lies 6km to the N.

   The road up Strath Vaich is private, and the shortest approach is from the A835 road at the NW end of Loch Glascarnoch, starting at the bridge over the Abhainn an Torrain Duibh. From this point the route to Am Faochagach is trackless, and the first 1½km across the level strath is over rough boggy ground normally very wet underfoot, and includes the crossing of the Abhainn a' Gharbhrain. In normal conditions this crossing will entail wet feet; in wet conditions (which some might regard as normal) the crossing is likely to be impossible, and a diversion upriver to try a higher crossing may be no more successful. Am Faochagach is, therefore, a mountain for dry conditions, or a hard winter's day when frost grips the ground.

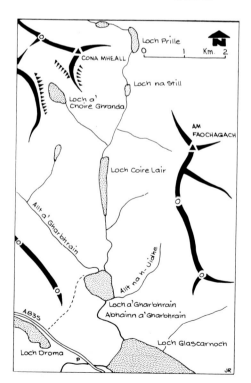

   Apart from these obstacles, the ascent is straightforward. A course NNE from the road across the bog leads to the river crossing, then bear NE, keeping on the side of the Allt na h-Uidhe. The going becomes easier as bog and tussocky heather give way to smoother grassy slopes, and the col on the main spine of the range 3km S of Am Faochagach is reached. From there the going is very easy along the broad grassy ridge, over barely perceptible rises, past a few cairns until the final steeper slope, where the effects of solifluction are evident, leads to the flat summit of Am Faochagach crowned by two cairns a few metres apart (7km: 690m; 2h 50min).

*The approach to Beinn Dearg (left) and Cona' Mheall from the south-east*          *J. Renny*

**Cona' Mheall;** 980m; (OS Sheet 20, 275816); M170; *hill of the meeting or joining.*

This mountain is one of the Beinn Dearg group, and although it can be climbed from the north-west with the others of the group (see p214), the character of Cona' Mheall can only be appreciated if it is climbed from the south, and the extra effort needed for this rather rugged approach is well worthwhile. The finest feature of Cona' Mheall is its narrow SE ridge, on both sides of which the mountain drops precipitously. Coire Ghranda on the W side is the finest corrie of the Dearg group, a remote and impressive sanctuary; on the E side of the ridge and slopes of Cona' Mheall above Coire Lair are extraordinarily wild and rocky.

The approach from the south has very much the same character as the mountain itself, rough and wild. A path leaves the A835 road 9km NW of Aultguish Inn near the SE end of Loch Droma, climbs slightly to the NE and continues N, descending to the ruins of an old shieling at the NW corner of Loch a' Gharbhrain. Cross the Allt a' Gharbhrain, notoriously difficult or even impossible in spate, and continue N over trackless peat and heather towards Loch Coire Lair. Half way along the loch start climbing towards the lip of Coire Ghranda where the stream comes down over bare slabs; a very faint path helps in places, but the climb is steep, traversing grass ledges between the slabs.

The Coire Ghranda is in a superb setting with the cliffs of Beinn Dearg across the loch. Climb directly towards the S end of Cona' Mheall's SE ridge, scrambling steeply up grass and easy rocks to reach the more level upper ridge. This is narrow, but quite easy with two short descents and occasional scrambling, and the ridge becomes broader as it leads up to the bouldery summit. (8km; 800m; 3h 40min).

The descent may be made by the same route, but great care is needed on the lower part of the SE ridge. A very interesting alternative is the E ridge which drops steeply a few metres NE of the cairn. The route leads down by a series of wide ledges and shelves, but care must be taken, particularly in misty weather, as these shelves, formed by the strata of the rock, tend to lead too far S onto steep ground. It is necessary to check the correct route towards the outflow of Loch Prille. The descent S down the Allt Lair is steep at first, and lower down the corrie the uphill route is rejoined on the W side of Loch Coire Lair.

*Coire Ghranda below the cliffs of Beinn Dearg*                    *A. Thrippleton*

**Beinn Dearg;** 1084m; (OS Sheet 20; 259812); M55; *red hill.*
**Meall nan Ceapraichean;** 977m; (OS Sheet 20; 257826); M172; *perhaps from ceap, meaning a back or hilltop.*
**Eididh nan Clach Geala;** 928m; (OS Sheet 20; 257843); M249; *web of the white stones.*

These mountains, known collectively as the Deargs, lie to the south-east of Loch Broom. From Ullapool, Beinn Dearg itself appears as a great high dome rising above its neighbours. From elsewhere, distant views of this group show it as an undulating plateau rather than separate mountains, and its many superb corries are hardly seen. Only by penetrating into its heart can the true character be appreciated.

The best approach is from the A835 road at the head of Loch Broom where, a few hundred metres N of Inverlael House, a private road leads for 3km through the Lael Forest into the lower part of Gleann na Sguaib. Beyond the forest follow a stalker's path up this glen on the NE side of the River Lael past some fine falls and a beautiful little lochan nestling below the cliffs of Beinn Dearg to the col at the head of the glen. There another lochan lies in a desolate stony landscape.

To climb Beinn Dearg first, go S to reach a dry stone dyke of massive proportions and climb up on its W side. Towards the top, where the dyke turns W, go through a gap and bear SSW for a few hundred metres across the flat dome of Beinn Dearg to its summit. (10km; 1070m; 4h).

Return to the col by the same route and climb the easy-angled ridge of Meall nan Ceapraichean. (12km; 1190m; 4h 40min). Continue NE along a broad stony ridge to Ceann Garbh (967m). Descend NE, easily at first, but lower down small crags and rock bands have to be circumvented and the next col is reached at (265838). From there an easy grass slope leads to Eididh nan Clach Geala where there are two cairns, the NW one being the summit. (14½km; 1370m; 5h 30min). Just below the cairn, on the NW side, are the white quartzite boulders which may well give the mountain its name.

Descend W down a grassy slope for ½km, then turn SW into the corrie W of Lochan na Chnapaich where a stalker's path is joined and followed downhill to the main path in Gleann na Sguaib.

**Seana Bhraigh;** 927m; (OS Sheet 20; 281879); M254; *old upper part.*

Seana Bhraigh competes with A' Mhaighdean for the title of most distant Munro, and like that mountain it occupies a remote, lofty, cliff-girt situation in true wilderness country. A good path helps with access for most of the way to what is one of the best summits in Scotland, hidden in the hinterland of the Inverlael Forest far to the east of Loch Broom.

Start from the A835 road to Ullapool as for Beinn Dearg (qv) through the Lael Forest as far as Glensguaib. Then take the stalker's path out of the forest onto the Druim na Saobhaidhe ridge, crossing the wide western corrie of Gleann a' Mhadaidh and rounding a spur of hills above to continue up Coire an Lochain Sgeirich which has a peculiar succession of lochans in it.

The path vanishes in a boggy wilderness at about 750m, and in poor visibility very careful navigation is

*Seana Bhraigh summit looking towards Creag an Duine*                    H.M. Brown

required for the continuation to Seana Bhraigh across rough terrain. There are crags above the S bank of the burn flowing into Loch a' Chadha Dheirg, and peat hags and minor bumps abound. In bad visibility one way is to find the lochan at (271856) near the end of the path, navigate to Loch a' Chadha Dheirg and the tiny lochan at (288860) from where a course due N leads up easy slopes to the 906m dome. Follow the cliff-edge of Luchd Choire NW to Seana Bhraigh, whose cairn stands right on the edge of the corrie. (13½km; 1100m; 4h 50min).

The spur of Creag an Duine on the E side of the Luchd Choire appears as a fine sharp peak from the S, and the cliff edge of the Cadha Dearg is an impressive place with a view down lonely Glen Douchary. The quickest return is by the outward route.

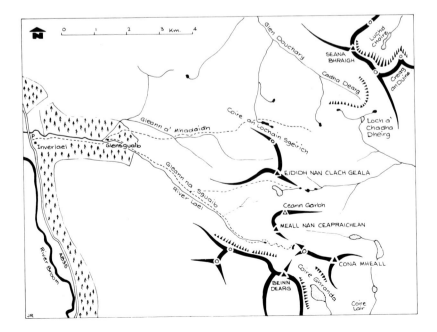

*Ben More Assynt from Conival*

D.J. Bennet

**Conival;** 987m; (OS Sheet 15; 303199); M154; *hill of the meeting or joining.*
**Ben More Assynt;** 998m; (OS Sheet 15; 318201); M140; *the big hill of Assynt (Norse: ass, a rocky ridge).*

These two mountains are the highest peaks of wild Assynt, but they have a hidden, secretive character compared to bold neighbours like Suilven or Quinag. They are rough, rocky peaks at the heart of an unusually rough part of the harsh, empty northlands. Inchnadamph is the usual starting point, and the hotel there is a favourite with hill-goers, fishermen, botanists, cavers and scientists who all delight in this geologically interesting region.

Leave the A837 road just N of Inchnadamph Hotel by a farm track on the N bank of the River Traligill. Beyond Glenbain cottage a good track continues to a small plantation. Just beyond this point the main path crosses the river to reach the Traligill Caves. The route to Conival, however, continues on the N side of the glen with a rising traverse up the SW face of Beinn an Fhurain. Progress is easy over grassy, heathery slopes with occasional animal tracks; aim fairly high up, but keep below the line of crags to reach the high grassy alp below the Beinn an Fhurain - Conival col at 750m. From the col the final ascent of Conival is up rough quartzite scree, followed by a fairly level ridge to the large summit cairn. (7km; 920m; 3h 10min).

Ben More Assynt lies 1½km E along a dipping crest of the same rough, demanding terrain: a mixture of scree and crag, narrow in places, steep flanked and exposed to all the storms that blow. In poor visibility it may be difficult to decide which of two shattered bumps is the summit of Ben More; it is the N one. (8½km; 1050m; 3h 40min). The simplest return is by the same route.

A more interesting continuation is to go out along the SE ridge for 1km to the South Top of Ben More Assynt (960m). This traverse involves a narrow, rocky section of ridge sometimes compared with the Aonach Eagach; however its 'bad steps' are no more than exposed slabs. Continue ½km S from the Top and descend steeply W to Dubh Loch Mor. Bear NW, climbing 60m, to the fine narrow pass between Conival and Breabag Tarsuinn, and continue by a narrow path towards Gleann Dubh and the Traligill Caves.

*On the ridge from Conival to Ben More Assynt*                    D.J. Bennet

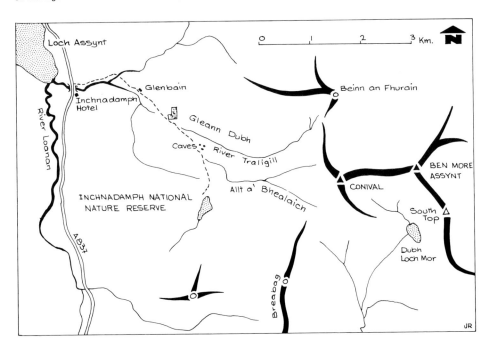

*Ben Klibreck from the South*                                                    *W.B. Young*

**Ben Klibreck**; 961m; (OS Sheet 16; 585299); M190; *hill of the speckled cliff.*

This great isolated mountain rises above the desolate moorland of central Sutherland. The extraordinarily vast and featureless character of the landscape in this part of Scotland gives to Ben Klibreck an equal impression of remoteness, though in fact its summit is only 4 kilometre from the A836 road between Lairg and Tongue. The spine of the mountain is a long curving ridge between Loch Naver and Loch Coire, and the summit, Meall nan Con, is the highest of several tops along this ridge. The NW side of the mountain facing Altnaharra is quite steep, and on the W side, some distance below the summit, there is a steep prow of broken crags. The SE side of the mountain is carved into wide grassy corries above Loch a' Bhealaich and Loch Coire.

The inns at Crask and Altnaharra are possible starting points for the ascent, but the shortest and easiest route starts from the A836 road through Strath Vagastie near (545303) where there is a good roadside parking place near the river. Cross the river (no footbridge, difficult in spate) and continue E across the moorland to the S end of Loch na Glas-choille. From there the route continues ESE, following the line of a fence, to reach the outflow of Loch nan Uan. The face of Ben Klibreck immediately ahead is very steep, with crags to the NE under Meall nan Con. The easiest ascent goes SE from the outflow of the loch to climb steep grassy slopes to the main ridge at its lowest point 1km SW of the summit. Finally an easy walk along the smooth grassy ridge and a short pull up a bouldery slope lead to the cairn. (5km; 790m; 2h 30min).

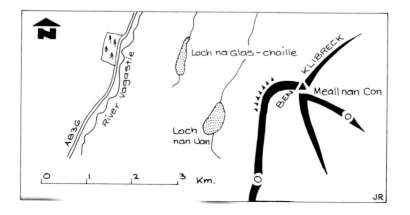

*Ben Hope from Loch Eriboll*                                                    K. Rezin

**Ben Hope**; 927m; (OS Sheet 9; 477502); M253; *hill of the bay.*

Ben Hope, with its Viking name and splendid isolation, is a worthy peak for the most northerly Munro. Its long west flank above Strath More and Loch Hope is double-tiered and has plenty of crags, but the ascent up this side is not unduly difficult. The easy southern and eastern slopes can only be reached by long approaches, so are seldom used. It would not be difficult to climb both Ben Hope and Ben Klibreck in a single day, with a short drive by car between them.

To reach the mountain, branch west at the crossroads north of the hamlet of Altnaharra on the A836 road from Lairg to Tongue and follow the narrow road westwards over the moors to descend into Strath More. After several kilometres the interesting broch of Dun Dornaigil is reached, then the farm of Alltnacaillich. About 2km north of Alltnacaillich park near the sheep shed by the stream which descends from the Dubh-loch terrace on the west flank of Ben Hope.

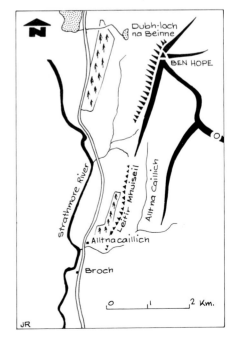

Climb up beside the stream for ¾km NE and continue up the E tributary which comes down from the vast bowl of the mountain's southern slopes. This leads through a break in the line of cliffs which is clearly seen on the OS map, and the cliff edge can then be followed to the trig point on the summit dome. The setting is spacious and majestic. The best viewpoint is slightly to the N, but this does not lead to a descent route. (3½km; 920m; 2h 20min). Return by the route of ascent, or by the Alltnacaillich variation mentioned below.

This slightly longer alternative starts at Alltnacaillich farm and takes the path up the S bank of the Allt na Caillich (the old woman's burn). After crossing the stream above a fine waterfall, the ridge of Leitir Mhuiseil is followed N to join the route described above.

*Sgurr Dearg and the Inaccessible Pinnacle, the hardest Munro*          *J.E.S. Bennet*

# SECTION 17

### The Islands of Mull and Skye

*Ben More and A' Chioch from the east*                                    *D.J. Fabian*

**Ben More;** 966m; (OS Sheet 48; 526331); M185; *big hill.*

The only island Munro outside Skye, Ben More dominates the western group of hills on Mull and gives them their impressive form, especially when seen from the south. Splendid views of the Ben More group are also obtained from the B8035 road along which the climber comes from Salen to reach Loch na Keal and the foot of the moutain. Ben More itself is a fine isolated peak, its summit at the apex of three ridges. Of these the finest is the north-east which leads to A' Choich, a sharp subsidiary top, and the traverse of this ridge is the best route to Ben More.

Start from the shore of Loch na Keal at the foot of the Abhainn na h-Uamha and follow the S bank of this stream past many attractive pools and waterfalls up the grassy Gleann na Beinne Fada to reach the bealach between Beinn Fhada and A' Chioch. Turn S and climb towards A' Chioch; as height is gained the ridge becomes steeper and rockier, and gives a delightful scramble up a rocky staircase without any difficulty. The continuation to Ben More maintains the interest, and the connecting ridge can look impressive when framed by cumulus clouds or sharpened by snow on the N face of Ben More. On the final ascent from the col the climb is reminiscent of the Aonach Eagach or Liathach, but there are no comparable difficulties, just the same exhilaration and unforgettable views from the summit if the day is clear. (6km; 1060m; 3h 10min).

The quickest descent route is down the broad NW ridge, keeping to the N of the shallow hollow of the Abhainn Dhiseig to return directly to the day's starting point by Loch na Keal.

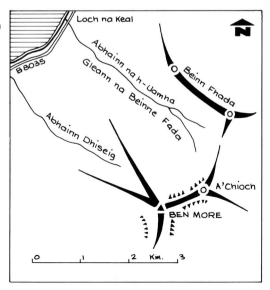

*The Cuillin Ridge in winter, a view south-west from Am Basteir*                    R. Robb

The Cuillin are the most challenging mountains in Scotland, with airy crests, girt with precipices, and with only a few walking routes to their tops. Climbing these mountains is very different from the perfectly simple hill-walking which is involved in the ascent of all but three or four of the mainland Munros. Most of the Cuillin require some scrambling to reach their summits, and one - The Inaccessible Pinnacle - calls for rock-climbing. Much of the scrambling is fairly easy, but there are places where, for a few metres, the difficulties are more akin to easy rock-climbing. There are also many places where the narrowness of the ridges and their exposure are such that a slip might have serious results. In such situations surefootedness and a good head for heights are essential.

In spite of the fact that the Cuillin are composed of gabbro, one of the finest of climbing rocks, there is a great deal of loose rock, and care should be taken at all times. There have been many accidents over the years due to loose rock in otherwise straightforward situations.

There are a number of places on the Main Ridge and close to it where the compass is unreliable due to local magnetic anomalies. Thus in mist one should at all times retain a firm sense of one's whereabouts. These anomalies do not occur on lower ground.

The OS 1:50000 map is not really adequate for navigation except on the lower ground and in the corries. The Ordnance Survey produces an excellent 1:25000 map of the Cuillin, and the Scottish Mountaineering Trust publishes a 1:15000 chart, with walking routes marked, which is most helpful.

All the routes described (except that for Bla Bheinn) are on the Sligachan and Glen Brittle side of the Main Ridge. This is for two reasons: first, these places are easily accessible and can provide accommodation, and second, the Loch Coruisk side of the Ridge, though magnificent, is remote and forbidding, and is left for the climber who is able to find his way without the aid of a guidebook.

**Sgurr nan Gillean**; 965m; (OS Sheet 32; 472253); M187; *peak of the young men.*

A superb mountain from all aspects, offering from its summit on a clear day one of the world's greatest mountain views. Even by the easiest route the final ridge is an airy scramble. It may be seen to advantage from the roadside at Sligachan, and its conical tip is visible from the slipway at Kyles of Loch Alsh as one crosses to Skye.

Because of the featureless nature of the lower ground, and the precipitous terrain higher up, this route should not be attempted in poor visibility.

Start 200 metres SW of Sligachan Inn at a car park. Opposite, on the S side of the road, a faint path leads in 200 metres to, and then crosses, the Allt Dearg Mor. Thereafter it meanders SSW amongst peat hags, endeavouring without much success to avoid the boggiest terrain until in 1 ½km it reaches the Allt Dearg Beag. The path, now much improved, follows the W bank for ½km to a bridge, where it branches. Ignore the path which continues up the burn, but cross the burn and follow the path which heads S and climbs slightly. By now the crags of Nead na h-Iolaire are slightly to the left (E) with a

*Sgurr nan Gillean from Sligachan*                                                  *H.M. Brown*

plateau visible beyond. At about the 300m contour the path crosses an oval area of small stones 15 metres in diameter. Ignore the faint path to the right and continue S, dropping slightly as one enters Coire Riabhach, and pass some 200 metres W of a lochan over the side of some rocky hummocks. Ahead may be seen a band of rocks broken by a scree-filled gully. The path, now well worn and clearly visible, ascends this scree. Above the steep section, on easier terrain, the well cairned path leads to the SE ridge of Sgurr nan Gillean at 750m.

This ridge, not visible from Sligachan, is at first broad and rises to the NW. Higher up it narrows, and care is required for the final scramble to the summit. (6km; 950m; 3h).

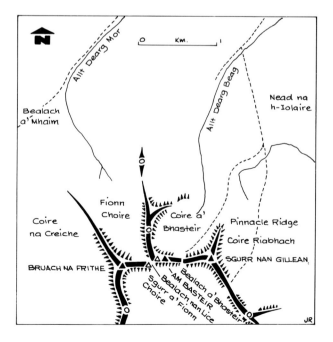

*Am Basteir from Sgurr a' Fionn Choire*                                        *H.M. Brown*

**Am Basteir**; 935m; (OS Sheet 32; 465253); M236; *meaning obscure, but probably not, as is commonly supposed, the executioner.*

A blade of rock, vertically sided to the north and very steep on the south, which may nevertheless be ascended relatively easily by its east ridge. However, it is no place for those without a good head for heights, and no place to have a slip. The setting is dramatic, and much to be recommended.

From Sligachan follow the route for Sgurr nan Gillean as far as the oval area of stones at 300m, where the Sgurr nan Gillean path continues S. Branch rightwards on a faintly discernible but adequately cairned path rising SW towards the broad rocky spur that falls from the N side of Sgurr nan Gillean. This spur is obvious even when seen from Sligachan.

Once on the crest of this spur impressive cliffs fall away on one's right to the Basteir Gorge, but the path keeps well away from the edge. The spur flattens out a little below the level of the lip of Coire a' Bhasteir from which a delightful tumbling burn emerges. At this height one can see Portree harbour to the N.

Beyond the flattening the slope steepens towards the base rocks of the Pinnacle Ridge. Climb towards the rocks for 70m, seeking a faint line departing upwards and rightwards. It follows more or less the base of the rocks along the top of the screes of Coire a' Bhasteir, and leads to the Bealach a' Bhasteir (833m). Am Basteir and its broad but steeply sided E ridge now lie immediately to the W.

From the bealach the route to Am Basteir goes directly up its E ridge, easy at first, but becoming narrower and more exposed higher up, and giving a good scramble with one place of slight difficulty near mid-point where an awkward descent of a few steps has to be made. (5½km; 930m; 2h 50min). The summit of Am Basteir is a spectacular place with vertical drops to the N and W. For the walker the only route of descent is back down the E ridge to the Bealach a' Bhasteir.

From the bealach, if returning to Sligachan by the ascent route, beware of dropping too low into Coire a' Bhasteir, for there may be difficulty in regaining the crest of the spur that leads back to Sligachan. Alternatively, the continuation W along the Main Ridge from the bealach goes down on the Coire a' Bhasteir side of Am Basteir, following a path in the screes below its N face. This path leads back up to the ridge just W of the Basteir Tooth at the Bealach na Lice. From there one may either continue along the ridge to Bruach na Frithe, traversing the little peak of Sgurr a' Fionn Choire (930m), or return to Sligachan by descending NW into the Fionn Choire, as described on the next page.

*Bruach na Frithe*                                                      *H.M. Brown*

**Bruach na Frithe;** 958m; (OS Sheet 32; 461252); M198; *slope of the deer-forest.*

A fine viewpoint and a peak whose outline would excite attention in any other less imposing environment. The only peak in the Cuillin which is not defended by cliffs.

From Sligachan take the road to Alltdearg House and follow the path leading SW towards Glen Brittle by the Bealach a' Mhaim. It holds to the NW side of the Allt Dearg Mor. At about 250m above sea level the path bears S and the ground becomes exceptionally soft as the top of the pass is approached. To the SE lies a smooth grassy corrie known as the Fionn Choire. The terrain is quite featureless until an elevation in excess of 450m is gained. From the top of the pass head S and climb onto the NW ridge of Bruach na Frithe, and continue without difficulty to the summit. The route traverses onto the W side of the ridge, overlooking Coire na Creiche, at one point where the crest steepens and becomes excessively shattered. (7km; 940m; 3h 10min).

Bruach na Frithe may also be ascended by a more complex but more interesting route by way of the Fionn Choire. Leave the Allt Dearg Mor path 1km before reaching the Bealach a' Mhaim and bear S up the corrie to its head at the Bealach nan Lice. There is no path, but the going is easy and there is a spring high up towards the Main Ridge. Impressive views may be had from the col down into Lota Corrie on the S and up to the overhanging blade of rock forming the Basteir Tooth. From the col head SW over Sgurr a' Fionn Choire (930m) to reach Bruach na Frithe without difficulty.

For the inexperienced it cannot be stressed too strongly that finding the way back to Sligachan can be a problem if the mist is below 500m because of the featureless nature of the lower ground. In such conditions the following directions may help:- From the summit of Bruach na Frithe descend due N towards Fionn Choire for 15 minutes, then bear left on 330° magnetic. Any stream encountered will be flowing N and if followed will lead down to Sligachan.

*Sgurr a' Ghreadaidh*                                                      R. Robb

**Sgurr a' Mhadaidh**; 918m; (OS Sheet 32; 446235); M266; *peak of the fox.*
**Sgurr a' Ghreadaidh**; 973m; (OS Sheet 32; 445232); M181; *peak of torment, anxiety.*

The central part of the Cuillin Main Ridge is dominated by Sgurr a' Ghreadaidh, a great twin-topped peak which on its Coruisk side has the longest rock-climbs in Skye on its huge buttresses. Just to its north along the Main Ridge Sgurr a' Mhadaidh shows an elegant outline of four peaks, but only the south-west one, that nearest to Sgurr a' Ghreadaidh, reaches Munro height. These two mountains are central in the view up Loch Coruisk towards the Cuillin. On the Glen Brittle side Sgurr a' Ghreadaidh and the highest top of Mhadaidh overlook Coire a' Ghreadaidh, and it is by the northern arm of this corrie, the Coire an Dorus, that the ascent of both is most easily made. In the north-east corner of Coire an Dorus an easy-angled scree slope runs up to An Dorus (the door), the col between the two peaks, and it gives the easiest route to both. However, a more interesting though more difficult route is described which gives a fine traverse of them.

Leave Glen Brittle at the Youth Hostel and follow the path up the Coire a' Ghreadaidh on the S side of the stream for about 2½km. Cross to the N side and beyond a grassy alp follow the tributary stream which comes down from the innermost NE corner of Coire an Dorus. (Traces of paths on both sides of the stream). When the last grassy patches are reached below An Dorus bear N and climb scree towards the col between Sgurr a' Mhadaidh and Sgurr Thuilm. Some broken rocks and slabs just below the col are climbed by zig-zagging up ledges.

From the col traverse a narrow horizontal ridge SE to the foot of a steep buttress bounded on both sides by dark gullies. The ascent of this buttress is a very fine but in places difficult scramble, with considerable exposure. After about 80m the angle relents and easier scrambling leads up to a cairn from which a ledge goes right and diagonally up to the summit of Sgurr a' Mhadaidh. (4km; 900m; 2h 30min).

Descend easily from Sgurr a' Mhadaidh down broken rocks and boulders to the An Dorus col. The last few metres of the descent are steep and awkward, as are the first few metres of the ascent of Sgurr a' Ghreadaidh on the opposite side of this narrow gap. Continue up the crest of the ridge, soon bearing over to the left side to cross, with hardly any drop, the top of the Eag Dubh (the black notch), from which steep gullies fall on both sides. Immediately traverse right again to regain the crest and continue towards an impressive looking tower which appears to block the ridge. It is something of an imposter, however, as a broad easy scree ledge leads round its right (W) side and a short distance higher the summit of Sgurr a' Ghreadaidh is reached. (5km; 1030m; 3h).

The lower South Peak (969m) is a hundred metres away, but the connecting ridge is very narrow and exposed, and the continuation of the Main Ridge southwards gives no easy descent to Glen Brittle for a long way. Unless one wants to embark on a long traverse, therefore, one should return to An Dorus and descend its screes and boulders to Coire an Dorus where the uphill route is rejoined.

*The Innaccessible Pinnacle, Sgurr na Banachdich and Sgurr a' Ghreadaidh from the top of*    R. Robb
*The Great Stone Shoot.*

**Sgurr na Banachdich**; 965m; (OS Sheet 32; 440225); M186; *meaning obscure, according to Forbes may be smallpox peak from the pitted appearance of some of its rocks, or perhaps from banachdag, a milkmaid.*

This fine peak of three summits, of which the northern one is the highest, fills the head of Coire na Banachdich, and it is by this corrie that the ascent from Glen Brittle is usually made. The Bealach Coire na Banachdich is one of the few easy passes over the Main Ridge, and the path to it is well marked.

Starting near the Glen Brittle Memorial Hut, take the path on the N side of the Allt Coire na Banachdich and in ¾km cross this stream just above the Eas Mor waterfall. Leave the obvious Coire Lagan path and follow another one on the S side of the Allt Coire na Banachdich to pass below the prominent Window Buttress and reach the wild and rocky inner corrie. In front great slabby walls bar progress directly upwards, and the path, now only a faint trail but well cairned, bears right beside the southernmost tributary stream. Aim to the right (S) of the slabby cliffs where an open gully filled with scree and boulders provides the way, still well cairned. Above the gully bear left (NE) on a rising traverse and finally go directly up scree to the Bealach Coire na Banachdich.

From the pass climb directly along the SSE ridge of Sgurr na Banachdich over its two subsidiary tops, either scrambling along the crest which is narrow and shattered in places, or traversing easy ledges on the W flank just below the crest. (4½km; 950m; 2h 40min).

On the descent from the Bealach Coire na Banachdich to Glen Brittle, do not go straight down, but after the first 100m traverse left (SW) where cairns indicate a slightly rising passage where the path is clear.

Map on page 228.

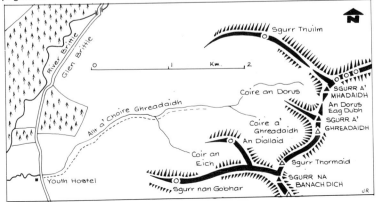

*Sgurr Dearg and the Inaccessible Pinnacle*                                    R. Robb

**Sgurr Dearg; The Inaccessible Pinnacle;** 986m, Cairn 978m; (OS Sheet 32, 444215); M159; *red peak.*

The most notorious peak in Skye, the Inaccessible Pinnacle is a vertical blade of rock which just overtops the nearby cairn of Sgurr Dearg. It is the only Munro that calls for rock-climbing ability, and most Munro-baggers have to call for help from their rock-climbing friends to get to the top of this one. The ascent of the Pinnacle should not be attempted without at least one experienced climber in the party, a rope and some previous practice in the art of abseiling, and it should probably be avoided on a wet and windy day when the ascent of the Pinnacle's narrow and exposed edge might be distinctly unnerving.

Follow the path from the Glen Brittle Memorial Hut towards Coire Lagan as far as Loch an Fhir-bhallaich, then strike up the great boulder-strewn W shoulder of Sgurr Dearg past bands of crags. Higher up the ridge narrows and there is some exposure as one scrambles along the crest over some minor bumps to reach the cairn on the scree-covered dome of Sgurr Dearg. (3½km; 970m; 2h 30min).

A short distance to the E is The Inaccessible Pinnacle, showing no easy way to its top. Technically the easiest route is by the E ridge, whose foot is reached by descending scree along the bottom of the S face. Though only Moderate in standard (in rock-climbing terms), and fairly easy-angled, the E ridge is narrow and remarkably exposed, with vertical drops on both sides and a disconcerting lack of really reassuring handholds. On the descent it is usual to abseil down the short W side, and it may be desirable to have a spare safety rope for the reassurance of those members of the party who are unfamiliar with the technique or overawed by the exposure on this, the most spectacular of Munros.

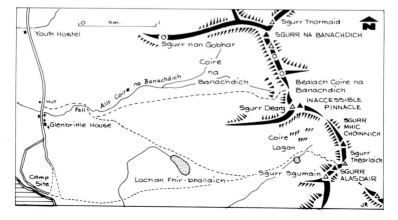

*Sgurr Mhic Choinnich (left) and Sgurr Alasdair above Coire Lagan*                    R. Robb

**Sgurr Alasdair**; 993m; (OS Sheet 32; 449208); M147; *Alexander's peak, named after Sherrif Alexander Nicolson who made the first recorded ascent in 1873.*

**Sgurr Mhic Choinnich**; 948m; (OS Sheet 32; 450210); M211; *MacKenzie's peak, named after the well known Cuillin guide, John MacKenzie.*

By common consent Coire Lagan is the grandest of all the Cuillin corries, and the peaks which enclose it — Sgurr Dearg, Sgurr Mhic Choinnich and Sgurr Alasdair — are a superb trio. All three are guarded by steep buttresses and gullies, and the screes of An Stac and the Great Stone Shoot are the most notorious in Skye. High above, the crest of Coire Lagan is one of the most dramatic sections of the Main Ridge, both in appearance and in the quality of the climbing along it. Sgurr Alasdair, the highest of the Cuillin, is a sharp-pointed peak commanding an unexcelled view over its neighbouring mountains to the islands on one hand and the mainland on the other. Sgurr Mhic Choinnich, though much lower, is an impressive wedge of rock with steep cliffs falling from its narrow summit ridge into the depths of Coire Lagan, and it is one of the more difficult peaks of the Cuillin from the hillwalkers' point of view.

Both peaks share the same approach walk from Glen Brittle into the heart of Coire Lagan, where the ascent routes diverge. Starting either at the Glen Brittle Memorial Hut or at the camp site, take one of the many worn paths eastwards over rising moorland past Loch an Fhir-bhallaich and below the cliffs of Sron na Ciche to reach Loch Coire Lagan, set amid huge glaciated slabs. Ahead, great curtains of scree and rock drop from the rocky crest above to the depths of the corrie. Walk round the N side of the loch and beyond it reach the innermost recess of Coire Lagan.

The route to Sgurr Alasdair goes up the big stony gully, the Great Stone Shoot, that rises in the SE corner of the corrie between steep walls to the high col between the peak and its neighbouring Top, Sgurr Thearlaich (984m). Once a highly mobile scree, now nearly all the small stones have been shifted to the foot of the slope by thousands of scree-runners, and the upper part of the gully consists of medium-sized boulders and big lumps of rock in a fairly stable state. A worn path zig-zags up the gully and gives a tiring and tedious ascent which is hardly worthy of the Cuillin's highest peak. From the col at the top of the Stone Shoot a short easy scramble leads W to the summit of Sgurr Alasdair. (5km; 1000m; 2h 50min).

Going to Sgurr Mhic Choinnich from Coire Lagan, bear NE from the loch to the foot of the huge scree slope which plunges down from the Bealach Coire Lagan, the col between Dearg and Mhic Choinnich. This slope is ascended with considerable effort, trying to find the most stable stones and boulders up which to make progress; very much a case of two steps up and one step down. Do not aim for the gap about 120 metres SE of the true bealach as it involves rock climbing. Once on the col turn SE and ascend the NW ridge of Sgurr Mhic Choinnich, which is airy and exposed and involves some difficult scrambling in places. (5km; 950m; 2h 50min).

*Sgurr Dubh Mor and Sgurr Dubh na Da Bheinn from the north-west*    R. Robb

**Sgurr Dubh Mor**; 944m; (OS Sheet 32; 457205); M222; *big black peak.*
**Sgurr nan Eag**; 924m; (OS Sheet 32; 457195); M259; *peak of the notches.*

Sgurr Dubh Mor is a fine sharp topped peak lying to the east of the Main Ridge on a long subsidiary ridge which rises from the edge of Loch Coruisk. The lower part of this ridge above the loch is formed by a huge expanse of bare gabbro slabs which sweep up to Sgurr Dubh Beag, from where a narrow crest continues to Sgurr Dubh Mor and on to join the Main Ridge at Sgurr Dubh na Da Bheinn. The ascent of this, the Dubhs Ridge, is one of the great Cuillin scrambles, (it is hardly a rock climb in the accepted sense, although a rope should be taken for one short abseil), and it is without doubt the finest route up Sgurr Dubh Mor. For the Glen Brittle based climber, however, the approach to this peak by Coir'a' Ghrunnda ia much shorter and easier.

Sgurr nan Eag, the southernmost Munro on the Main Ridge, is not a particularly distinguished peak by Cuillin standards, although it does have some steep crags overlooking An Garbh-choire. It too is most easily climbed from Coir'a' Ghrunnda.

From the Glen Brittle campsite take the well-worn route to Coire Lagan (see Sgurr Mhic Choinnich) for 1km and diverge ESE across the moor towards the lower end of Sron na Ciche. If coming from Glenbrittle House follow the Coire Lagan path to Loch an Fhir-bhallaich and strike SE across the Allt Coire Lagan along quite a good path to join the former route. Continue contouring SE below Sron na Ciche, and reach the foot of Coir'a' Ghrunnda. Climb into the corrie by a well cairned path on the W side of the burn and reach Loch Coir'a' Ghrunnda. Go round its NW side and climb easy slopes to the col on the Main Ridge ¼km NW of Sgurr Dubh na Da Bheinn. Climb this peak easily and descend E along the ridge to Sgurr Dubh Mor, whose ascent requires some scrambling. (6½km; 990m; 3h 10min).

Retrace steps to Sgurr Dubh na Da Bheinn and descend S along the Main Ridge. The col between Coir'a' Ghrunnda and An Garbh-choire has a prominent gabbro castle astride it - the Caisteal a' Garbh-choire. Do not attempt to climb over the castle, but traverse below it on either the E or W side where there are ledges. Continue along the Main Ridge, now easy, to Sgurr nan Eag. (8km; 1170m; 3h 50min).

Return down the ridge as far as the S end of Caisteal a' Garbh-choire, then descend W into Coir'a' Ghrunnda to rejoin the uphill route.

*Sgurr Dubh na Da Bheinn, Gars-bheinn and Sgurr nan Eag from Sgurr Alasdair*      D.J. Bennet

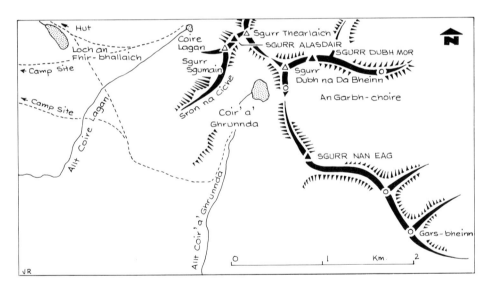

*Bla Bheinn from Bruach na Frithe*

*H.M. Brown*

**Bla Bheinn (Blaven)**; 928m; (OS Sheet 32; 530217); M251; *perhaps blue hill from Old Norse bla blue, and Gaelic bheinn hill, or possibly warm hill.*

A magnificent isolated mountain massif, capturing the heart of the lover of mountain scenery. Girt with precipices and rising directly from sea level, it gives the feel of a hill far higher than it actually is. Though of gabbro rock like the main mass of the Cuillin, it stands apart and so offers a superb perspective of the main range. Exceptionally accessible.

Take the road from Broadford to Elgol. As the head of Loch Slapin is approached near the village of Torrin, the great massif of Bla Bheinn fills the western view. Leave the road at an Allt na Dunaiche, 1km S of the head of Loch Slapin on its W side. Follow the path along the N bank of this stream, first past a beautiful wooded gorge and then up the moor toward the foot of Coire Uaigneich. Cross to the S side of the Allt na Dunaiche and follow the path which climbs more steeply holding to the NW side of the burn tumbling out of Coire Uaigneich, first on heather and then grass to reach a delightful little grass alp at 400m. At this point two great slabby buttresses rise to the right (NW), and between them are steep grass and rocks bounded on the left (S) by a vertically walled gully. The path, rather indistinct, zig-zags up the slope to the right of the gully. At about 600m the grass gives way to scree, and the path, now well cairned and clearly visible, continues to a shoulder at 780m. This shoulder is followed WSW on rocks with occasional scrambling to merge with the main ridge of Bla Bheinn and gain the summit dome. (4km; 930m; 2h 30min).

The return may be made by the same route. Alternatively, a rapid but unattractive descent is to continue S from the summit for 150 metres to the col between the N and S tops and then plunge down the scree gully to the E to regain eventually the grassy alp of the upward route.

*Bla Bheinn above Loch Slapin*                    D.J. Bennet

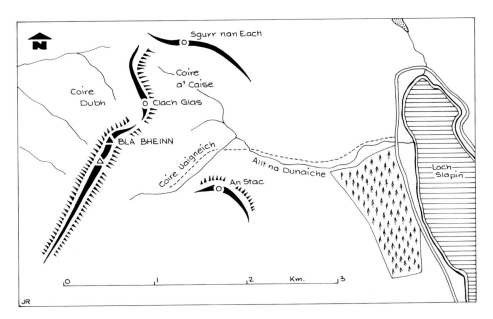